Advertising Dolls
Identification & Value Guide

By Joleen A. Robison
and Kay F. Sellers

COLLECTOR BOOKS
P.O. Box 3009
Paducah, Kentucky 42001

Dedication

To Art and Richard

The labor of this book was divided with Kay doing the photography and owning the majority of the dolls, me doing the research and writing.

Joleen A. Robison

The current values in this book should be used only as a guide. They are not intended to set prices, which vary from one section of the country to another. Auction prices as well as dealer prices vary greatly and are affected by condition as well as demand. Neither the Author nor the Publisher assumes responsibility for any losses that might be incurred as a result of consulting this guide.

Additional copies of this book may be ordered from:

COLLECTOR BOOKS
P.O. Box 3009
Paducah, Kentucky 42001

@ $9.95 Add $1.00 for postage and handling.

Copyright: Joleen A. Robison, 1980
ISBN: 0-89145-134-X

Printed by IMAGE GRAPHICS, Paducah, Kentucky

Acknowledgments

Being our first and only book we learned much by trial and error. The most rewarding thing we learned is the special nature of most doll collectors--they are interested, generous, helpful, encouraging and kind.

Starting back two years ago when we first began amassing the information for this book we want to thank Elizabeth Fisher, who sent us her little cloth **Nestle Baby Food** doll all the way from Connecticut to be photographed. That was the first doll we photographed from a collection other than Kay's. Many more followed.

Our first response from a company, C & H Sugar, arrived about the same time as the Fisher doll. They answered all my questions and sent a copy of their ad used to advertise the cloth Hawaiian girl and boy dolls.

At that point I thought how easy the book would be and expected all collectors and companies to respond promptly and with full information. I supposed Kay and I would always be full of enthusiasm and dedication for finishing the book. Bouts of pneumonia, major surgery, car accident, two children married, heart attack and a stray manuscript slowed us down, sometimes for months at a time, but we continued to plug ahead.

Collectors such as Marge Meisinger, Juanita Ciolek, Karen Miller, Janie Varsalona, Alma Wolfe, Pam Coghlan, Loretta Zablotney, Kathlene Lyons, Sharon Ricklefs, Sue Russell, Ken Lansdowne, Anneruth Pfister, Sally Esser, Jo Keelen, Elizabeth Wright and Betty Welch cooperated especially generously, sending dolls to be photographed, photos, and providing information. They gave us the incentive to see the book to the end.

A special thanks to Frances Walker and Margaret Whitton for allowing us to use photos from their book, Playthings by the Yard, published in 1973. Margaret also provided several dolls from the Margaret Woodbury Strong Museum in New York. The dolls were photographed by Barbara Jendrick.

Some companies were exceedingly generous and helpful. The complete listing of Kellogg's dolls is due to material sent by Rolfe Jenkins of the Kellogg's Company.

Help with the Campbell Kids came from Dean Blair and Fran Bush of the Campbell Soup Company. They provided a list of their premium dolls plus sent a copy of Harvest, Spring 1975, that contained a feature on the history of the Campbell Kids. Loraine Burdick's Celebrity Doll Journal, Year Nine, Issue Three for May, 1975 and two articles in Toy Trader, November 1967 and December 1968 by Patricia N. Schoonmaker also helped with the Campbell Kid section.

History on Nabisco came largely from the book, Out of the Cracker Barrel: the Nabisco Story, from Animal Cracker to Zuzus, by William Cahn. Nabisco sent photos to complete the story, an extra thanks to Jerry Glen, of that company.

Gerber Products sent a photo of their original cloth Gerber Baby premium and also a list of their dolls and a history.

Information on the Quaker Oat Company including the history of Cream of Wheat came from the book, <u>Brands, Trademarks and Goodwill: the Story of the Quaker Oat Company</u>, by Arthur F. Marquette.

Other companies that made mail delivery time rewarding were: Atlas Van Lines, Miles Labratories, American Beauty Macaroni, Pizza Hut, McCall Corporation, Chiquita Brands, Clairol, Club Products Company, Coca-Cola Company, Brunswick Corporation, H.D. Lee Company, Carnation Company, Dairy Queen of America, Topps Chewing Gum Company, Vlasik Pickles, Eskimo Pie Corporation, Faultless Starch Company, H.J. Heinz Company, RJR Foods, Libby's, Armour & Company, Long John Silver, Georgia -Pacific Paper Company, Sun-Maid, RCA, McDonald's, Nestles, Planters/Curtiss Confectionery, Philip Morris, Ralston Purina, Revlon, Sambo's, Scott Paper Company, Seven-up Bottling Company, National Icee Corporation, Glenbrook Labratories, Purity Mills, Levi Strauss & Company, Sylvania, Westinghouse Electric, Travelodge International, Western Union, Galeski Photo Center, Premier Malt Company, Facit-Addo, Gillette Company, Frito-Lay Company, Phillips Petroleum, Doyle H. Spencer Company, Lion Uniform, Eastman Kodak, Beatrice Foods, Little Crow Foods, Exxon Company, Colgate-Palmolive Company and CPC International.

Other helpful people were: Frances L. Charman, curator of Buster Brown Musuem, Melba Quick, Deloras Bultje, Marcile Kolterman, Vickie Anguish, Loraine Edmonson, Linda Yagatich, Nancy Ricklefs, Lois Shearer, Rosemarye Bunting, Kathy Brunnell, Doris Stilwell, Georgia Cannon, Alice Leonard, Winona Dingman, Mary Ann Beahon, Berneice Glass, Helen Walas, Betsy Beisecker, Lila Murnan, Mary Lowe, Naomi Wolfe, Vivian Rasberry, Rinda Coons, Edna Rogers, the late Laura Maxfield, Ruth Eagles, Margaret Rice, Isabelle Mather, and Melba Hiter.

Ralph Griffin, Elmer Bell and Paul Johnson were cooperative allowing Kay and I access to the dolls in the museum section of the Parkview, Missouri shop; Ralph's Antique Dolls.

My admiration, respect, and thanks to the Coleman's who wrote the <u>Encyclopedia of Dolls</u>, a most valuable reference book on dolls manufactured prior to 1929.

Information on later dolls was aided through the research of Johanna Gast Anderton in her books, <u>Twentieth Century Dolls</u> and <u>More Twentieth Century Dolls</u>.

Tidbits concerning various advertising trademarks, names and origins came primarily from <u>Famous American Trademarks</u>, by Arnold B. Barach.

Many times when a question arose I picked up the phone and asked for the reference desk at the Lawrence Public Library.

I have undoubtedly forgotten people or companies who should be thanked. Much input is necessary to compile a book, it becomes impossible to list them all.

4

Introduction

Generally speaking, the dolls in this book are listed alphabetically by the product they represent. **Speedy** is under Alka Seltzer and **Li'l Softee** is under Zee Toilet Tissue--to give an A to Z example.

If a company or product changed names or merged, the doll is listed as the product or company was listed at the time the doll was offered. For example, in the late sixties Atlantic Richfield service stations sold dolls for 99¢ with the purchase of gasoline. Since that time the company's name was changed to Arco. The dolls are listed under Atlantic Richfield, rather than Arco.

When a product has offered several dolls, they are described chronologically. For instance, the **Mr. Peanut** doll made of wood beads is discussed first because it is the oldest, followed by the paper mache nodder, the older cloth doll, and finally the recent cloth **Mr. Peanut**.

There are two exceptions to listing alphabetically by product. Dolls offered by a cereal are listed under the company that produced the cereal rather than the cereal itself. **Cap'n Crunch** dolls are listed under Q for Quaker Oats Company rather than C for Cap'n Crunch cereal. **Toucan Sam** is with other Kellogg's cereal's dolls rather than under F for Froot Loops.

Another exception is when several products from a company offer a doll. The company is listed rather than each product, such as Procter & Gamble, which in 1975 included Pogo cartoon characters with several of their products. Instead of listing each product and the Pogo characters, it is listed only under Procter & Gamble.

Every collector has a different idea of what should be included in an advertising doll book. At one end of the spectrum is the purist who would only include dolls with a product tie-in. I am of that inclination. For example, of the Post cereal dolls a purist would include the **Sugar Crisp Bear** but not the series of **Storykin** dolls.

The opposite of the purist is what I'll call the "conglomeratist," one who collects a wide variety of advertising items. A conglomeratist would include all plastic hand puppets, containers in the shape of a doll, display characters, figurals, and commercial premiums. Kay is of this inclination. Between the two of us we tried to hit a happy medium.

Deciding what constitutes an advertising doll was often debatable. We followed no iron-clad rules, often letting whimsy and availability be our guide. Dolls we included are:

1. Premiums. We included premium items offered by a product, with or without a company tie-in. Premiums with a company connection include the **Chiquita Banana** doll, Seven-up's **Fresh-up Freddie** and Travelodge's **Sleepy Bear**. Premiums with no tie-in include Kellogg's **Miss America**, which is a Barbie doll manufactured by Mattel and sold commercially in the Miss America outfit. Others with no relationship to the company are Tide's teddy bear, Scott's plush elephant and donkey, and Carnation Milk's **Cry Baby** doll.

2. Trademark Symbols. The book includes any doll that represents a trademark symbol whether the doll sold commercially or by premium. Commercially sold trademark symbol dolls include the early **Campbell Kids**, Pillsbury's **Poppin' Fresh** and **Rice Krispies' Snap, Crackle and Pop**.

3. Tradename dolls. Dolls have been manufactured by toy companies and have been named for a product, such as the **Toni** dolls, manufactured by Ideal and American Character, which were named after a home permanent. Along that same line is the **Harriet Hubbard Ayer** doll named for a line of cosmetics and the **Sun-Maid Raisin** doll.

4. Display Figures. In the early stages of the book we planned to omit display figures, but several collectors gave such convincing arguments we reconsidered and have included some. One collector reminded us these were the true advertising dolls. In the book will be found a **Miss Curity** that stood on a drug store counter to remind customers to purchase Curity first-aid supplies. Several figures that were used in taverns to encourage patrons to purchase their brand of beer are included--Miller High Life, Duquesne, and Stoney's. Many of these are attached to a base and are figurals.

5. Animals, Banks, and Puppets. Not only dolls and display figures are included, but also animals **(Fresca Rabbit)**, banks **(Big Boy)**, and many puppets. The puppets range in quality from the plastic ones that are given free at restaurants (Church's Fried Chicken) to plush ones with moveable mouths **(A&W Great Root Bear)**.

Dolls we chose to exclude are:

1. Subscription Premiums. We omitted dolls offered for magazine subscriptions because practically every doll manufactured prior to world War II has been offered in this manner, even Shirley Temple.

2. Advertisement for an organization. Also omitted are dolls that represent organizations such as Scouting, Red Cross, or the Military.

3. Entertainment Personalities. Strictly speaking, dolls that represent radio, television, or movie characters are advertising a program from that media. We chose to exclude that category--an entire book could be devoted to entertainment personalities: **Amosandra Doll**, from the radio show Amos and Andy; **Kotter and the Sweat Hogs Dolls** from television; and **Our Gang Dolls** from the Our Gang movies.

4. Salt and Peppers. Doll-like salt and pepper shakers are excluded. Again they are for some one else's books.

5. Paper Dolls. Advertising paper dolls is a large category we left to others who are experts in the field.

6. Famous Endorsers. One gray area includes dolls that represent people used extensively for advertising a product. For example, the Dionne quintuplets were used, for many years, to advertise

Palmolive Soap, Quaker Oats, and Karo Syrup, and there were many Dionne quintuplet dolls. Along this same line--Kewpies and Jello were inseparable for over a decade and Kewpies are also made as dolls. We chose to exclude this type of doll.

Defunct companies were a major problem in compiling this guide. When dealing with advertising dolls, it is important to know the product and company it represents, in addition to the identity of the doll and its manufacturer. Often it was difficult because the product or company of some older advertising dolls is no longer in business. Companies and products such as Malt Breakfast Cereal, Korn Krisp, Textile Bluing, and Sea Island Sugar are no longer advertising; whether they merged, went out of business, or changed names is difficult to trace down. Usually the only information known comes from the advertising doll itself.

Some products have been owned by more than one company or have changed names. Aunt Jemima Pancake Flour was originally a product of Davis Milling Company, then the company became Aunt Jemima Mills, and later was purchased by Quaker Oats Company. Along the way, records of the dolls were lost, or packed away, and are not available. Multiple owners were often a problem.

Occassionally a product fails to sell well and is dropped from a company's line. Some of these products are: Zuzu ginger-flavored cookies, Quake cereal, Raisin Bran Chex, and Yukon Flour. When this happens the dolls give the only information available.

Advertising dolls help keep track of many products that have become phased out and quickly forgotten. Who but an advertising doll collector remembers: Quaker's Crackles, Dy-o-la Dye, or Arbuckle coffee?

One of the biggest surprises when accumulating the information for this book was to learn that many companies keep no records of their premiums. It is true that premiums are usally rather inconsequential items although a look at today's antique market should prove, to the most causal investigator, that interest in advertising memorabilia is significant.

Some companies who have been leaders in premium promotion have no information to release to interested consumers. When a company provides no information it is almost impossible to learn about the premium. Most of the advertising was done on a carton and it was usually discarded.

Being unimportant toys, many advertising dolls were never patented. Some exceptions are the **Aunt Jemima Dolls** (1914, 1916, and 1917), **Toni** (1949), and **Miss Curity** (1951).

If an advertising doll proved popular, it was often reissued. The reissue almost always resulted in some minor change. The companies consider that they have one premium doll, discerning doll collectors consider each variation different and desire an example of each. During the last decade **Bracho the Clown** was issued three times, each time the collar being the only thing changed.

History of the Advertising Doll

The earliest advertising dolls were cloth dolls with such names as **Dolly Dimple, Flossie Collingbourne, Miss Flaked Rice,** and **Trena.** Later, when trademark figures became so important, dolls were copied to resemble the trademark figure, such as the **Ceresota Boy, Aunt Jemima,** and **Anty Drudge**.

To a company, their product's trademark symbols are serious business. Often large amounts of time and money are spent to find a satisfactory symbol.

Years ago companies relied heavily on their symbol. At one time it was legal to manufacture a product of inferior quality, package it similar to a successful product, and market it under a name that was almost the same. For instance, someone could produce an oval bar of soap that looked like Fairy Soap, but was made of inexpensive ingredients. They could copy the label, and name their soap Fariee Soap, taking advantage of Fairy Soap's advertising and reputation for having a top quality product. At that time many Americans were unable to read because they had no education or were from a non-English speaking country. They could be tricked into purchasing a bar of inferior soap, thinking it was the product they'd purchased and liked in the past--the name looked the same.

Here is where the value of the symbol played such an important role. Only Fairy Soap used the symbol of a little girl in a big hat. A person might not be able to distinguish between the words Fairy and Fairee, but would learn to watch for the little girl.

Before laws were passed to protect manufacturers, there were many infringements. One was the Y'u Needa Biscuit, but it didn't use the antique printer's symbol of the cross with two bars, nor the figure of a little boy in a yellow slicker, which represented NBC's quality controlled biscuit. People soon learned it was important to watch for the symbols.

Trademark symbols were widely advertised in magazines and were usually printed prominently on the product's package. Ceresota Flour's small boy slicing a piece of bread was used on their package from the time the flour was first milled in the 1800's until today. Many of America's residents had grown up in a country that used ground flour much like Ceresota's. When shopping for flour they searched the shelves for the sack stamped in purple ink with a little boy, that way they could be assured of purchasing a brand of flour similar to the kind they'd used in the old country.

Today trademark symbols and names are protected by law and it is a serious offense to illegally copy a symbol for a doll or any other purpose unless authorized by the company.

Chronology

The oldest advertising dolls we found were cloth, used in the early 1900's. They were printed on sheets of fabric to be cut, sewn, and stuffed by the owner. The cloth cutout doll first appeared on the market in the late 1880's. If there were advertising dolls that early, we did not find them. By 1905 the **Aunt Jemima, Miss Flaked Rice,** and **Punch and Judy** could be ordered for a few stamps or coins and the designated proof of purchase. The appeal of the cloth doll has been enduring--today advertisers continue to offer cloth premium dolls.

Some of the old cloth dolls had darts, such as **Miss Korn Krisp,** with darts at the thighs and neck. Some early cloth dolls had parts of the costume cut separately. The **Ceresota Boy's** hat brim and the **Cream of Wheat Chef's** hat and apron were separate.

Instructions and identification were usually printed on the background fabric that was cut away when the doll was assembled.

According to early magazine ads, cloth dolls between 1900 and 1930 were printed on linen, muslin, art cloth, sateen or cambric. The features were described as: "stamped on, lithographed, or painted in oils that will not crack". Ads often emphasized the durability by saying, "never loses its head, its eyes don't fall in, doesn't suffer mishaps common to other dolls."

At the turn of the century Arnold Print Works of Massachusetts and Art Fabric Mills of New York were the two largest producers of cloth dolls. Arnold was strictly a wholesale company, while Art Fabric Mills allowed customers to order directly from them. Both printed advertising dolls. Two other companies producing cloth dolls in the early 1900's were Grinnell Lithographic Company of New York City and Niagara Lithographing Company of Buffalo, New York. Grinnell redesigned the **Aunt Jemima Doll** series in 1924 and issued other advertising dolls. Niagara manufactured the early cloth **Sunny Jim Doll** used by Force cereal.

The firm of Selchow & Righter was an agent for both Art Fabric Mills and Arnold Print Works in about 1910, in addition to manufacturing some cloth dolls of their own. Later they imported bisque dolls. This company became the successor to Art Fabric Mills.

Cloth dolls gained renewed interest in the 1970's. Many cloth advertising dolls were introduced during this decade. The dolls were constructed of two flat pieces of fabric, lithographed, and prestuffed, being two dimensional with no darts or separate pieces. Prior to 1960 cloth advertising dolls were never prestuffed, to my knowledge.

Today the major cloth advertising doll manufacturer is Chase Bag Company of Reidsville, North Carolina. Some of the dolls manufactured by Chase are: **Burger King, Bunny Bear, Cheetos Mouse Man, Hecker's (Ceresota) Boy, Keebler Elf, Baby Magic's Snuggle Sam** and **Snuggle Susie, Eskimo Pie**

Boy, George and Martha Washington from Gillette products, Franklin Life Insurance's **Benjamin, Gingerman** and **Razzle**. Plastic dolls are also dispersed by Chase Bag Company, whether they are manufactured by them also is not known.

From about 1910 to 1930 toy manufacturers sold composition dolls copied from famous trademark figures. Taking advantage of the extensive advertising used to present the trademark figure, toy firms were quick to issue **Campbell Kids, Jap Rose Kids, Fairy Soap Girl, Skookum Apple Indian, Uneeda Biscuit Boy, Crackerjack Boy, Sunny Jim, Babbitt Boy,** and others. Composition advertising dolls were usually made from a formula that was very hard and held up well. Bodies were usually cloth with gauntlet hands and sometimes composition lower leg with molded boots or shoes.

Prior to World War II children often received a little Japanese bisque doll for purchasing a new pair of shoes at certain stores. The 2 to 4-inch dolls were stamped or incised with the brand name of the shoe such as Poll Parrot or Weather Bird. World War II changed that pleasant practice--shoes were rationed and Japan was the enemy.

Few advertising dolls of any material were offered in the 1940's, probably because most supplies and people were helping with the war effort. Latex foam was perfected in Britain in the 1930's, but it was later that the precious rubber could be used for dolls. In the 50's American Companies were allowed to use the patented foam material for dolls; the **Mobil Oil Man** doll and later the **Budman** Doll were made from this substance. The dolls proved great for teething, but unfortunately harden and disintegrate.

From 1945 to 1955 was the decade of the rubber squeak toy doll. The advertising dolls were skillfully molded and painted and most have retained their shape much better than unpainted rubber dolls of the same decade, as noted with the **Tillamook Cheese Cow**, the **Cal-Neva Indian**, and the **Campbell Kid** dolls.

By 1950 plastics had replaced composition as the material used for most commercial dolls. The quality varied from a sticky soft formula to brittle hard product. Some were tinted a garish pink while others had a sickly yellow cast. Plastic was definitely an ideal subatance for dolls--it was almost unbreakable, washable, pliable, held paint, and was realistic looking. The quality of plastic was soon perfected.

Beginning in the 1950's many companies and products used a commercial 8-inch plastic doll for a premium. The doll actually varies from 7 to 8-inches tall. Early ones have mohair wigs, while the later ones use synthetic wigs; both are glued on the head. Eyes on the older dolls are painted, later ones open/shut. Some of these dolls are jointed at the shoulder. Most have painted shoes. The costumes are made from taffeta with braid and lace trim. Many are stapled to the doll. To encourage customers to purchase several, the dolls are often part of a series such as International Dolls, Americana Dolls, Story Book Dolls, or Dolls of the World. What is a Swiss doll in one series, may be Goldilocks in another, and Southern Belle in the third--identity is interchangeable.

Prior to the 1960's these dolls were free or cost 50¢ . By the 1960's they cost 99¢ , then the price began to climb--today they sell for $2.25 on packages of Good Value Margarine. Companies who have offered this type of commercial doll include: Little Debbie Cakes, Atlantic Richfield, Blue Bonnet, Armour Products, Frito-Lay, Reddi-Wip, Peter-Paul Candy, Lucerne Ice Cream, Manor House Products, Tastee Freez, and Fab detergent.

Today the major producer of plastic advertising dolls is probably Dakin & Company of California. This company has produced: **Smokey Bear** for Aim, **Big Boy, Jolly King**, Close-up Toothpaste's **Dumbo** and other Disney cartoon characters, **Li'l Miss Justrite**, and several tigers and Sambo's Dolls for Sambo Restaurants. The Dakin dolls are well marked and high quality.

Reasons for Collecting Advertising Dolls

There are probably as many reasons for collecting advertising dolls as there are collectors. Two major reasons might be because they are interesting and inexpensive. One of the interesting things about advertising dolls is how they reflect fashions. Early cloth dolls show girls wearing demure white frocks with drop waists and big bows in the back. They wear long stockings and high button shoes. Collingbourne's **Flossie** dresses quite differently from Atlas Van Lines' **Atlas Annie** in her lithographed pant suit.

To learn of America's eating habits, take a look at the advertising dolls. The early ones advertise such commodities as cooked cereal--Imperial Granum, Malto Rice, and Flaked Rice. It was many years later that the first cold cereal was developed and presented to the consumer. In 1926 Kellogg's of Battle Creek, Michigan sold **Goldilocks and the Three Bears** dolls to promote their flakes made of corn. Recent dolls reflect a new trend in cereals--the presweetened cold cereal. Outer space character **Quisp, Cap'n Crunch,** the rabbit **Trix, Count Chocula,** and many others have become immediately recognizable to the preteen consumer.

Judging from early advertising dolls, America did much baking prior to 1930. Flour sack dolls abound: Arkadelphia, Puritan, Voights, and Istrouma all printed a doll on their sacks of flour.

Today's flour comes in paper bags and is stored in a canister on top of the counter. Consumers are inclined to purchase baked goods as reflected by the dolls for Hostess Ho Hos and Dunkin Doughnuts.

The evolution of packaging is another interesting sidelight that can be observed through advertising dolls. Until the 40's flour and sugar came in cloth bags, sturdy paper replaced cloth, then plastic replaced the paper.

During the time of the cloth bag, companies figured if they were going to print something on the sack it might as well be something that would help sell the product. Then, as now, the power of a child's plea to the parent was recognized. The choice of a product often depends, not on the product itself, but on the premium included or the packaging. Today children walk up and down the grocery aisle selecting a cereal from the offers described on the box, with no thought of the taste or nutrition of the cereal.

In the 1930's Western Refineries, the company who produced Sea Island Sugar, had a good thing going with their dolls printed on the back of every sugar sack. What fun it was to pull the string just right and allow it to unravel all around the sack! Then cut the dolls, sew them up, except across the bottom, turn them right side out, stuff them with cotton, sew the gap across the bottom closed and--surprise--**Little Franz** or **Gobi** or **Fifi**.

More than a pretty face or an advertising doll, the advertising doll captures a slice of time, so we can glimpse another era. The historical attitudes of our nation toward its black citizens, its morals, its women, are reflected in advertising dolls.

To obtain an idea of what the average white citizen's attitude toward black was, we can look at the **Aunt Jemima** dolls. The Davis Milling Company meant no put-down in 1908 when it depicted in doll form a black family that included a toothless husband, and barefoot ragged clothed children. To the company's credit, the next issue of the popular doll series was improved. By 1929 they were a family of dandies with high top hat, gold watch chain, and shoes. Still they were a stereotype.

To illustrate how advertising dolls mirror morals look at the Faultless Spray Starch dolls. The Kansas City company had no intention of being humorous or judging the morals when it offered **Miss Lilly White** and **Miss Phoebe Prim**. In the early 1900's it was admirable to be lily white and being prim was a compliment.

Besides being interesting the other major reason for collecting advertising dolls is probably the cost factor. As new doll collectors become enthusiastic about their hobby, they soon find out that many dolls, especially the antique ones, are out of their budget range. For the price of one molded hair Schoenhut, bisque Bye Lo, or china Jenny Lind they can purchase many advertising dolls.

That old human desire to get something for nothing enters in. You will probably never find a Bru, a Heubach, or even an Armand Marseille at a garage sale or thrift store, but you may find an unmarked **Baby Ruth**, and for perhaps one dollar. Its that something-for-nothing thrill that keeps a stream of cars pulling over at garage sales and using precious gas to patronize local thrift stores.

In 1979 premium dolls cost within a range of $1.00 for the **Wizard of O's** to about $6.00 for **Cap'n Crunch**. For the patient shopper of flea markets and garage sales, these advertising dolls can often be purchased for less, a year or so after being issued. By then their owners have tired of them.

Campbell Soup's **Colonial Kids** dolls, issued for the bicentennial, were available into 1978. Their value has taken a jump. They cost about $10 for the pair when purchased from Campbell; today lists show them at $35. Not all recent dolls have increased that dramatically. Many seem to stay valued at the issue price for five or six years.

Cloth dolls of the late 1960's are becoming scarce and therefore demand has increased the price. The **C & H Sugar Twins**, some of the **Jolly Green Giant** dolls, **Charlie Chocks** and others of this decade cost from $8 to $18, when clean and in good condition.

The paper mache and plaster nodder dolls of this decade bring from $8 to $30, and most were sturdy and remain in good condition. The rubber dolls or squeak toys of this decade can often be found at bargain prices--at a doll shop expect to pay about $10. Composition advertising dolls such as Philip Morris' **Johnny** and H.D. Lee's **Buddy Lee** bring good prices. **Johnny** will probably cost from $50 to $100. The composition **Buddy Lee** is selling for from $75 to $200 depending on condition and which uniform it is wearing. At a 1979 auction the Coca-Cola doll brought $200. Coca-Cola collectors drive Coca-Cola memorabilia prices high. At doll shows the usual cost is $70 to $90 for the cowboy, farmer, or service station uniforms. The doll is less when damaged or missing parts of the uniform.

The pre-1930 cloth dolls are difficult to find and especially in good condition. They range in price from $30 to $200. Uncut cloth dolls usually bring $10 to $20 more than cut and assembled dolls. With cloth dolls much depends on the condition. A ragged, faded doll no matter how rare is not going to bring much over $25. The top dollar I have seen was a **Ceresota Boy** in perfect condition for $200. At the UFDC Convention in Denver, 1978, I recorded the following prices: **Miss Flaked Rice** for $65, **Goldilocks and the Three Bears from Kellogg's** for $150 in excellent condition, **Lena** from Premier Malt for $75, and **Ceresota Boy** in poor condition for $75. At these prices some did not sell.

The composition dolls made during this thirty year period are the most expensive of all the advertising dolls. The **Campbell Kids** made in 1929 and in original clothes sold for $260 at a doll show in 1978. The **Babbitt Boy** is close to $200, **Skookum Indian** is nearing $80.

Like a car, an advertising doll must hold its value to be a bargain. If you send in a coupon and $2 for a doll in 1974, can you expect to double your money by 1976, when it is no longer being offered? As interest in advertising dolls increases, the answer is bably yes.

Molded vinyl dolls such as **Keebler Elf**, Pillsbury's **Poppin' Fresh**, and the **Trix Playmate** will surely increase as time passes. I doubt that dolls like the Voortman Cookie doll and the 8-inch commercial dolls used by many products will increase at all in value.

Cloth dolls with minimal distribution, such as **Mr. Galeski** are sure to always be sought after by collectors living in other areas. Their price will reflect the demand and supply. Dolls with wide dispersal, such as **Mr. Peanut** and **Burger King** will be lucky to increase at all.

Premium dolls with no relationship to the product they represent are usually offered at a bargain price. Post cereals have offered Mattel dolls at about 30% less than retail cost. They are a bargain but have little trade-in value compared to dolls that represent a trademark figure. Their inflation rate is the same as the rate of similar commercial dolls.

Companies usually make no profit on their premium dolls. Cost of manufacturing the doll, handling, and postage combined is what the consumer is charged. A good example is the Close-up Toothpaste Monkeys offered in 1976 for $3.98--the 1977 Christmas season at toy stores they cost almost $12.00. Mattel has made several talking advertising dolls such as **Libby** and **Charlie the Tuna**. These cost considerably less than comparable Mattel talking dolls manufactured for the commercial market.

A very few premium dolls are no bargain. They cost the same or more than the retail level. It is debatable whether the 8-inch plastic dolls used by so many products are a bargain. Today the undressed dolls sell for from 49¢ to 79¢. The dolls cost $2.25 when ordered with a proof-of-purchase. Does the clothing make them worth $2.25? Many collectors think so, or the dolls wouldn't have been so popular for so many years. Each collector must decide whether a doll is worth the price. Generally speaking advertising dolls are a bargain.

How To Build A Collection Of Advertising Dolls

When a doll is promoted it is often for a very short period of time. To paraphrase a saying often seen in antique shops, "The time to buy an advertising doll is when you see it." For instance, the **Trix Playmate** ad was only on Trix cereal boxes in my grocer's shelf about three months, when the box was changed to carry a new offer.

In 1979 an offer for Pillsbury's **Poppin' Fresh** and **Poppie** ran in a February magazine with a February 28th expiration date. My request was mailed two days late and was returned, marked "offer expired."

It is true that other dolls are offered over a long period of time and remain available after the expiration date. To be on the safe side it is best to order a doll as soon as the offer is made.

Some dolls are offered in limited areas, such as **Li'l Miss Justrite**, which was a promotion that centered in Indiana. If you see a regional offer, buy it, and a few extras to trade if possible.

When traveling don't pass up a doll at a restaurant or service station, planning to pick it up later. The next restaurant, even though the same chain, may not even know the doll exists.

If you hear of a doll offered in an area that you will be unable to visit, write the company and see if they'll mail one, or try to remember some friend who lives in the area and ask them to send you one. Be sure to include money for the doll and postage. Also send a stamped self-addressed envelope.

Antique and older advertising dolls are difficult to find. Make it known that you specialize in advertising dolls. Realize that you will have to pay the price, (which will be high if you want to acquire old dolls in good condition). Again trading is often an excellent way to build your collection.

It is helpful when building a collection of advertising dolls to correspond with collectors in various parts of the country. They often know of dolls that are not offered in your area.

Advertising dolls can be found everywhere and anywhere. Keep your eyes open when shopping, in back rooms, in church toy boxes, and of course at antique shops, flea markets, garage sales, thrift shops and doll shows.

When building any collection the care of the items is important, and especially advertising dolls. If a cloth doll is dirty it poses a problem because it can't be washed like vinyl or bisque. When purchasing a dirty cloth doll, one should ask, "For the price is the doll worth it?" Sometimes yes.

You might benefit from a personal experience. I purchased a dirty **Ralston Purina Squarecrow**. It has a vinyl head and a long cloth body stuffed with foam rubber. I put it in the washer on the delicate cycle with other clothes and it came out clean. It dried after a couple of days outdoors. Only do this if the doll is filled with foam rubber.

Another washing experience concerns an old **Miss Korn Krisp**. She was water stained, filled with lumpy cotton, and smelled stale. I found where she'd been stuffed and the gap sewn shut and carefully cut the threads. After pulling out the old stuffing, I soaked her a few hours in cool water then hand-washed her. I could see some red color coming from her shoes so stopped washing. She came out much better looking. Dacron batting solved the odor problem.

Plastic dolls can be cleaned with a toothbrush that has been dampened and rubbed over a bar of soap. Afer scrubbing in all the little creases rinse with cool water and dry. If the features have been painted rub them very lightly if at all because the paint can flake off.

Be sure the inside of the doll is not filled with water. Either take care not to allow any water to seep inside or shake thoroughly to remove all water.

Mechanics hand cleaner will remove crayon and other ground-in filth from plastic dolls.

Pre-laundry spot removers will often remove crayon or grease pencil from cloth dolls. Thrift stores are notorious for marking the price of a doll with a black grease pencil.

Storing advertising dolls is a problem. They take lots of space. Many, being cloth, will mildew if damp and will fade if in the sun. When visiting different collectors to photograph their advertising dolls it was interesting to see how they handled the problems. Several ideas were worth passing along. Kathleen Lyons leaves hers in their plastic bags and attaches them to a peg board. Dolls that didn't come in plastic she has found sacks for. The dolls are hung close together so the peg board is hidden.

Kay Sellers does a similar thing. She hangs her advertising dolls in plastic bags with shower curtain rings on shower rods hung in her basement.

The Ricklefs have floor to ceiling shelves filled with advertising dolls along one wall of their young daughter's bedroom. How charming for an upstairs bedroom in their pre-1900 house!

Storing the early cloth dolls printed on flat fabric is fun, easy, and takes little space. They can be put in clear folders in a loose-leaf notebook or album. They look wonderful framed or thumb-tacked to a bulletin board.

This brings up the debate of the cutters vs. the non-cutters. If you are so lucky to own an old, or even a new (Mennen dolls, 1975), sheet of uncut cloth dolls, please leave it uncut. The printing on the background fabric is often the only information known about the doll. Some feel strongly the doll should be cut and assembled. Here is where the debate begins.

Some advertising dolls look especially attractive when displayed with related items. My Campbell Kids are displayed on top of a secretary, along with various Campbell mugs, spoons, a Drayton valentine, note paper, and paper dolls.

It is always important to identify your dolls. When you order a new doll try to obtain an extra coupon and label for your records. If it is a cereal offer, cut the description from the box. Keep any magazine or newspaper ads about the doll.

For each doll have a page, a card, or a folder with the description of the doll, its costs, marks, and any other material available.

Unidentified dolls, found at a garage sale, can be a delightful challenge. Pursue it as you would any mystery. Write down everything you can learn from the doll itself. Ask friends, especially younger ones, if they know who the doll is. If you belong to a doll club take it to a meeting: someone is likely to know or give you a clue. If the doll is old browse through old magazines looking for ads that carry a trademark; see if any match your mystery doll.

Old cloth dolls that are unmarked usually wear a lithographed chemise. Note the edging, if it wears jewelry, ribbons in the hair, what the shoes are like. Each detail will help match it to the dolls found in ads.

When writing a description for your records, you may find discrepancies in the sizes of your dolls and the ones listed in this book. We found sizes varied. Two 1977 Burger King dolls varied an inch. If your doll is a bit larger or smaller than the size given, it probably means the seam allowance varied, not that you have a totally different doll.

Colors also vary from printing to printing. We found oranges that were almost red on one doll and almost yellow on another. This may be due to mixing the dye for the colors. Some dolls were intentionally different color combinations. For instance one **Ben Franklin** was pink and gray, another found was blue and green.

Collecting Advertising dolls can get in your blood. Soon you find yourself looking at all trademarks as potential advertising dolls. Some seem perfect for a doll, for instance Roto-Wash, the car wash symbol, and the doughnut man used on Carol Lee Doughnut advertisements.

If you become hooked you'll find the family eating Spaghettios every day for a week to obtain the necessary labels to purchase the **Wizard of O's** doll. Most mornings you will be eating presweetened cereal because that is the type that offers premium dolls. Oh, the price advertising doll collectors pay. Yet, it's worth it.

For a hobby that combines history, mystery, fashion, and fun--we recommend **advertising dolls**.

A

A & P.

In the early 1970's, some A & P Grocery Stores gave a 5" x 2½" red plastic bank in the shape of a pig. Marks: "A & P", indented on sides. $1.00.

A & W Root Beer, a subsidiary of United Brands. Two sizes of a brown plush bear and a hand puppet have been sold from A & W Root Beer stands. The **Great Root Bear**, 13-inches, was offered during the Christmas season 1975, for $3.95. The bear wears an orange jacket and cap and is marked on the chest with an A & W patch. A larger size was also offered at some stands.

This advertisement for the *A & W Great Root Bear* was placed on trays at the restaurant.

The **Great Root Bear** hand puppet, 10-inches, was sold at stands the following year, 1976, for $1.00. It is made of brown and tan nylon stretch fabric with an orange hat and cuff. Below the mouth it is marked with an A & W patch.

A & W Drive-in Restaurants sold the *A & W Great Root Bear* during the Christmas season in 1975. The 13-inch brown plush bear is dressed in an orange jacket and cap. This size usually sold for $3.95. Other sizes were available. Marks: "A & W", on oval patch on chest. $4.00.

These posters at the A & W Restaurants were the primary method of advertising the hand puppet.

A & W Great Root Bear hand-puppets were available in 1976. Marks: "A & W", on oval iron-on patch below mouth. $1.00.

A.P.W. Paper Company.

All six lines of the company's toilet tissue used the same trademark figure, a little girl wearing a black and white checked dress. A.P.W. offered: Satin Tissue, Pure White, Bob White, Cross Cut, Fort Orange, and Onliwon. A cloth doll was available for 10¢ and any one of these wrappers according to ads in 1925 magazines.

The 12-inch cloth doll was lithographed in black and yellow on white fabric. Her yellow hair is cut in the popular dutch-cut of the 20's. The facial features are very simple, two widely spaced black dots for eyes and a black rosebud mouth, no nose. The dress is a bit different from the doll seen on the

wrappers, it has a wrap-around over skirt with a romper suit underneath.

The doll was printed on a flat sheet to be assembled. All identification was printed on the background fabric.

A small cardboard doll house was also available from the same 1925 ads. It was a 10-inch house printed to resemble a white clapboard with red-shingled roof, green shutters, and red flower filled window boxes.

The trademark figure of the A.P.W. Paper Company was sold as a 12-inch cloth doll in 1925. The doll is lithographed in two colors, yellow and black, on white. The doll is unmarked. Courtesy of "The A.P.W. Paper Company Premium Offers Circa 1925" by Alma Wolfe, THE DOLL READER, Volume VI, Issue 3, April 1978, Copyright Hobby House Press. $35.00.

Abbot Ice Cream. This

New York company sold a clown bank in the early 1970's for $1.50.

19

Adam's Black Jack Gum, a product of the American Chicle Company. Back when gum sold for 5¢ a package, twelve cloth zoo animals were advertised by this gum company. The only animal doll of the series found is an 11-inch rabbit lithographed in profile with a package of that wonderful tasting Black Jack Gum sticking out of one pocket. The exact date of the cloth doll is unknown, a calculated guess is 1930, judging from the style of clothing and the request for a 2¢ stamp on the offer; two-centers were used from 1926-32.

The twelve zoo animals were also made in tin for store displays. Whether all twelve were also made as cloth dolls is unknown. The rabbit is marked number nine, so one would suppose that at least nine had been made in cloth. It does seem odd that none of the others have appeared in doll literature or in our search for advertising dolls.

Thomas Adams' Black Jack gum is the oldest flavored gum on the market today. For several years before Adams had the idea of flavoring chicle with licorice he sold unflavored chicle labeled "Adams' New York Gum-- Snapping and Stretching."

According to the book *Why Did They Name It . . .?* by Hannah Campbell the person actually responsible for the chewing gum industry is General Antonio Lopez de Santa Anna, of "Remember the Alamo" notoriety. After the war Santa Anna came to New York and he brought with him a chunk of chicle, the dried sap of a Mexican jungle tree. The story here is a bit hazy, but one way or another he met a Yankee inventor Thomas Adams. According to Campbell's book: Santa Anna induced Adams to experiment with the chicle as a rubber substitute. The experiments were a total failure and after weeks of futile effort, Adams

gave up, and discovered that Santa Anna in the meantime had been granted political amnesty and had returned to Mexico, leaving his Yankee inventor friend to pay expenses and the warehouse bills for storing the chicle.

"In the course of his conversations with Santa Anna, Adams noticed that the diminutive General occasionally took a small pinch of chicle from his pocket and chewed it with a great deal of gusto. Adams' own son, Horatio, had also enjoyed chewing the chicle. One afternoon in a Hoboken drugstore, Adams saw the druggest sell a piece of paraffin and spruce to a little girl, paraffin and spruce being about the only such items available in that day. It reminded Adams of Santa Anna's "chewing" and also Horatio's enjoyment of the exercise. Adams asked the druggist if he'd like a better cud to sell and the druggist assured him he would, and agreed paraffin wasn't really a very good chew.

"At home Adams and Horatio went to work on Santa Anna's chicle. (Horatio died in 1956 at the age of 102, although this may be entirely irrelevant to his gum chewing habit.) Father and son mixed the chicle with hot water until it was about the consistency of putty. They rubbed, kneaded and finally rolled it into little balls, which they presented to the amiable druggist. A day or so later the druggist reported the chews were selling at a penny apiece."

Adams' suspected he'd hit on a good thing so invested in more chicle. It was tasteless and was put up in boxes with the legend: Adam's New York Gum--Snapping and Stretching.

"Another Adams' son, Thomas, Jr., a traveling salesman, took the gum west as far as Mississippi, and by the time he returned home, orders were flowing in in spite of puritanical outcries of "Vice!"

Snuff habituates and pro-tobacco pluggers dismissed it as "sissy." Parents outlawed it, in vain of course, and schoolteachers condemned it bitterly as unfair competition in the class room.

"In a more scientific vein, rumors spread that it was really made of horses' hooves and glue. Indigestion was not the worst thing that would result, "they" prophesied gloomily, if a piece were accidentally swallowed. It could cause appendicitis at best and make the intestines "stick together" at worst. Anyone knew "stuck-together" intestines would result in certain death. There must have been hundreds of children who believed their lives were spared in some miraculous fashion as they sat patiently waiting for the Grim Reaper to arrive after swallowing their wad, only to discover he wasn't coming after all. As late as 1932 Nikola Tesla, the electrical genius, solemnly warned: 'By exhaustion of the salivary glands, it puts many a foolish victim in the grave!' On the other hand, five years ago, Dr. James H. Doggart told the American Medical Association convention that Jack Dempsey had so strengthened his jaw by his gum-chewing habit that when Georges Carpentier hit him in 1921, Carpentier's thumb was broken instead of Dempsey's jaw, and that was why Dempsey won the fight."

Adams and later others experimented adding flavoring and sweetener to the chicle, apparently making gum irresistible to the public because today a person chews an average of 168 sticks of gum a year.

From Campbell's book we learn: "The gum we chew today is mostly polyvinyl acetate, a synthetic plastic, supplied almost entirely by Hercules Powder Company--primarily explosive manufacturers. Until recently the chewing gum industry has been rather cagey about publicizing its use of synthetic gum bases because it feels there's more romance in the sap of a jungle tree, gathered by chicleroes deep in the mysterious jungle than in a scientist's sterile test tube in an immaculate laboratory."

The 11-inch cloth rabbit is one of 12 cloth premium animals offered by the Adams' brand of chewing gum. Marks: "This is No. 9 of the Chiclet Zoo. There are 12 in all. You get any of the others by mailing five 5¢ wrappers of either Adams Chiclets, Adams Pepsin, Adams Black Jack or Beemans Pepsin gum and a 2¢ stamp to American Chicle Company, Metropolitan Tower, New York, City." P. Coghlan collection, Harry Sykora photographer. $45.00.

Adorn Hair Spray, a product of Gillette Company. Cloth **Martha** and **George Washington** dolls were offered by the

Gillette Company to commemorate the nation's bicentennial. Proof-of-purchase from their products was needed. (See Gillette)

Aim Toothpaste, a product of Lever Brothers Company. Five Loony Tune cartoon characters were offered with a December 1974 expiration date. **Tweety Bird, Bugs Bunny, Road Runner, Wile E. Coyote,** and **Sylvester** were available for $1 each. The figures are vinyl, 4 to 6-inches high, and have moveable heads, legs, arms, and tails.

In 1976 Aim Toothpaste offered one of the best buys ever in advertising dolls. It was an 8-inch **Smokey Bear** doll manufactured by R. Dakin and Company and sold for only $1.00. The fur and other features are carefully molded into the vinyl. **Smokey** wears denim jeans, a yellow hat, and carries a shovel. The well-made clothing is detailed down to **Smokey's** name on the tiny belt buckle.

In 1976 Americans were thinking about Smokey. The 27-year old bear was very ill and died in November of that year. A new Smokey had been selected the year before to replace the original ailing Smokey, but in the hearts of many there could only be one real Smokey Bear. That was the cub found in June 1950 clinging to a charred tree in New Mexico after a forest fire. His burned paws were treated, but he limped for the rest of his life. Little Smokey was brought to Washington, D.C. where he became known to Americans as the living representative of the Forest Service. Smokey brought in thousands of dollars in residuals from the Smokey Bear items sold. Smokey is the only animal in the country with its own zip number, 20252. A usual week brings 13,000 letters.

Loony Tune cartoon characters were offered by Aim Toothpaste in 1974. The 4 to 6 inch tall characters photographed are: *Wily E.* *Coyote, Sylvester the Cat,* and *Roadrunner.* J. Ciolek collection, Visual Images photographer. $2.00.

Magazine ads and these point-of-sale coupons were the only forms of advertising used by Aim for their *Smokey Bear* promotion.

Special Aim offer!

Aim Toothpaste offered a *Smokey Bear* doll until March of 1976, the 8-inch hard vinyl doll wears denim pants with a tiny belt, a hard hat, and carries a shovel. Marks: "Smokey", on hat, belt buckle, and shovel; shovel is also marked "Prevent/Forest/Fires"; "Smokey Bear", plus other information is on a cloth label on pants: "R. Dakin & Co./Authorized User/San Francisco/Product of Hong Kong", is printed on bottom of feet. K. Lyons collection. $4.00.

Official Smokey Bear Doll for $1.00 —plus *one* net-weight statement from *one* Aim® carton, any size.

Smokey's made of sturdy, *nontoxic* vinyl, except for his pants which are denim-like cloth. He's 8 inches tall. Both head *and* arms move.

Several magazines carried a small ad for the *Smokey Bear* doll.

A close-up photo of the *Tweety Bird* character given by Aim Toothpaste.

Air-India.

Air-India used this small 4½-inch doll wearing a turban to advertise their airline. J. Ciolek collection, Visual Images photographer. $5.00.

Alaska-Yukon-Pacific Exposition.

In 1909 an exposition was held on the campus of the University of Washington in Seattle, Washington. Seven permanent buildings were constructed to use later as student classrooms. The exposition was designed to acquaint the rest of the country with the resources and potential of the Pacific Northwest and the commerce possibilities of the countries in the Pacific Ocean.

The Alaska, Yukon, Pacific Exposition sold a 5-inch souvenir doll in 1909. Marks: on tag says, "STORK & COMPANY/IMPORTERS OF INFANTS"; other side says "WELL BEHAVED INFANTS FURNISHED/CITY OR COUNTRY/OUR CHILDREN ARE GUARANTEED/To go to bed when sent/Can also be used as a pin cushion./Any infant not satisfactory can be returned at our expense. /This will be found a great convenience to mothers;" stamped on the front of the doll, "THE NEW MAIL BABY. /Pat. Applied for/Art Fabric Mills, N.Y.; a second tag reads, "Souvenir of/Alaska, Yukon, Pacific/Exposition/Seattle, 1909. Courtesy of Ralph's Antique Dolls. $50.00.

Because so many fairs were opened before they were fully prepared, this one vowed to be ready, and emphasized it with the slogan, "The Fair that Will Be Ready."

An adorable cloth baby doll was mailed and also sold to advertise the exposition. The 5-inch doll was made like a sack of tobacco with a drawstring at the top. The printed face resembles a photograph of a cunning child. It is well marked.

Alberto VO5. This company in 1965 offered the 8-inch International Dolls.

Alka Seltzer, a product of Miles Laboratories, Inc. This remedy for indigestion has used a series of extraordinary successful commercials. Long before the lilting jingle: "Plop, plop, fizz, fizz, oh what a relief it is," and before, "I ate the whole thing," there was a little fellow called **Speedy** doing commercials.

The "Speedy" doll is copied from the trademark figure. It is a 7½-inch one-piece vinyl boy holding a large Alka Seltzer tablet. It is presumed the doll was used in the late 1950's or 60's because that is when **Speedy** was seen in Alka Seltzer advertising.

A **Speedy** bank was also offered at this time. It is a 5½-inch pliable figure with an Alka Seltzer tablet hat with a slot for money. **Speedy** wears a molded/painted blue shirt with another tablet held in front. These were available in limited areas.

Allied Van Lines. In the 1970's this moving company used a 17-inch cloth doll that represented a girl about eight years old. The doll's arms and legs are cut free from the body. She wears a lithographed orange jumper over a long-sleeved blouse. The hair is brown and a few freckles are sprinkled across the cheeks.

Speedy, a 5½-inch vinyl bank, was offered by Alka Seltzer. They also offered a Speedy doll. The suit is blue, hair red, and the tablets are white. Marks: both tablets have raised letters spelling "ALKA SELTZER; "SPEEDY" is across the front of the tablet hat. A. Pfister collection. $7.50.

Allied Van Lines offered this 17-inch cloth doll. Marks: "Allied Van Lines", under the company logo on the front of the jumper. K. Miller collection. $6.00.

Amana Woolen Mills. This company used one of the ordinary 7-inch plastic dolls for a promotion. The doll wears a black outfit copied from the clothing worn by Amish women. Date unknown.

American Airlines. In 1967 a 12-inch plastic doll much like the Barbie doll could be ordered for $4.00 from the American Airlines catalog. The doll is dressed as a stewardess in uniform and a pillbox hat. It is the same doll as Mary Make Up. $8.00.

A 12-inch *American Airline Stewardess* doll, manufactured by American Character, could be ordered from the airline catalog in 1967. The doll has a blonde wig, pale pink lips, blue eyes with no lashes, and light brown eye shadow. Her uniform is a two-piece suit with double-breasted buttons and a pillbox hat. L Yagatich collection, Donald G. Vilsack photographer. $2.00.

American Beauty Macaroni Company. According to recollections of a company official a cloth doll named **Roni Mac** was offered about 1937. The 11-inch doll was printed on a flat sheet of cloth, to be cut, sewn, and stuffed by the owner. The doll is unique, the head is cylinder shaped with side-glance eyes, a wide smile and no ears. A strap worn around the neck holds a stack of books and a ruler. A bow tie and shirt are the only clothes, of course all detail is lithographed.

Roni Mac was a mail-in premium advertised on packages of American Beauty Macaroni for 25¢ plus the box top.

The 11-inch cloth *Roni Mac* doll was a premium of the American Macaroni Company in 1937. Marks: "American Beauty/Roni Mac" on top of head. J. Varsalona collection. $25.00.

American Federal Savings and Loan Company of Tacoma, Washington. A cloth **Uncle Sam** doll was an advertising promotion of this company during the bicentennial. The doll is 14-inches high, clothing is lithographed in the traditional red, white, and blue.

A 14-inch bicentennial *Uncle Sam* doll was a promotion for American Federal Savings and Loan. Marks: "American Federal Savings and Loan. J. Ciolek collection, Visual Images photograper. $6.00.

American Rice Food and Manufacturing Company.

To my knowledge this New Jersey cereal company is no longer in existence. Apparently it was a thriving business in 1901 because several magazine ads from the Ladies Home Journal have been found for the company's two products: Cook's Flaked Rice and Cook's Malto Rice.

Several cloth premiums were offered near the turn of the century by this company. According to an old coupon, with the purchase of

Flaked Rice and Malto Rice, a free teddy bear was available. The 15-piece cloth bear was printed on a flat sheet and rather complicated to assemble, but resulted in a three-dimensional bear. Fur features of the bear were printed on shades of brown. A cloth collar said, **Cook's Teddy Bear**. It was patented in 1907 by Oliver C. Grinnell, Jr. of New York.

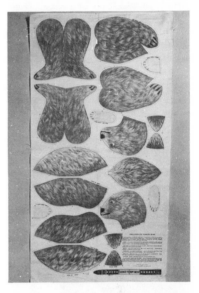

Cook's Teddy Bear required more sewing than the usual cloth premium, but it resulted in a three-dimensional bear when finished. The fur was printed in shades of brown. Marks: "COOK'S TEDDY BEAR", on collar. Playthings by the Yard, 1973. $45.00.

Ads describe two cloth **Miss Flaked Rice** dolls, sizes 21-inch and 25-inch. The smaller was copyrighted in 1899 by the American Rice Foods Manufacturing Company. It has black hair, a photographic type face and wears a gray chemise. The doll is marked across the front of the chemise.

The 25-inch doll is similar, except the chemise is white and it has no writing. The face looks sketched with water color details. To

27

quote the 1901 magazine ad for this doll: One will be mailed (doll) to any address upon receipt of the coupon contained in every box of COOK'S FLAKED RICE and 10¢ to cover expenses of mailing etc. Address Cook's Flaked Rice Co. Union Square, New York City." (We did not find this doll.)

We did find a 27-inch **Miss Flaked Rice**. It has the lithographed look of today's dolls. the construction of the doll is more elaborate than the other two **Miss Flaked Rice** dolls. It has seams at the neck, crotch, and shoulders to give it a more three-dimensional look.

Similar to the **Miss Flaked Rice** dolls is an 18-inch **Miss Malto Rice**. It is cloth and probably about the same date. **Miss Malto Rice** also wears a chemise with her name printed across the front.

This old *Miss Flaked Rice* is larger, 27-inches tall and is printed with a different process than the previous doll. It looks like today's lithographed dolls. The construction of the doll has several seams to give the body contours. Courtesy of Collector's House. $25.00-50.00.

Miss Flaked Rice was copyrighted in 1899 by the American Rice Food Manufacturing Company to promote their Flaked Rice cereal. The 21-inch doll is showing her age. The face is done with a photographic process and is in better condition than the body. Marks: "My name is/Miss Flaked Rice", across her gray chemise. K. Miller collection. $40.00.

The 20-inch *Miss Malto-Rice* doll was a premium of the American Rice Food & Manufacturing Company near the turn of the century. She wears button shoes and lace trimmed chemise. Marks: "My name is/Miss Malto-Rice". M. Rice Collection. $25.00-50.00.

For those curious about this old cereal, the ad says it can be prepared on the table in less than a minute, "Absolutely no cooking. It is not a new food, simply the very best Rice, sterilized and steam cooked."

Anahist. This allergy remedy is no longer on the market, but will be remembered for its 12-inch **Hello Dolly** doll. The doll was dressed in a reproduction of the stage costume worn by Carol Channing in the broadway play "Hello Dolly." An extra gown was included for the price of $1.95 plus an Anahist box top. The offer expired in January, 1966.

Arbuckle Brothers (later Yuban). This old brand of coffee, which is no longer found on grocery shelves under that name, would likely sink into oblivion if it weren't for collectors who seek their premiums. Besides interesting trading cards, Arbuckle Coffee enclosed cards advertising their cloth doll premiums.

In 1931 four 14½-inch dolls, characters from nursery rhymes, were offered. The dolls came in sets of two, **Mary** and her lamb with **Tom** the Piper's son, and **Jack** of course was paired with **Jill**. The dolls are printed on sheets of cotton fabric, to be completed by the owner. The dolls have particularly sweet faces and the colors are clear and varied.

An interesting explanation of how Arbuckle Coffee changed names was reported by a former employee. On green coffee shipments of bags containing the beans for Arbuckle's special blend were marked: $^{AB}_{NY}$ for Arbuckle Brothers, New York. When a brand name was to be chosen an effort was made to form a word out of the letters on the bags. Abny, Naby, and Bany has no appeal, Yban was no better, until someone

suggested adding the letter "u" making the sound Yuban, which we see on grocery shelves today.

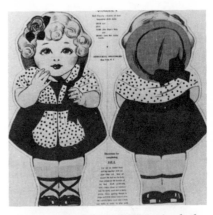

Jill is one of four 14½-inch cloth dolls offered by Arbuckle Coffee in 1931. Marks: "Jill", on back of waist; background fabric identifies the doll as a premium of this old chicory-flavored coffee. P. Coghlan collection, Harry Sykora photographer. $40.00.

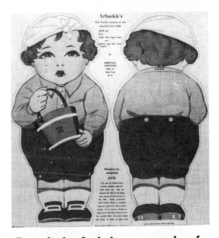

Poor little *Jack* has a couple of tears caused by a "broken crown" that is bandaged in "vinegar and brown paper." Marks: "Jack", on back of collar; "Jack/and/Jill", on bucket; other information on the background fabric. J. Varsalona collection. $40.00.

Mary and Her Little Lamb was a companion doll to *Tom the Piper's Son*. The 14½-inch doll has been cut from the sheet of fabric, sewn, and stuffed. J. Varsalona collection. $35.00.

Archie Comics. An 18-inch cloth **Archie** doll was advertised inside Archie Comic books during the early 1970's for $2.25 plus the coupon. Archie is a teenage character who has been popular for about 40 years. He remains the same age, about sixteen or seventeen, but he has changed with the times in order to remain interesting to the ever changing "new generations."

Archie and his friends were manufactured in 1976 and sold in retail stores, but these dolls are not included in this book because they are not advertising dolls.

Archie Comic books included this ad for a cloth *Archie* doll. K. Miller collection.

The 18-inch *Archie* doll was available through Archie Comic books in the early 1970's. K. Miller collection. $8.00.

Arco. See Atlantic Richfield.

Arctic Circle Drive-In Restaurant. The trademark of this fast food franchise is the **Acey** bird, which has been used for at least two promotions, once as a cloth doll and once as a bank. **Acey** is the Hop-a-long Cassidy of birds, complete with cowboy hat, holster and chaps.

The cloth bird is 15-inches tall with a large red felt rooster tail.

The **Acey** bank, 6-inches, is made of a hard substance, either plastic or plaster of paris, and wears the same cowboy outfit which is molded/painted.

Arctic Circle Drive-In Restaurants use *Acey* a cowboy rooster, for their trademark figure. We found a 15-inch cloth doll and a 6-inch bank of *Acey*. Both wear brown and tan cowboy attire with red accessories. J. Ciolek collection, photographed by Visual Images. $6.00 cloth.

Argo Corn Starch, a product of Corn Products Refining Company. For many years this company has used the trademark of an Indian girl with an ear of corn body. Her long-sleeved gown resembled the green husk, and opens to reveal yellow kernels of corn. She wears a red ribbon and two feathers in her long black hair. The trademark was used for Argo Starch, Mazola, Karo Syrup and perhaps other products.

In 1919 the American Ocarina and Toy Company manufactured an **Indian Princess** doll to represent this trademark. The 10-inch doll is very similar, but looks younger and pudgier. Features are handpainted in subdued shades. See also Corn Products Refining Company.

Arkadelphia Milling Company of Memphis, Tennessee. At least four **Dolly Dimple** dolls, 11, 17, 18, and 20-inches tall, were stamped on cambric sacks filled with flour from this old milling company.

The 17-inch *Dolly Dimple* doll is from the Arkadelphia Milling Company. As with many of the old cloth dolls, *Dolly* wears the stains of much loving and age. Marks: "DOLLY/DIMPLE", in very large letters across front of untrimmed chemise. M. Rice collection. $30.00-45.00.

31

After the sack was empty the doll could be washed, cut, sewn, and filled. The dolls were stamped in few colors, usually only three, and they were often rather faded. Each doll wore lithographed underwear. They were probably printed at different times because each varies slightly from the other.

One of Armour & Company's 8-inch plastic International Dolls, this one represents England. The doll wears a blue rayon dress with small cape and a gold braid crown. Many companies use this type premium doll. Unmarked. A. Leabo collection. $2.25.

The Arkadelphia Milling Company printed this 18-inch *Dolly Dimple* doll on their sacks of flour. She is flesh color with dark red hair and blue eyes. Her underwear is white with blue trim. Marks: "DOLLY/ DIMPLE/Highest Patent Flour", across front; "D", on the locket worn around the neck. Courtesy Ralph's Antique Dolls. $40.00.

Armour and Company.

This meat packing company has offered 30 International Dolls made of hard plastic continuously since 1972. At that time the dolls cost 99¢. The price has increased by steps. It is $2.00 at present. The dolls are 8-inches tall, have synthetic wigs, open/shut eyes, and moveable arms. Each one is dressed in a colorful native costume.

This same type doll has been offered by the product lines of many other companies. The costumes vary to fit the ad; some depict American Heritage, others story book characters.

Arthur Murray Dancing School.

This nationwide dancing school received publicity from an Arthur Murray Dancing Doll sold through Sears in 1952. The 14-inch plastic doll with open/shut eyes, saran wig, and dancing costume could be attached to a revolving music platform.

Atlantic Richfield.

Dolls of the World were sold for 99¢ with the purchase of gasoline from Atlantic Richfield service stations in 1971. The dolls were the usual 8-inch plastic type, but these had mohair wigs. Since that promotion the company has been reorganized and uses the name Arco. These are the same dolls offered by Armour.

Atlas Van Lines. This long distance moving company began the advertising promotion of **Atlas Annie**, a prestuffed cloth doll, in 1977. According to the company, "The idea was conceived because of a recognized need for assistance to children facing the unknown and often frightening aspects of moving." Hopefully by giving a child a new doll or a toy moving van the trauma of moving would be diminished.

Atlas Van Lines created their 15½-inch *Atlas Annie* doll for children who were going to move, but she has found her way to the shelves of many advertising doll collectors. Marks: "Atlas Annie", on cap: a trademark on pocket; and a tag with, "Hi! i'm Atlas Annie i'm here to make moving fun, with my special friend _____." $5.00.

Ads were placed in the March and April 1977 issues of Family Circle. Upon receipt of the coupon from the ad and $3.00 an **Atlas Annie** would be mailed. The nearest agent would receive a card with the name of a prospective mover. Agents probably soon learned that not only did lonely little girls, who were moving, order **Atlas Annie** but also adults who collect advertising dolls, with no intention of moving.

A toy box, which contains the Atlas Annie Coloring Book and some special decals is offered by the agent if the family moves with Atlas Van Lines. A miniature Atlas Van was also available for boys for $3.00.

Atlas Annie has the features of a young woman; red hair, full lips, and large eyes. The 15½-inch doll wears a lithographed two-toned blue pantsuit. Two letters come with "Annie", one for the child and one for the parents.

Aunt Jemima Pancake Flour. Aunt Jemima's dolls are as desirable to avid doll collectors as her pancakes are to fussy eaters. Nothing is quite like them-- dolls or pancakes--each has that special something. The flour and the dolls have had a long and varied history. First they were products of Aunt Jemima Manufacturing Company, the R.T. Davis Milling Company, next Aunt Jemima Mills Company, all of St. Joseph, Missouri. In 1925 they were sold to their present company, Quaker Oats Company of Chicago.

Aunt Jemima Pancake Flour's history began back in the late 1880's when newspaperman Chris Rutt and his partner Charles Underwood needed an exclusive and novel way to sell their flour. St. Joseph, Missouri, had long been one of the most important milling centers on the frontier. Once the western migration via wagon had slackened, the area was faced with an overproduction of flour.

What took lots of flour? Pancakes. What did almost everyone eat? Pancakes. What was difficult to mix with any consistency from batch to batch? Pancakes. Here was an opportunity for a new product, a pre-mixed pancake flour.

Batch after batch of experimental batter was griddled on an old kerosene stove in Rutt's home. Finally a recipe evolved that made light fluffy pancakes from hard wheat flour, corn flour, phosphate of lime, soda, and a bit of salt.

The first commercial batch of pancake flour was packaged in paper sacks. The Aunt Jemima name had not yet appeared. It was simply a self-rising pancake flour.

Mr. Rutt needed a trademark for his new product. While sitting at a minstrel show one evening he saw the trademark he wanted. The show stopper of the night was a jazzy cakewalk to a tune called "Aunt Jemima," which was performed by a character in an apron and a red bandanna in the tradition of the southern cook.

Here it was—southern hospitality personified. The next one-pound sacks had a wide-eyed grinning caricature of a black cook and the words "Aunt Jemima" stamped across the front. However, the novelty was not enough to insure success, and so Charles Underwood's brother Bert was brought into the company as financier and promoter. He registered the Aunt Jemima trademark and formed the Aunt Jemima Manufacturing Company. Unfortunately the company soon collapsed, but Rutt and the two Underwoods held on to their valuable recipe. Charles went to work for the largest flour miller in St. Joseph, the Davis Milling Company.

Possibly at Charles suggestion, R.T. Davis bought the recipe and the Aunt Jemima trademark. The R.T. Davis Milling Company is responsible for improving the mixture by adding rice flour and corn sugar; then it was simplified by adding powdered milk, so that the cook need only add water. Even a novice cook could successfully make the Aunt Jemima pancakes.

Davis was a master at fashioning publicity. He latched on to the idea of a gentle friendly Negro woman to sell his new Pancake mix. He told his food brokers to watch for such a woman, and that is how he found attractive 59-year-old Nancy Green, a magnificient cook, friendly, and gregarious in the extreme. It was as though Nancy Green was Aunt Jemima and Aunt Jemima was Nancy Green. She loved people and loved talking. For thirty years Davis made good use of her appeal: Nancy presided over pancake demonstrations at stores in cities around the country, and was the hit of the Chicago World's Fair in 1893.

The story of Aunt Jemima's befriending rebel troops by serving her pancakes, was part of the folklore narrated by Nancy Green and printed in a pamphlet entitled "The Life of Aunt Jemima, the Most Famous Colored Woman in the World." The pamphlet included many stories plus the factual material of her personal triumph at the fair.

The story of a soldier's returning to buy the recipe from the poor family and suddenly transforming them to riches was better known than the facts. The tale was nurtured by the company with a promotional cutout. A paper doll family showing Aunt Jemima Davis, her husband Rastus, and children Abraham Lincoln, Dilsie, Zeb, and little Dinah, all holding hands. The family is dressed in ragged clothing and all are barefoot. The caption says: "Before the Receipt was sold." An overlay of elegant clothing that fits over the old clothes has this caption: "After the Receipt was sold." Thus the rags to riches tale was encouraged.

Wherever Nancy Green went, her visit was announced by a billboard poster of Aunt Jemima with the slogan, "I'se in town, honey." As women witnessed the ease of cooking with the prepared

This uncut paper doll strip was a very early premium used by Aunt Jemima Pancake Flour. The characters: Aunt Jemima, Rastus, Abraham Lincoln, Dilsie, Zeb, and little Dinah are illustrated wearing ragged clothing and barefoot. Beside each paper doll is its name and the words: "Before the Receipt Was Sold." On the bottom of the strip each doll has an elaborate outfit of clothing that includes shoes, stockings, and fine accessories. Beside the fine clothes is the doll's name and the words, "After the Receipt Was Sold."

mix, the era of "convenience" foods began and sales of Aunt Jemima Flour rose.

In 1895 to popularize a new container, Davis printed a cutout paper doll of Aunt Jemima on it. The promotion was tremendously successful.

After R.T. Davis died in 1900, the company he had organized suffered many ups and downs. To pull itself out of financial chaos in 1905, the company issued an **Aunt Jemima** rag doll. In July and December 1908, four dolls were registered at the patent office. In 1910 magazine ads for "Funny Rag Dolls" were advertised for four Aunt Jemima Pancake flour coupons and 16¢. The same ad showed a climbing **Aunt Jemima** doll that could climb a string. (We were unable to find the climbing doll.)

The cloth doll family names were different from the paper doll family. **Aunt Jemima** was the same, but she was married to **Uncle Mose** now, not Rastus. Dinah became **Diana** and there were no dolls named Dilsie, Abraham Lioncoln, or Zeb. The only son was named **Wade**.

Two sets of **Aunt Jemima** dolls were found marked Davis Milling Company; therefore, they pre-date 1914 when the company changed names. One set appears older. The faces on this set are almost ugly. The mouths are abnormally wide with toothy grins. **Uncle Mose** is missing a front tooth. **Aunt Jemima** and **Uncle Mose** have their arms folded.

Wade has his hands in his pockets, and **Diana** has one hand up to her face and the other pulling a bit at her dress.

This set was cut out and assembled, thus eliminating the background fabric that often provides the cost, date, and other information. For identification purposes this group will be referred to as the ca. 1905 set.

The earliest *Aunt Jemima* cloth doll, ca. 1905, is 15-inches tall and wears a yellow dress with black dots under a red and white striped waist apron. The neckerchief is red with white dots; the head bandana is red with yellow O's. She has a wide, wide smile with upper and lower teeth showing. Marks: "Aunt Jemima's Pancake Flour Pickaninny Dolls/Davis Milling Company/St. Joseph, Mo.," in lower corner of apron. Courtesy Ralph's Antique Dolls. $50.00-75.00.

The other pre-1914 set marked Davis Milling Company is a noticable improvement. The faces are more kindly looking, almost photographic in appearance. The dolls have realistic proportioned mouths and limbs.

These dolls are uncut, so provide the cost as printed on the background fabric: "4¢ in stamps and one Aunt Jemima coupon. We want every child to have one of these Aunt Jemima Pancake Flour Pickaninny Dolls. Aunt Jemima's Pancake Flour is composed of the three great staffs of life--wheat, corn, and rice." The dolls could be purchased separately or as a set for 16¢. This set will be referred to as the ca. 1910 set.

Uncle Mose, ca. 1905, 15-inches tall, is dressed in brown and black pants, red and white striped shirt with a pipe in the pocket. His wide smile shows a missing front tooth, white brows and hair. The arms are folded. The doll holds a spoon in one hand. Marks: "Aunt Jemima's Pancake Flour Doll/Uncle Moses/The Davis Milling Co. St. Joseph, Mo.", on the front of shirt. Courtesy Ralph's Antique Dolls. $50.00-75.00.

In 1914 the company was renamed the Aunt Jemima Mills Company. This is a help in dating the cloth dolls because all of them are marked with the name of the milling company.

Wade, the son, is also part of the ca. 1905 set. The 12-inch cloth doll wears red and yellow checked pants and a white shirt with red circles. Marks: "Aunt Jemima's/Pancake Flour/Pickaninny Doll/Wade Davis/The Davis Milling Co./St. Joseph, Mo.," on front of shirt. S. Ricklefs collection. $35.00.

The 1910 *Aunt Jemima* is an improvement over the earlier doll. It is also 15-inches tall and wears apron, red neckerchief (this one tucked into the front of the dress), and a red bandana with yellow O's. The arms are to the side and cut free from the body. Marks: "Aunt Jemima's Pickaninny Dolls/The Davis Milling Co./St. Joseph, Mo.," in lower corner of apron. Courtesy Ralph's Antique Dolls. $50.00-75.00.

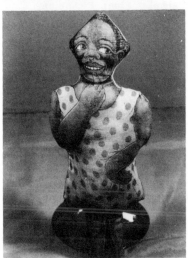

Diana, the daughter is ca. 1905 too. The 12-inch doll wears a yellow dress with red dots. One hand is pointing to her mouth, the hair is three tufts, making the head triangular. Notice the heavy arms. Marks: "Diana". S. Ricklefs collection. $35.00.

Wade, ca. 1910 is similar to the ca. 1905 *Wade* doll except for improved proportions and facial expression. The doll is 12-inches tall. Marks: "Aunt Jemima's Pancake Flour/Pickaninny Doll/Wade Davis/The Davis Milling Co./St. Joseph, Mo.," on shirt front. S. Ricklefs collection. $35.00.

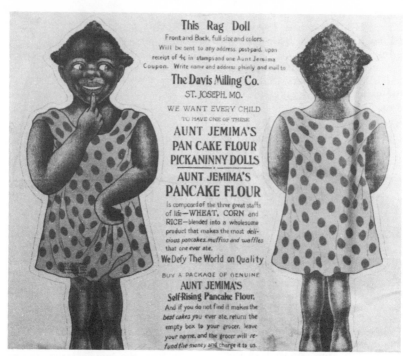

Diana, ca. 1910, is almost identical to the ca. 1905 *Diana* doll on first glance, but the arms are thinner and the facial expression is less ex- aggerated. Marks: Aunt Jemima's/ Pancake Flour Pickaninny Doll/ Davis Milling Co./St. Joseph, Mo.," $35.00.

During World War I the recipe had to be modified to comply with government restrictions on wheat flour, and the sales fell alarmingly. After the war, when the product had been restored to its traditional quality, customers were badly needed. A series of magazine advertisements from the mind and pen of James Webb Young spun new tales of Aunt Jemima lore. Young's advertisments, illustrated by N.C. Wyeth, have become popular collector's items today. The novel advertising proved suc- cessful, and sales for Aunt Jemima Pancake Flour soared for a short time.

In the early 1920's Grinnell Lithographic Company hired a commercial artist to redesign the four **Aunt Jemima** dolls. The new series was advertised in 1925 Ladies Home Journal: "If you want the jolly family of four rag dolls--**Aunt Jemima** and **Uncle Mose** (each 15-inches tall), little **Wade** and **Diana**--printed in bright colors, ready to cut out and stuff-send 25¢ in stamps or coin." (13-inches tall).

The sponsor was bombarded with requests, many of the writers saying they had owned one of the earlier **Aunt Jemima** dolls and now they wanted their children to have one of the new ones.

The 1924 dolls depict a hand- some family. **Uncle Mose** has grown a white fringe beard, wears a tie, but has a patch on his pants. He has unfolded his arms, one is in his pocket, the other holds a pipe.

It might be noted here, another **Uncle Mose** doll was found with the Aunt Jemima Mills Company mark. It was probably printed after 1914, but before 1924. This **Mose** has a white beard, folded arms, and closed lips.

The 1924 **Aunt Jemima** looks much like the others. She wears the same yellow dress with black dots, red and white striped apron, and she has folded arms.

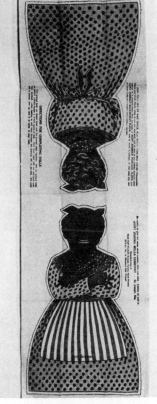

In 1924 the *Aunt Jemima* rag dolls were redesigned and printed by Grinnell Lithograph Company. The dolls in this series are marked "Aunt Jemima Mills Company" rather than Davis Milling Company; the company changed names in 1914. "Aunt Jemima," 15-inches tall, wears her usual attire, her arms are folded, and her smile shows upper and lower teeth. The uncut fabric includes front and back view. Marks: "Aunt Jemima," centered on lower edge of apron. Playthings by the Yard, 1973. $25.00-45.00.

Another 15-inch *Aunt Jemima* doll from the Aunt Jemima Mills Company wears the same clothing as the others, has arms folded, but her slight smile shows only upper teeth. Marks: "Aunt Jemima" centered on lower edge of apron. Courtesy Ralph's Antique Dolls. $25.00-45.00.

Three **Wade** dolls were found marked Aunt Jemima Mills Company, they will be referred to as 1924 dolls. One is dressed much like the earlier Wade dolls, except the legs of this doll are separated, and the face is more pleasant. The second **Wade** doll holds a straw hat in front of his body and wears a shirt with a window-pane design. The third Wade doll is almost identical to the second one, except the shirt is a diamond print and the hand that holds the hat is totally hidden behind the hat.

Two **Diana** dolls were found marked Aunt Jemima Mills Company. One wears a blue flowered dress and holds a kitten, the other **Diana** holds a little black doll.

This larger, 17-inch, *Aunt Jemima* doll is similar to the other ca. 1924 dolls, except for the wrinkled face, which is especially apparent on the actual doll. Marks: "Aunt Jemima Mills." L. Maxfield collection. $25.00-45.00.

Three *Uncle Mose* dolls were found that are marked "Aunt Jemima Mills Company." This *Mose* doll 15-inches tall, and has unfolded arms. One hand is in his pocket, and the other holds a pipe with smoke curling out the top. He wears blue patched pants, straw hat, red shirt, yellow suspenders, and a yellow tie with blue dots. The kindly face looks ready to speak. Marks: "Uncle Mose/Aunt Jemima's Husband," on back of shirt. $25.00-45.00.

This *Uncle Mose* doll was printed before 1924, when the dolls were redesigned by Grinnell Lithographers. "Mose" wears a red shirt with a pipe in the pocket and yellow suspenders hold up the brownish black pants. Marks: "Uncle Mose," on back. S. Ricklefs collection. $25.00-45.00.

This third set, known as the redesigned issue, was patented October 1923 for **Mose, Diana,** and **Wade**; April 1924 for **Aunt Jemima**. The slight variations between dolls are due to reprinting and were unimportant to the company, but of interest to the careful advertising doll collector.

An **Aunt Jemima** and **Uncle Mose** were found marked: "Aunt Jemima Mills Co." that are larger than the ones advertised in 1924 magazines. This pair is 17-inches tall and is slightly different from any of the other dolls. **Aunt Jemima** has a wrinkled face, otherwise she is similar to the others of this period, yellow dress with black dots, red and white stripe apron, and arms folded.

Uncle Mose has a gray felt hat, red shirt with white circles, and a pipe in the pocket.

A 17-inch *Uncle Mose* marked "Aunt Jemima Mills Company". This *Mose* has put his pipe back in his pocket and holds his left suspender. He wears a polka dot shirt and patched trousers. L. Maxfield collection. $25.00-45.00.

The second *Wade* doll marked from Aunt Jemima Mills Company is noticably different from previous *Wade* dolls and probably is part of the redesigned set sold in 1924. Ralph's Antique Dolls. $25.00-35.00.

Three *Wade* dolls were found that are marked "Aunt Jemima Milling Company". One is dressed like the earlier *Wade* dolls and he also keeps his hands in his pockets. The major difference in the doll is it stands with legs apart. Marks: "Wade Davis," on back of shirt. Playthings by the Yard, 1973. $25.00-35.00.

The third *Wade* doll marked "Aunt Jemima Mills Company" is almost exactly like the first, except one hand has a finger pointing and the shirt has a window-pane print. L. Maxfield collection. $25.00-35.00.

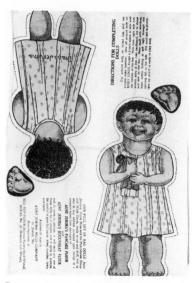

Diana wears a polka dot dress with Marks: "Diana Jemima", on the back of the dress (other Jemima rag dolls have used the surname Davis); the background fabric identifies this as an Aunt Jemima Mills Company doll. **Playthings by the Yard, 1973. $25.00-35.00.**

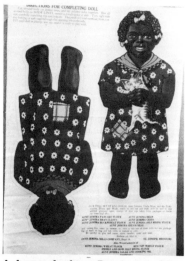

A happy looking *Diana* is holding a kitten. This is the doll pictured with a daisy print and a few patches. Marks: "Diana/Aunt Jemima's /Little Girl," on back of dress. Courtesy Ralph's Antique Dolls. $25.00-35.00.

Financial troubles hit again in 1925, and by 1926 the company was sold to Quaker Oats Company. Quaker was able to more thoroughly distribute Aunt Jemima products to stores across the country and soon business exceeded the best years of the Aunt Jemima Mills Company.

Then came the depression, the company sought a way to revive the public's interest in pancakes. Remembering the success of Aunt Jemima's Nancy Green at the Chicago World's Fair, the advertising planners decided to find a new living Aunt Jemima who could circulate among the people and to the places which were making the news of the day. Beloved Nancy Green had been killed by a car in 1923 when 89-years old, so the company had been without a living Aunt Jemima for seven years.

The search was on. Black women from Chicago needing a job with good pay swamped the company's employment department. According to the company, "One stood out among all the rest. She was a massive woman with the face of an angel. Her name was Anna Robinson." For 21 years she promoted Aunt Jemima products. Her magnetic smile gleams from packages of Aunt Jemima Pancake Flour today. She died in 1951 after many years of service as the personification of Aunt Jemima.

In 1929 Quaker Oats offered a fourth set of **Aunt Jemima** dolls. These dolls were made to represent a more affluent family, "after the receipt was sold." **Mose** is a southern dandy with top hat, bowtie and cane. **Aunt Jemima**, for the first time, wears a white apron, not the usual red and white striped one of all the previous sets.

The 1929 **Wade** doll wears striped trousers and a polka dot bow tie. A rather pudgy **Diana** all decked out in a dotted dress with sash and scalloped collar is much different from the 1905 Diana.

In addition to **Aunt Jemima** dolls the Quaker Oats Company offered plastic Aunt Jemima kitchen accessories. The company says, "Latter-day promotions (ca. 1945) have distributed four million sets of Aunt Jemima/Uncle Mose salt and pepper shakers in polystrene, 150,000 cookie-jar premiums shaped like Aunt Jemima, and one-million housewives bought a plastic syrup pitcher." There was also a spice set and more than one size salt and pepper shaker. These items are often found at flea markets and antique shops.

Uncle Mose is a dandy in his top hat, bow tie, long jacket, and watch chain. The new affluent looking set came out in 1929. Marks: "Uncle Mose", on white rim of collar showing above jacket in back. S. Ricklefs collection. $25.00-45.00.

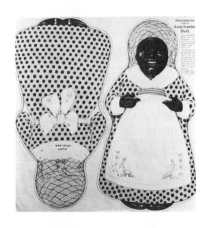

An entirely new looking set of Aunt Jemima rag dolls came out in 1929. From the looks of their clothing, it was after the "Receipt" was sold. *Aunt Jemima* is dressed similar to the earlier cloth "Aunt Jemima" dolls, but the other members of her family are considerably better attired. *Jemima* holds a plate of pancakes in front of her new waist apron. Instead of the old red and white striped apron, this one is white with rabbits in the corners. Uncut fabric shows the front and back. Background fabric is marked from Quaker Oats Company--it was renamed this in 1922. Marks: "Aunt Jemima", on back of collar. S. Ricklefs collection. $25.00-45.00.

Wade doll from the 1929 set. K. Miller collection. $20.00-30.00.

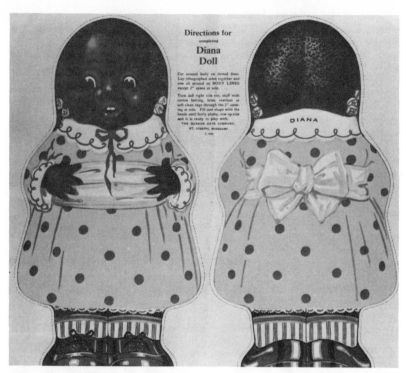

Directions for
completing
Diana
Doll

Cut around body on dotted lines.
Lay lithographed sides together and
sew all around on BODY LINES
except 2" space at side.

Turn doll right side out, stuff with
cotton batting, bran, sawdust or
soft clean rags through the 2" opening at side. Fill and shape with the
hands until fairly plump, sew up side
and it is ready to play with.

THE QUAKER OATS COMPANY,
ST. JOSEPH, MISSOURI
© 1929

DIANA

The most dramatic change in the dolls occurs with *Diana*. The 1929 doll is totally unlike the predecessors; compare it to the ca. 1905 *Diana*. For the first time *Diana* wears shoes and stockings. Her dotted dress has a scalloped collar and cuffs, and a sash spans her pudgy middle. Her hair is worn in braids tied with flowers. She has a startled expression. Marks: "Diana", on back of collar. S. Ricklefs collection. $20.00-30.00.

For almost 20 years Aunt Jemima offered no dolls. In 1950 a totally different set were offered. These were made of an oilcloth-like plastic with bonded seams. The faces were similar to a scarecrow's with printing that looked like stitched on facial features, for instance **Aunt Jemima's** nose is a triangle of checked print.

The dolls were mailed flat, to be stuffed and sewn across the bottom by the owner. A set of four cost $5.00 probably plus some labels from Aunt Jemima Pancake Flour.

Neither the 1929 nor the 1950 sets are listed on the patent records.

The prices asked for the four cloth sets of **Aunt Jemima** dolls do not seem to vary greatly even though in time they span from 1905 to 1929. A collector is willing to pay the same price for the scarce dressed up set as the more plentiful earlier issues. The oilcloth type set brings considerably less. During the past two years these have sold for $25.00 per set in mint condition and less on occasion. A problem with this set is the seams, the bonding tends to split and they have to be hand stitched together.

Today's collectors pay premium prices for the cloth **Aunt Jemima** dolls. A set in good condition, 1924 vintage, sold for

$150.00 in California recently. Single dolls sell from $25.00 to $50.00, usually more for the **Aunt Jemima** and **Mose** in mint condition.

in 1925. There were undoubtedly many other dolls named Aunt Jemima.

The 12-inch *Uncle Mose* in the 1950 set is dressed in a yellow jacket, striped blue and white pants, and holds a top hat. S. Russell collection. $7.50.

The 1950's set of Aunt Jemima dolls is made of a plastic oilcloth-like material with bonded seams. The faces bear no resemblance to the previous cloth dolls--more like a scarecrow face with stitched on features. *Aunt Jemima* wears a checked dress and white apron with cross-stiched letters spelling "Aunt Jemima" across the bottom. The 12-inch doll holds a plate of pancakes. J. Varsalona collection. $7.50.

In addition to the five sets of Aunt Jemima dolls offered as premiums by the company, Aunt Jemima dolls were manufactured by toy companies to sell in retail stores and catalogs. Sears listed a composition **Aunt Jemima** doll with cloth body in their 1931 catalog. In 1940 Effanbee made one, and the Toy Shop of New York City made an **Aunt Jemima** and a pickaninny baby

Wade from the 1950 set of dolls is 9-inches tall and wears a red and white striped shirt, blue patched pants, and carries a yellow lollipop. $7.50.

Diana **from the 1950 set, 9-inches tall, wears a patched polka-dot dress with three ribbons in her hair. J. Varsalona collection. $7.50.**

In 1955 when the first Aunt Jemima Restaurant was opened in Disneyland a new living Aunt Jemima was selected. Aylene Lewis is the last Aunt Jemima used by the Quaker Oats Company.

Verifying dates and facts concerning the Aunt Jemima dolls is almost impossible because the Quaker Oats Company was unable to provide any information. The historical data used here is largely from the book Brands, Trademarks, and Goodwill by Arthur F. Marquette.

In the advertising field, Aunt Jemima represents the zenith of coordination between a trademark and a product. For over three-quarters of a century families have looked to Aunt Jemima for superb pancake flour and delightful dolls.

Chronology of Aunt Jemima Pancake Flour

1888 Chris Rutt and Charles Underwood, owners of Pearl Milling Company, St. Joseph, Missouri, developed a self-rising pancake flour.

1889 Selected name Aunt Jemima from a song by that title and used the trademark of a Negro woman.

1889 Rutt and Underwood organized the Aunt Jemima Manufacturing Co. with Charles' brother Bert, who registered the trademark.

1890 Business collapsed; sold trademark and recipe to R.T. Davis Milling Co., which improved the flavor and simplified the mix by adding powdered milk.

1893 Nancy Green chosen to represent Aunt Jemima; made her debut at the Chicago World's Fair.

1895 Paper doll cutout on new cartons.

1900 Owner R.T. Davis dies.

1905 First Aunt Jemima Rag Doll offered to customers.

1908 Family of four Aunt Jemima dolls - Aunt Jemima, Uncle Mose, Wade, and Diana -were patented in America.

1910 Ads for the dolls ran in women's magazines.

1914 Renamed the Aunt Jemima Mills Company.

1919 Beginning of series of James Webb Young ads illustrated by N.C. Wyeth.

1923 Nancy Green, 89, killed in car-pedestrian accident.

1923
to
1924 Aunt Jemima rag dolls redesigned and registered at patent office.

1923
to
1925 The Toy Shop of N.Y.C. manufactured Aunt Jemima dolls.

46

1925 Redesigned rag dolls advertised in Ladies Home Journal.

1926 Quaker Oats Company buys Aunt Jemima Mills Company.

1929 A new set of Aunt Jemima dolls are printed.

1930 Anna Robinson selected as new Jemima; her portrait becomes trademark on all Aunt Jemima products.

1945 Aunt Jemima doll family made of bonded plastic that resembles oil cloth; available through stores or mail-in.

1951 Anna Robinson dies.

1955 Aunt Jemima Kitchen Restaurant opens at Disneyland in California.

1957 Aunt Jemima at Disneyland is Aylene Lewis.

Aunt Sarah's Pancake House of Fredericksburg, Virginia. In 1973 this restaurant sold a cloth doll made to resemble Aunt Sarah. The 15-inch doll

A cloth *Aunt Sarah* doll was offered in 1973 by the Aunt Sarah's Pancake House. The doll is dressed in a black and white dress and a hat with yellow trim. Marks: "Aunt Sarah ® ", on front of apron. A. Wolfe collection, David Nelson and James Giokas photographers. $6.00.

wears eyeglasses. She holds a yellow bowl presumably filled with pancake mix in one hand, the other hangs to her side. Legs are cut free and the shoes turn out.

Automatic Gas Range Company. A cloth doll designed by Spence Wildery and printed on flat sheets of muslin were used to advertise the Automatic Gas Range Company. **Kookie** is a chubby chef doll complete with tall white hat, tie-around apron, and for some strange reason white gloves. Ca. 1960.

Harriet Hubbard Ayer.
In 1953, shortly before this line of cosmetics disappeared from the market, Ideal named a doll after the founder of the company. The **Harriet Hubbard Ayer** make-up doll had pale facial coloring; her new owner was to provide make-up from the assortment of cosmetics in the accompanying kit. The beauty aides were washable so could be reapplied with many effects.

The **Harriet Hubbard Ayer** doll is a modified reissue of Ideal's very successful **Toni** doll, manufactured a few years before. It came in the four **Toni** sizes: 14, 15, 18½, and 20½-inches and has a hard vinyl body and legs. Eyes open and close independently and it wears a glued on wig, in a variety of colors. The long-tapered fingernails are polished red.

It is interesting that Ideal chose to name their "Doll of Beauty", as it was called, after that particular line of cosmetics. In 1953 **Harriet Hubbard Ayer** cosmetics were definitely on the decline, few stores stocked their products. Perhaps the doll was named after Harriet Hubbard Ayer herself. She was certainly an unusual woman. In the late 1880's she began selling a product that became very successful, cold cream. When the new business became solvent and

The *Harriet Hubbard Ayer Make-up Doll* came with a vanity and a generous supply of cosmetics. The doll wears the original gray dress with matching panties sewn to the waistband and striped apron. Marks: "Made in U.S.A. by Ideal Toy Corporation, Hollis 23, N.Y." on vanity; "MK 14/IDEAL DOLL", on doll head; "IDEAL DOLL/P-90", on body. A. Wolfe collection, David Nelson and James Giokas photographers. $45.00.

destined to making a fortune, family members had Mrs. Ayer declared insane and she spent over a year in a mental institution. At her trial the plucky lady appeared to defend herself and the court was convinced she was able to manage her own company with no help from anyone. To vindicate her character, she toured the country to relate her experience of forceably being taken and held in a "madhouse."

By the time Ideal introduced the **Harriet Hubbard Ayer** doll, the company had no connection with the original Mrs. Ayer.

Azar Nut Company. In 1974 a 9-inch stuffed squirrel was offered by this Texas nut company. The squirrel, manufactured by Animal Fair bears little resemblance to the bright-eyed **Azar the Terrific** as seen on packages of nuts.

B

Babbitt Cleanser, (later called Bab-o) a product of B.T. Babbitt Co. In 1916, Modern Toy Company manufactured a doll representing the trademark figure used by Babbitt Cleanser. The **Babbitt Boy** doll, 15-inches, has molded/painted composition head, boots, and gauntlet hands. One arm is bent at the elbow to hold a miniature can of cleanser. The other is straight in a saluting position, just like the figure on the label. The body is cloth filled with excelsior.

The *Babbitt Cleanser Boy* doll, 15-inches, is a representation of the trademark figure used on cans of Babbitt Cleanser. The 1916 Composition and cloth doll wears original clothing, but is missing the hat. Small "B"s stamped with blue ink on the collar washed out when the jacket was washed for the first time for this photograph. The suit is white with a blue belt. Marks: "Babbitt's Cleanser", on button; doll carries a replica of the old Babbitt Cleanser can. $175.00.

He wears a two-piece white uniform with a blue belt and a button. The doll itself is unmarked, but having such distinctive features it can readily be identified.

Baby Magic baby products, products of the Mennen Company. In 1975 two large, 24-inch cloth doll kits were offered. The dolls, **Snuggly Sammy** and **Snuggly Suzie** were printed on a flat sheet of cloth, like premium dolls of the past. The dolls cost $1.00 plus 25¢ postage and a proof-of-purchase from Baby Magic lotion, oil, or bath lather.

The doll's lithographed mouth and eyebrows resemble pieces of rickrack. The predominant colors used are green and yellow.

The kits were manufactured by Chase Bag Company of Reidsville, North Carolina.

In 1975 *Snuggly Sammy*, a large 2-foot tall doll, was offered by Mennen's Baby Magic products. *Sammy* and a companion doll, *Snuggly Suzie* are lithographed primarily in yellow with touches of blue, green, orange, and flesh. Marks: "© 1975 The Mennen Co.," on back of one foot. S. Esser collection, Bruce Esser photographer. $8.00.

Snuggly Suzie. S. Esser collection, Bruce Esser photographer. $8.00.

Made to advertise the delicious Baby Ruth candy bar, this *Baby Ruth* doll was possibly sold in 1927 when the Curtiss Confectionery Company registered a patent for a doll. Marks: "BABY RUTH", on ribbon worn diagonally across body. K. Miller collection. $12.00.

Baby Ruth, a product of Curtiss Confectionery, a division of Standard Brands, Inc. This candy bar's name makes it a natural for an advertising doll, yet only three dolls and a listing for a patent were found.

The doll that appears the oldest is 14½-inches tall, cloth with features that look hand-painted. It has a 1920's look: small heart-shaped mouth, wide side-glance eyes, and wisps of hair in the wind-blown style showing below her cloche hat.

This doll may be the one whose patent was registered January 27, 1927, by Curtiss Candy Company of Chicago, Illinois. The listing only says, **Baby Ruth** for wax, china, celluloid, fabric, and stuffed.

The second "Baby Ruth" doll is similar, 16-inches tall, and made of orange flannel fabric, solid color for pants and hat, print for bodice and ruffle on the hat. The face and hands are knit fabric. Again the face appears hand-painted.

Baby Ruth doll is constructed of orange flannel fabric. Buttons and buckle are black oilcloth. Marks: "BABY RUTH", on ribbon worn diagonally across body. $12.00.

Hasbro's *Baby Ruth* doll was available for three months in 1973 as a premium. Later Hasbro placed the doll and three others, also named after candy products, on the retail market. Marks: "BABY RUTH" on heart in front; the box was also well-marked. K. Lyons collection. $8.00.

In 1973, for a three-month period, a **Baby Ruth** doll was advertised on the back of six-pack packages of Butterfinger and Baby Ruth candy bars. The doll was manufactured by Hasbro and is the bean bag type. The face mask and hands are plastic; body and limbs are a nylon tricot suit filled with styrofoam pellets that allow the doll to sit easily. Three tufts of rooted hair protrude from the sewn-on hood that forms the back of the doll's head.

As a premium, the doll was available for $3.50. Later when Hasbro placed them on the retail market, the price was $5.50. Only 2,500 premium dolls were redeemed.

Most people probably suppose the Baby Ruth candy bar was named for the home-run champ, Babe Ruth. Not so, the name honors a White House baby, the eldest daughter of President and Mrs. Grover Cleveland.

The Curtiss Candy Company selected the name after it was suggested by an employee in a naming contest. Prior to that time the nut roll candy bar had been named Kandy Kake.

The logo was copied from the engraved lettering of the name used on a medallion struck at the time of the Chicago World's Columbian Exposition in 1893. The medallion pictured the President, his wife and daughter Baby Ruth.

To familiarize the public with the Baby Ruth candy bar the company used many ingenious promotions. In Pittsburgh a plane was hired to drop candy bars suspended by tiny parachutes. A 26-plane aerial circus, a Scottish Kiltie Band, hockey and bowling teams and a six-pony team toured the country boosting the tasty nut roll candy bar that continues to be sold today.

Baggies Food Storage Bags. In 1974 an inflatable alligator was offered for $2.00 and

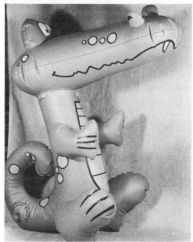

A green inflatable alligator was offered by Baggies storage bags. Marks: "©1975 Colgate-Palmolive Co.." $4.00.

the end flap from a package of Baggie plastic storage bags. The first offer expired January, 1975. The offer was extended to April 1976.

Baker's Chocolate, a product of Walter Baker and Company. Way back in 1780 Walter Baker purchased the first chocolate mill in America that had been built a few years earlier. From that start in Dorchester, Massachusetts the company expanded to become one of the leading makers of fine chocolate.

It was almost 100 years after its beginning that a trademark was selected. One of the world's loveliest trademarks is Baker's "La Belle Chocolatiere." From two of the many small recipe booklets Baker's offered come two slightly different stories about the story behind the trademark. The 1916 version states that Jean-Etienne Liotard painted the famous painting, "La Belle Chocolatiere," then goes on to say, "There is a romance connected with the charming Viennese girl who served as the model, which is well worth telling. One of the leading journals of Vienna has thrown some light on the Baltauf, or Baldauf, family to which the subject of Liotard's painting belonged. Anna, or Annerl, as she was called by friends and relatives, was the daughter of Melchior Baltauf, a knight, who was living in Vienna in 1760, when Liotard was in that city making portraits of some members of the Austrian Court. It is not clear whether Anna was earning her living as a Chocolate bearer at the time or whether she posed as a society belle in that becoming costume; but, be that as it may, her beauty won the love of a prince of the Empire, whose name, Dietrichstein, is known now only because he married the charming girl who was immortalized by a great artist. The

marriage caused a great deal of talk in Austrian society at the time, and many different stories have been told about it. The prejudices of caste have always been very strong in Vienna, and a daughter of a knight, even if well-to-do, was not considered a suitable match for a member of the court. It is said that on the wedding day Anna invited the chocolate bearers with whom she had worked or played, and in 'sportive Joy at her own elevation' offered her hand to them saying, 'Behold! now that I am a princess you may kiss my hand.' She was probably about 20 years of age when the portrait was painted in 1760, and she lived until 1825."

The 1932 account sounds a bit fictionalized, but makes a more interesting story. "Her (La Belle Chocolatiere) story is another delightful version of Cinderella and Prince Charming. He is Prince Dietrichstein, brilliant young Austrian nobleman. She is a waitress in a new Viennese chocolate shop--Babette Baldauf, daughter of an impoverished knight!

"One frosty afternoon in 1760, the dashing young hero demands his chaise to stop before this quaint chocolate shop, first of its kind in Vienna. He must discover for himself the merits of a rich new beverage--that romantic drink from the tropics which is the topic of conversation among all the young fashionables.

"He enters, seats himself at a table, orders "hot chocolate" and promptly discovers not only the glories of this mellow fragrant drink, but also the prettiest girl in all Vienna.

"Day after day, he returns for more chocolate and more demure glances. The bewildering enchantment grows and grows . . .until his daily cup of chocolate becomes the most important thing in his life. He completely forgets that a Prince may not look at a waitress . . .And the rest you've already guessed!

"As a betrothal gift, Duetrichstein engaged a talented artist, Jean Etienne Liotard, to paint his winsome beloved in the simple costume in which she first bewitched him. This portrait now hangs in the Dresden Museum . . .and its well-known replica graces every can of Walter Baker's Breakfast Cocoa."

Instead of using the common model poses, the imaginative artist choose to draw her serving chocolate. For more than 100 years the painting hung in the Dresden Gallery in Germany. In 1862 the president of Walter Baker's toured Europe and while visiting the gallery was captured by the painting, "La Belle Chocolatiere." He knew that it would make an appropriate and attractive trademark. In 1872 the chocolate girl made her debut for Walter Baker's Chocolate and has been used for over 100 years. Baker's Chocolate is a product of General Foods today.

It might be noted the painting was reproduced on a postage stamp by East Germany in 1963.

Many beautiful half-dolls representing "La Belle Chocolatiere" were manufactured near the turn of the century by unknown manufacturers. One we located is an exquisite china doll wearing a white cap with only a bit of hair showing at the forehead. Her graceful hands hold a china tray with a cup and saucer and a glass. The facial features are small and delicate. It measures about 7-inches from waist to head.

The Baker's girl was used for many small premium trinkets: a metal pencil sharpener about 2-inches high, a tiny mirror, and a broach. The girl was also pictured on Baker's cards and cookbooks.

One, of several china pincushion dolls, representing "La Belle Chocolatiere," the trademark used by Baker's Chocolate for almost 100 years. This example is one of the most exquisite. The hands, tray, and cap are carefully detailed. N. Wolfe collection. $300.00.

La Belle Chocolatiere was used for many small premiums such as this 2-inch high metal pencil sharpener. M. Kolterman collection. $12.00.

Barker's Department Stores. This chain of stores has sold a white plush dog named **Barky**. Sitting, the dog measures 15-inches tall. It wears a royal blue knit shirt that is also the upper body. Lining on ears and bottom of feet match the shirt. The dog was sold in the stores.

Barky advertises the Barker's Department stores. It is white plush with royal blue shirt. In a sitting position the dog is 15-inches tall. Marks: "B", on front of shirt. B. Welch collection. $8.00.

Bazooka Bubble Gum, a product, of Topps Chewing Gum, Inc. In 1973 wrappers on Topps' new sugarless bubble gum announced the promotion of a **Bazooka Joe** doll. The 18-inch doll is made of prestuffed cotton fabric with lithographed features and clothing.

Bazooka Joe, offered on wrappers in 1973. Marks: "BAZOOKA/JOE ® ", on front of shirt. $6.00.

Bear Brand Hosiery Company. A family of three

Papa Bear doll, 9-inches, is one of three cloth dolls used to advertise Bear Brand Hosiery. Marks: none, except the hosiery box held is an exact replica of the ones used by the company years ago. K. Miller collection. $25.00.

54

Mama Bear, 9-inches, wears a blue skirt with yellow dots, and a white blouse with a red bow at the neck. Marks: only those on the box she is holding which says "Bear Brand Hosiery". K. Miller collection. $25.00.

Boy Bear, 9-inches, wears blue trousers and a red shirt with a yellow stripe. Marks: replica of box in bear's paws. K. Miller collection. $25.00.

cloth bear dolls were used by this company probably sometime prior to 1930. The 9-inch dolls are printed in bright colors on heavy muslin. Each bear holds a replica of one of the boxes used for Bear Brand Hosiery.

The company continues to manufacture hosiery, but has had no other dolls to our knowledge.

Beaver Enterprises. In 1972 this company created a plush **Beaver** toy 12-inches tall to promote its company. The beaver trademark was first introduced in 1959.

Beaver Enterprises is also responsible for creating the Travelodge bear trademark.

The brown plush fabric *Beaver*, 12-inches, is the symbol of Beaver Enterprises. The teeth, tail, paws, and ears are felt; the eyes are plastic. A. Wolfe collection, David Nelson, James Giokas photographers. $8.00.

Beech-Nut Fruit Stripe Gum. A **Gum Man** and a **Zebra** doll have been advertising premiums of this brand gum. The 7-inch **Gum Man** is made from an enlarged replica of the Fruit Stripe

Gum package with plastic eyes, nose, and mouth attached. Legs and arms are made of plastic-coated wire and can be positioned to allow the doll to stand. The figure wears large plastic shoes and a cap. Date and cost unknown.

In 1972 a 12-inch cloth **Zebra** similar to the trademark on packages of Fruit Stripe Gum was offered by a coupon available in six-pack packages of gum. The **Zebra** could be obtained until March 31, 1975 by mailing the coupon, 5 outer wrappers, and $2.00.

Beach-Nut's *Fruit Stripe Zebra*, 12-inches, is a copy of the trademark found on packages of Fruit Stripe gum. The plush toy was available in 1972. $5.00.

The *Beech-Nut Fruit Stripe Gum* doll, 7-inches, is easy to identify because his body is a replica of the gum package. No other identifying marks are used. $5.00.

Beefeater's Gin. This brand of gin has used numerous display figures and dolls representing the English Beefeater to advertise their product. Some are small to be used on the counter of a bar. Others are six or seven feet high to use outdoors.

Benjamin Franklin Savings and Loan. A 15-inch cloth doll representing the man who coined the phrase, "A penny saved is a penny earned" was given as an advertising promotion in the early to mid-1970's. **Benjamin** wears a long coat, vest, and knee pants with long stockings. **Mr. Franklin** has a wide smile, white hair, and wears spectacles.

The *Benjamin Franklin* doll was an advertising promotion of the savings and loan company of the same name. Marks: "Benjamin Franklin Savings and Loan Co." $5.00.

Beta Fiberglass Company. A sad-mouthed cloth doll with a tiny bedspread was used by

The sad-faced *Bad Doll*, 10½-inches, was used by the Beta Fiberglass Company to advertise their "Well Behaved" bedspread. Marks: "Bad Doll", on removable dress. $8.00.

this company to advertise their "Well-Behaved" bedspread line. The 10½-inch doll with removable dress came with several miniature accessories: shopping bag, soap, mess kit, sponge, and a booklet that reads: "I'm a Bad Doll. I'm fun to play with."

Betty Bubbles, a product of Lander Dist. The container for this bubble bath is also a doll. It is 9½-inches high, and has a doll head with rooted wig, painted eyes, and mouth as the cap of the container. The hands and arms are molded/painted to the skirt, which holds the bubble solution.

Betty Crocker Products, a division of General Mills. Over fifty products use the name Betty Crocker--cake mixes, noodle dishes, frosting mixes, and potato flakes to name a few. Not until the 1970's was a doll sold to represent "America's First Lady of Food" as General Mills considers her.

The 13-inch tall **Betty Crocker** doll was manufacatured by a General Mill's division--Kenner Toys, and was sold only at the retail level. It is cloth, with side-glance eyes, line mouth, brown suede hair with yarn ponytails. The doll wears a red-checked dress, skirt sewn at the waist, apron, and black suede shoes.

Included in the box with the doll were an apron for a child, six baking mixes, panhandler, baking pan, cookie cutters, rolling pin, mixing bowl, and baking book.

The name Betty Crocker was selected many years ago by General Mills to use when signing letters in answer to customer inquiries. Requests for information poured in along with responses to a puzzle contest held to publicize Gold Medal Flour. Women wanted to know such things as: How long

The *Betty Crocker* cloth doll, 13-inches, is shown with her original box and baking kit. The hair is brown suede-cloth with yarn ponytails tied with red ribbons. Marks: a red spoon applique on pocket, which is the symbol used for Betty Crocker items. A. Wolfe collection, David Nelson and James Giokas photographers. $12.00.

do you knead sour-dough bread? And what is the best way to make a lattice-top pie?

The advertising staff were willing to answer the questions, but wondered how to sign the letters. They quickly chose a surname-- Crocker--the name of a popular employee who had recently retired. To complete the name they added a familiar, comfortable name--Betty. Today a large staff is needed to fullfill the duties of Betty Crocker.

Betty Rose. This quality brand of coat issued a rather clever cloth doll with a removable coat. The doll is 14½-inches tall. Its arms and legs are cut from a separate piece of cloth and sewn on. The yellow-haired **Betty Rose** doll wears a gray dress with red stripes and a red belt. Also printed on the sheet of fabric is a blue coat with cuffs and a large collar printed to resemble gray Persian lamb. A tiny Betty Rose label is provided to sew in the neck of the coat.

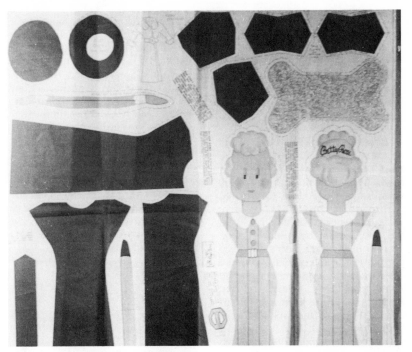

The 14½-inch *Betty Rose* doll has a separate coat and hat printed on the sheet of fabric. Marks: "Betty Rose", written in script on back of hair; label (as mentioned). K. Lyons collection. $15.00.

Bewley's Yeast. Two cloth dolls were found marked "Bewley's Best." The dolls found were alike except for size, one is 8-inches tall, the other is 11-inches. Both wear a red cape

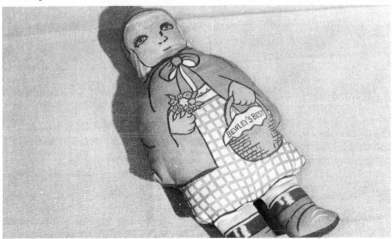

Little Red Riding Hood came in two sizes and advertised Bewley's Yeast. Marks: "Bewley's Best". A. Wolfe collection, David Nelson and James Giokas photographers. $30.00.

and carry a basket of goodies in one hand and a bouquet of flowers in the other. They undoubtedly represent **Little Red Riding Hood**. The date is unknown, as this company is no longer in business, but judging from the dolls, probably prior to 1930.

Big Boy Restaurant. This restaurant chain earned its name from the oversize hamburgers made by Bob Wain in 1936 at his restaurant in Glendale, California. Customers patronizing his restaurant began asking for "the big one," thus the franchise was started and called Bob's Big Boy Restaurant. Each owner could use his own name combined with the words Big Boy. Many of the restaurants in the west are named J.B.'s Big Boy after Jack Broberg, who opened a very successful restaurant in Provo, Utah. Other names include: Azar's, Fritz's, Kip's, Elia's, Elbie's, Shoney's, T.J.'s, and Vip's. Almost 1,000 restaurants have been opened in the United States and Canada.

In 1967 the franchise was sold to Willard J. Marriot. Since that time many promotional items have been manufactured with the Big Boy trademark on them such as key chains, T-shirts, glasses, banks, watches, ashtrays, and of course dolls. The trademark is a well-fed boy wearing red and white overalls. His dark hair is flipped up off his forehead, and he usually carries a hamburger or has his hands on his suspenders. Each restaurant used the trademark figure throughout the restaurant. Many have a larger than life-size figure in front of the restaurant entrance.

We found seven dolls and one bank. Each manager handles his own promotional items; therefore, it was difficult to obtain a complete record of what has been available and at what dates.

Except for the two new dolls available in 1978, a dog and a little girl, all the dolls and bank resemble the Big Boy figure. One doll is a 5-inch nodder to go on the dashboard of a car. Another is an 8½-inch vinyl doll made by R. Dakin and Co. with removable clothes. One cloth doll is 17-inches and was offered primarily in the Midwest. The 10-inch hard plastic doll with molded/painted features and clothes is much like the 10½-inch hard plastic bank except the figure is thinner and the legs are separated. The bank is made wide and straight across the bottom to hold lots of money.

Several dolls have been used to promote the trademark of the Big Boy Restaurants. One is the *Big Boy* nodder doll, 5-inches, with a shiny paper mache' head over a heavy base of undetermined material, possibly plaster of paris. Note the protuding ears on this doll. Marks: "Big Boy", on front of shirt; "Reg. U.S. T.M.", on base. $5.00.

Plastic *Big Boy* doll, 10-inches tall, which sold at counters in the restaurant, from 1974-78. Marks: "Big Boy", across front of shirt. $2.00.

Big Boy doll, 8½-inches tall, is not as pudgy as the others. The red and white checked cloth pants, white shirt, and white shoes are removable. The arms are in a different position than the trademark, one holds a hamburger and the other is at the side. Sold at counters in 1974. Marks: "R. Dakin & Co. #2040", on tag; "R. Dakin & Co.", on back of head; "Dream Dolls/R. Dakin & Co." on label on pants. K. Lyon collection. $8.00.

In 1978 the Big Boy doll family grew with three cloth pillow dolls being offered: **Big Boy**, a girl **Dolly**, and a dog **Nugget**. The dolls are 14-inches high and cost $3.98 each. The only advertising for these dolls is found in the free comic book given to children who eat at Big Boy Restaurants.

The **Big Boy** pillow doll is another copy of the trademark, wearing lithographed red and white checked pants. His hands hold the suspenders to the pants, so the outline of the doll has no appendages.

Vinyl *Big Boy* bank, 10-inches high, depicts the well-fed boy. Marks: "Big Boy", on front of shirt; "Big Boy is a Reg. U.S. Trademark," on back. $2.00.

61

A cloth *Big Boy* doll, 17-inches, has arms and legs cut free from the body, brown hair, and a single line mouth, not quite in a smile. Marks: "Big Boy® " K. Miller collection. $8.00.

A cloth *Big Boy* pillow doll, 14-inches, the arms are lithographed on the body with hands holding the suspenders, legs are not separated and it is a wider doll. Marks: "Big Boy® ", across front of shirt. C. Erickson collection. $4.00

Dolly is a new member of the family. She has yellow hair, circle eyes, and simple line mouth, nose and brows, and wears a red dress with white dots. The arms are behind her back.

Nugget is also new. The tan dog is printed in profile sitting on his back haunches. His big floppy ears are lined fabric sewn on the prestuffed head.

In 1978 *Dolly* was introduced. She is also 14-inches tall, has yellow hair, and wears a red dress with white dots. Marks: "I'm/Dolly . . / Who are/you?," lithographed on a disk on the front of the dress. $4.00.

A pet dog *Nugget*, 14-inches, was also introduced in 1978. The tan dog is in profile. Marks: "Nugget", around collar. $4.00.

Birds Eye Frozen Foods,
a product of General Foods Corp.
Three lithographed cloth dolls,
Merry, Minx, and **Mike** were
promotional features of Birds Eye
frozen orange juice in 1953. The
dolls were used extensively in their
advertising and were well-known
to the public according to an independent advertising survey
made in 1956. They were included
in the top four consumer recognized trademarks, right up there with
Borden's Elsie, Aunt Jemima, and
the Campbell Kids. How quickly
the consumer forgets without
advertising. Today few people
recall the Birds Eye trio.

Mike, 11-inches, wears green
overalls with his name on the bib
and a handkerchief in the hind
pocket. Marks: "1953 General
Foods Corp." Playthings by the
Yard, 1973. $10.00.

Merry, 11-inches, is one of three
cloth dolls offered by Birds Eye
orange juice in 1953. The color process used to print these dolls
resembles water color. *Merry*
wears red pants and a green shirt
with her name across the front.
This is the only doll with pigtails.
To extend the lower part of the
braid, an extra triangle of fabric
had to be sewn on. Marks: "1953
General Foods Corp.", on back.
Playthings by the Yard, 1973.
$10.00.

Minx, 11-inches, wears blue jeans,
shirt, and neckerchief. All three
dolls have a line smile with tongue
to one side. Marks: "1953 General
Foods Corporation", on back of
belt. Playthings by the Yard, 1973.
$10.00.

The smiling 11-inch dolls were printed on a flat sheet of fabric, one of the few cloth premium dolls sold this way in the past 25 years. The ad for these dolls ran in the October 1953 issue of Family Circle Magazine. They could be purchased for 25¢ plus one can top per doll. The dolls are well-marked with their named across the front and the company and date on the back.

The Birds Eye brand is taken from the name Clarence "Bob" Birdseye, known as the Father of Frozen Food. Bob was an explorer, scientist, inventor, businessman, adventurer, and individualist. On one of his sojourns in the sub-zero Labrador wilderness his young family subsisted on fish and local game. These were highly treasured and in order to make them last as long as possible Bob put such delicacies in a barrel with sea water and as they froze he added more water and more vegetables until the barrel was full. In the cold climate they froze quickly. For several months Bob could hack a chunk from the barrel and treat his family to a vegetable delicacy.

From this experience he developed an avid interest in trying to devise a method of preserving food by freezing. In time he perfected a quick-freezing process that could be used commercially. In 1923 he received a patent, but it was years before industry and the public were ready to trust frozen food.

General Foods Corporation took over the Birdseye company, retaining the Birds Eye trademark, which is, of course, derived from the Birdseye name. They sufferd losses the first few years, but shared Birdseye's faith in the ultimate succes of frozen foods.

Clarence Birdseye died in 1951 with many inventions to his credit

and a line of frozen foods using the original spelling of his name. The name came from an ancestor whose well-aimed arrow pierced the eye of a hawk that threatened an English queen and was thereupon dubbed Birds Eye.

Black and White Scotch. The figure of the little Scottie dogs used to advertise this liquor was made of paper mache and given as a promotional display item to bars. The 9½-inch high figural was manufactured by Displaymate.

Black and White Scotch's two Scottie dogs were a display item given to bars. L. Yagatich collection, Donald G. Vilsack photographer. $20.00.

Blatz Beer. Several dolls or figurals have been used by dealers selling this brand of beer for display. One is a 10-inch winking man with an actual Blatz Beer can for the body with hard plastic head, arms, legs, and bow tie. The doll holds pennants proclaiming the virtues of "Milwaukee's Finest Beer."

A second Blatz figure is a baseball player made from heavy cast iron. The doll is 10½-inches tall and has a barrel body, this time a keg of Blatz Beer. He wears a molded/painted blue suit and blue hat, and has a white mustache and hair. It is one of three baseball figures that were all attached to a base.

The third Blatz display figure is a waiter attached to a base. It has a Blatz Beer bottle body with plastic head, arms, and legs. One hand holds a tray with a mug of beer; the other arm has a towel folded over it.

The *Blatz Man* figure is made of cast iron and very heavy. It is a 10½-inch tall baseball player with a barrel body. The suit is molded/painted. Marks: "Blatz", on front and back of barrel. B. Welch collection. $25.00.

Blue Bonnet Margarine. For about five years packages of Blue Bonnet margarine advertised AMERICANA DOLLS. These were the ordinary unmarked 8-inch plastic doll dressed to represent a variety of characters such as: Yellow Rose of Texas, Indian Girl, Western Cowgirl, and Pilgrim. At the beginning of the offer a **Blue Bonnet Sue** doll was included in the list. This doll was dressed in blue like the trademark figure and had some relationship to the product, therefore making it appealing to the advertising doll collector. Unfortunately this doll was dropped from the list after a year or so.

The dolls cost $1.35 plus the coupon from a package of Blue Bonnet margarine, until 1976 when the price was raised to $2.00. The offer is still available.

Blatz Beer Man is a display item used in bars selling Blatz Beer. The only identification is the beer can used for the body. The figure is missing its arms and pennants which were attached to the hands. $15.00.

Three of the American Dolls offered on packages of Blue Bonnet Margarine: *Western Cowgirl, Girl* *Next Door, and Alaskan Eskimo.* No marks. Elizabeth Wright collection. $2.00.

Another three Americana Dolls offered by Blue Bonnet Margarine: *Frontier Woman, New Amsterdam* *Dutch, and Southern Belle.* Elizabeth Wright collection. $2.00.

Blue Bonnet Sue was one of the 21 American Dolls advertised on packages of Blue Bonnet Margarine. The 8-inch doll was sold for several years in the 70's. "Sue" wears a dark blue taffeta dress and a bonnet with braid trim, similar to the figure on packages of Blue Bonnet Margarine. Unmarked. K. Lyons collection. $2.00.

Blue Ribbon Malt Extract,

a product of Premier Malt Products, a subsidiary of Pabst Brewing Company. This product is on the market today and the label continues to carry the picture of **Lena,** their trademark almost since Premier Malt Products was formed in 1917. According to a company spokesman, "Lena was one of our first kitchen technicians and her robust and friendly Germanic form and countenance undoubtedly influenced the founding fathers to use her as a model."

A cloth doll representing the trademark was made prior to 1930. The 14-inch doll has no hair showing from the front, except a widow's peak, she has bulgy eyes, and apple cheeks. **Lena** wears a long green dress with yellow O's. She holds a can of Blue Ribbon Malt Extract.

The company was unable to provide additional information because their plant in Peoria was ravaged by fire in 1930 and many records were destroyed. No one at the company remembers the **Lena** doll.

Old-fashioned as she looks, *Lena,* 14-inches, is found today on labels of Blue Ribbon Malt Extract. The pre-1930 doll's dress is green with yellow O's, and the shoes are three-dimensional. Marks: "Lena", in corner of apron. Courtesy Ralph's Antique Dolls. $50.00-75.00.

Bluine Company.

This laundry product, that was considered indispensable in the past, offered a 30-inch doll printed on fabric, free for selling 12 packages of Bluine at 10¢ each. The doll had blond ringlets with a bow on top of the hair. She wore printed underclothes. The newspaper ad for this doll ran September 28, 1913.

Bondex. This hot iron mending fabric offered a 17-inch **Bondy** cloth doll the fall of 1960. One side had the face of a boy dressed in a jacket and pants. The other side was plain to be decorated by the owner with iron-on Bondex fabric. The doll cost 50¢ plus a Bondex label and coupon, found in packages of the mending fabric. The doll came flat to be stuffed after the plain side was completed.

Boraxo. Jennie, a 22-inch cloth doll was a mail-in promotion on boxes of the cleaning product Boraxo in 1974. The doll was lithographed on fabric, to be cut, sewn, and stuffed by the new owner. The distinguishing characteristic of this cloth doll is the eyes, which resemble rhinestones.

Borax, the major ingredient of Boraxo, has had an interesting history. In 1870 "cottonball" (ulexite, one of the borate minerals) was found in quantity on the Nevada desert. Prospectors by the score were picking, digging, and blasting the state in search of gold or silver, but only one, F.M. "Borax" Smith, saw any value in the shimmering white mineral. He set aside his pick and gold pan and began shoveling cottonball. One by one he bought out competitors until he became a powerful figure in the industry.

A few years later another even larger field of cottonball was discovered, this time in formidable Death Valley, California. William T. Coleman was the leader in this area. He had plenty of the product, but how to transport it across the desert was indeed a problem.

A young muleskinner solved the problem by designing a special wagon pulled by two ten-mule teams. From 1883 to 1889 the teams hauled borax out of Death Valley, over the steep Panamint Mountains and across the desert to the railroad junction at Mojave.

It was a 20-day round trip, often going only 15 to 18 miles a day--a tribute to the ingenuity of the designer and to the stamina of the teamsters and the animals.

The 20-mule teams became a world famous symbol incorporated into borax products advertising. Today we think of borax products primarily as cleaning agents. It is used in hundreds of products both in industry and agriculture. In grandmother's time it was advertised as a product that could do most everything, ads read: remove dandruff, wash carriages, the baby, and even cure bunion and epilepsy.

Borden Company. Since 1937 Elsie the cow has been the trademark figure of this company. At that time Bordens sold primarily dairy related products so Elsie was a fitting symbol. Prior to women's lib days Elsie was known, incongruously, as the "World's No. 1 Milkman."

Some trademark figures seem to especially catch the public's fancy, apparently Elsie is one of the successful ones. In 1939 a real life Elsie attended the World's Fair in New York. She gained further fame on stage, screen, and TV, even accumulating a few "honorary" college degrees.

In 1951 a survey was taken by an independent advertising firm to determine the consumer's ability to identify trademark figures to the product they represented. Elsie rated third, after Aunt Jemima and the Birds Eye Kids, ahead of the Campbell Kids. The survey was repeated five years later and Elsie continued to hold third place. In the 1940's, not only Elsie was being used to advertise Borden products, but also Elmer her husband and Beauregard her son. Elmer stayed in vogue long enough to have Borden's white glue named for him, then no more was heard about Elmer.

A doll collector, who grew up in Chicago in the 1940's remembers visiting an outdoor exhibit that featured the Bordon trio: a real cow, bull, and calf.

During this period of wide exposure plush toys were offered of all three Borden bovines. We found an **Elsie** toy from the early 1950's with a vinyl molded head and an aqua plush body. **Elsie**, 15-inches, is in a most uncowlike position, sitting on her tail with legs and hooves up in the air. The same **Elsie** was offered again in 1958 for $2.50 plus the flap from a package of Borden's Ice Cream.

A clever *Elsie* toy was manufactured by Mesyo Products. The wooden Elsie assumes different positions when the bottom disc is pressed. The base also houses a "Moo" box. Arlene Wolfe collection, David Nelson, James Giokas photographers. $18.00.

Borden's *Elsie* cow, 15-inches, has been popular with young consumers for over 40 years. This plush toy with vinyl head was offered twice in the 1950's, and again in 1977. The first two animals had soft aqua plush bodies. The latest *Elsie* is made of brown plush with yellow felt hooves. Because they look exactly alike in black and white photos, only the 1950 *Elsie* is shown. S. Ricklefs collection. $5.00-15.00.

In the 1950's Borden created *Elsie's* little calf, *Beauregard*. He is on all fours and comes in "Guernsey" colored plush fabric with a vinyl head. A yellow ring is in the nose. P. Harding collection, David Nelson, James Giokas photographers. $10.00.

The little calf, **Beauregard**, 8½-inches tall, of Guernsey colored plush was also offered in the 50's. It is on all fours like a respectable calf should be. We were unable to find an **Elmer**, but suppose one existed.

Another **Elsie** toy was found. It is made of wooden segments strung with elastic, much like the jointed bisque dolls. By pressing a disk on the bottom of the box the cow stands on, the elastic relaxes and tightens making **Elsie** shift into all sorts of unusual positions. The disk also activates a "moo" sound. This toy may have sold on the retail market.

To commemorate Borden's first hundred years, Elsie with the aid of an advertising crew, produced twin calves. The $25,000 prize for naming the pair went to a grandmother from California for the names Latabee and Lobelia. To our knowledge these twins were never made as toys.

In 1977 Elsie was reissued for $5.95, and was available until the expiration date December 31, 1977. It was manufactured by the R & R Toy Manufacturing Company and made of brown plush, yellow felt hooves, and the same vinyl head used on earlier Elsie plush animals. Both are 15-inches tall.

Boston Baked Bean. A 19-inch broadcloth doll shaped like a bean was offered by this product. The top half of the doll is brown, the lower half is black. It has white spindly legs with black feet and black velvet tubing arms with white felt hands. The only article of clothing is a felt hat with a ribbon that is marked: Boston Baked Bean.

Bounce Fabric Softener. This recently developed product which is used to take the static cling out of machine dried

clothes offered a **Bouncy** kangaroo doll. The prestuffed cloth doll is 17-inches tall, dark brown with a lithographed blue jacket and cap. Marked Bouncy on leg. Manufactured by Chase Bag Company.

Brach Candy and Brach Circus Peanuts, products of E.J. Brach & Sons, Inc. This confectionary company has offered two cloth advertising dolls: **Bracho the Clown** (three editions) and **Scarecrow Sam**. The exact dates for each doll are unknown, but probably span the years from 1968 to 1975. The dolls were mail-in offers advertised on candy wrappers and cans of Circus Peanuts.

Bracho Clown, 17-inches, a promotion for Brach Candy, was a mail-in offer advertised on the back of candy packages. He wears a yellow and orange suit, side-turned oversize shoes with purple stitching, purple hat, and pink hair. His collar is a white detachable ruffle. Marks: "Bracho/the/T.M. Clown", on front of suit. $5.00.

This *Bracho Clown*, 17-inches tall, has a lithographed ruffle collar and was probably the later edition. Marks: "BRACHO/the ® / CLOWN", on front of suit. $5.00.

All three editions of Bracho are 17½-inches tall, and have lithographed clown suits. The difference in each edition of **Bracho** is the ruffle around the neck. One is plastic (according to Johanna Anderton's More Twentieth Century Dolls), one detachable cloth, and the third is lithographed. To doll collectors these slight differences are worth noting; to the company there is only one **Bracho the Clown** doll. Although unverified, it is probable that the first clown had the plastic ruffle, the second was cloth, and the most recent was lithographed. **Bracho** sold for $1.00.

The **Scarecrow Sam** doll, 16-inches tall, and coloring book were available for $1.50 plus an empty Brach candy package or wrapper. The doll is unmarked except for the letters LUV on the front of the overalls.

Scarecrow Sam doll and coloring book were advertised on backs of Brach Candy packages. "Sam" wears blue patched overalls, red and white checked shirt, and a floppy yellow hat. Marks: "LUV" in heart on bib of overalls. $4.00.

Coloring book that came with the *Sam Scarecrow* doll.

Bradlee Stores. A 14-inch gold plush bear with big plastic eyes was offered by this chain of stores. **Bruff** was manufactured by Animal Fair; the date is uncertain.

Bruff, 14-inches, was offered by Bradlee Stores. The gold plush bear has round plastic eyes and an open mouth. The green shirt is also the upper body. Marks: "Bruff", stenciled on front of shirt. $8.00.

Bran Dandies. This old cereal, that is no longer on the market, used the **Sunny Jim** figure in their advertising. This cereal may have been produced by the same company that produced Force cereal. Force used **Sunny Jim** in their advertising and made numerous cloth and a composition doll representing the character.

Breast O' Chicken. A 19-inch Aqua and yellow plush bunny was offered in 1968 for three labels from a can of tuna fish plus $2.95.

Advertisement for plush bunny from Breast O' Chicken tuna from a 1968 magazine. The 19-inch bunny is blue and yellow. $12.00.

Breck Hair Products. **Bonnie Breck**, a 9-inch vinyl doll, was offerd in 1971 by the Breck Company to sell their Baby

In 1972 a well-made *Bonnie Breck* doll, 9-inches tall, was used to promote Breck Baby Shampoo. The doll wears a homemade looking dress, which is original. Marks: "Beautiful/Bonnie Breck/Made in Hong Kong", on a cloth tag inside dress. $10.00.

Shampoo to young girls. The advertising read, "Breck Baby Shampoo is gentle and kind for little girl's hair . . . and for their doll's."

The doll was available for $2.00 plus proof of purchase and the coupon from the October, 1971, McCall's Magazine. The well-made doll is fully jointed, even the knees. It has painted eyes with inset lashes and a closed mouth. The luxuriant rooted wig is made to withstand constant shampooing and combing by a child. It wears a nondescript long dress.

Brer Rabbit Molasses. In 1964 a 27-inch plush **Easter Rabbit** sold for $2.75 plus the label from a bottle of Brer Rabbit Molasses or syrup.

Brer Rabbit Molasses advertised a 27-inch *Brer Rabbit Easter Bunny* in 1964 magazines. $12.00.

Brown's Chicken. This fast food chain is located primarily in the Mid-west and South. A Farmer Brown trademark figure is used in the decor and also as an advertising doll. The first **Farmer Brown** doll was offered in the mid-1970's. It wore lithographed bib overalls of brown, the other predominant color was yellow. The 18-inch dolls were available at the restaurant for $1.00 and were marked Farmer Brown.

By 1978 the chain had expanded and introduced two new cloth dolls: a revised **Farmer Brown** doll and a chicken. The new doll is 16-inches tall, and wears lithographed denim colored bib overalls, a plaid shirt, neckerchief, and a straw hat. The smiling doll is well marked.

Farmer Brown doll, 18-inches tall, was a promotion used by Brown's Chicken restaurant franchise. The lithographed clothing includes brown overalls, yellow and white checked shirt, neck scarf, and a straw hat. Marks: "Farmer Brown" on front and back. $10.00.

The companion doll is an 11-inch high chicken **Brewster Rooster**, that is almost as wide as it is tall. The feather markings are black on a white background with a touch of color for accessories,

In 1978 a new cloth *Farmer Brown* doll was introduced. The new version, 16-inches, is well marked: "Brown's/ Chicken/It tastes better," under the trademark emblem on front of overalls; "Farmer Brown" on hat band. $2.00.

A companion doll to the 1978 *Farmer Brown* is *Brewster Rooster*. The 11-inch chicken wears tie, and dark red glasses and comb. Marks: "Brown's", on large emblem on chest. $2.00.

the beak, and feet. The pair of 1978 dolls were sold at the restaurants for $1.00 each during the holiday season.

Brunswick Corporation. To encourage bowling, this company began a promotion the summer of 1967 that involved a cloth doll named **iitywybts**, which is the acronym for "If I Tell You will You Bowl This Summer?" Only 2,000 were made. They sold over the counter for $1.25.

The following summer a female doll, **itylyti**, was added, that was the acronym for "I Told You Last Year, Try It." The third year the program included twins–**itybits** and **itygits**. These had no meaning, except "b" for boy and "g" for girl.

The Brunswick Corporation began a promotion the summer of 1967 using the 16-inch *iitywybts* dolls. The unusual name is the acronym for If I Tell You Will You Bowl This Summer? Marks: "iitywybts", across front in large letters; "Brunswick", in small print over one leg. $10.00.

The summer of 1968 Brunswick Corporation offered a female doll, 16-inches, named *itylyti*, the acronym for I Told You Last Year, Try It. Marks: "itylyti/Brunswick". $10.00.

itygits, 14½ inches, was offered in 1969 along with her twin brother "itybits". The four dolls in the Brunswick family are all prestuffed with lithograped bowling ball bodies and strange duck-like heads. Marks: "itygits/Brunswick". $8.00.

Budweiser Beer, a product of Anheuser-Busch, Inc. In the late 60's an artist for Budweiser Beer drew a character and named him Bud Man. The company had been looking for a figure that would appeal to the college crowd. The new character was tested on a group of students and it proved successful. The company lost no time dispersing banners, stickers, and a doll to distributors at college dorms.

The first doll was 18-inches tall and made of a foam rubber material. **Bud Man** wears a red hood that covers his head and eyes, exposing only the lower part of his face. He wears a removable blue-plastic cape; molded boots, gloves, and suit. The material the doll is made from was perfected by a British firm and they licensed an American Company to use the

The third year of Brunswick Corporation's promotion to encourage people to bowl in the summer, twin dolls were offered. *itybits*, 12-inches is the boy twin. These names have no acronym. Marks: "itybits/Brunswick". $8.00.

material. Many of the dolls are showing their age via cracking in the surface. The dolls cost Budweiser about $5.00, but were given free along with other Bud Man premiums.

The *Bud Man* rubber doll, 18-inches, was used primarily for a promotion involving college age consumers. This Superman-like trademark wears a red molded/-painted suit and mask, gloves and boots are blue, to match the removable blue plastic cape. Marks: "Bud/Man" on front of suit in large white letters; "Budweiser"on bow tie. S. Ricklefs collection. $20.00.

When a Budweiser official was asked about the cloth **Bud Man** doll he said, "Must be bootlegged, its impossible to control." When questioned further he felt certain that the company had not authorized a cloth **Bud Man** doll and some company had produced it contrary to trademark laws. It is puzzling that a company would violate the law to produce the doll. Yet one owner said her doll was purchased new at a gift shop.

The cloth *Budman* doll was called a "bootleg" doll by a company spokesman who was unaware of its existence. Marks: "Budman". B. Welch collection. $10.00.

Bumble Bee Tuna. A 24-inch inflatable replica of the bee used in Bumble Bee Tuna televi-

The inflatable *Yum Yum Bumble Bee* toy wears a blue and yellow striped shirt, brown pants, and has yellow transparent wings. Marks: 'Yum Yum Bumble Bee" across hat. $5.00.

sion commercials was available in 1974 for $2.25 plus two labels.

Bunny Bear Mattress Company. A 12-inch cloth **Bunny Bear** doll was advertised on coupons attached to Bunny Bear baby crib mattresses in 1973. The fabric is pale gold with speckles of brown, black, and white to represent fur. The bunny wears lithographed pants with suspenders. It is unmarked.

A plastic *Bunny Bread* hand puppet was given by the American Bakers Cooperative. $1.00.

Burger Chef. The trademark for this restaurant is a chef's head with a big white hat, two red dot eyes and a red line mouth. In the early 1970's the trademark was made in cloth and sold at their hamburger stands. It has a brown

In 1973 *Bunny Bear*, 12-inches, could be ordered from a coupon found on Bunny Bear Baby Crib Matresses. The cloth animal is lithographed with speckles of brown and black on pale gold, and wears blue trousers. $5.00.

Bunny Bread. A plastic hand puppet with a bunny face was given free with this brand of bread.

The *Burger Chef* doll-pillow is a copy of this hamburger chain's trademark. Marks: "Burger Chef ®." $5.00.

77

cotton fabric face with red printed smile and eyes, the hat is also lithographed and stuffed.

Burger King. "Have it your way at Burger King" is the slogan that distinguished this hamburger franchise from the many others.

During the holiday season Burger King has offered three prestuffed cloth dolls in the years 1972, 1973, and 1977. The 1972 **Burger King** doll is a 16-inch cartoon rendition of a king with unrealistic proportions. The $1.00 doll wears lithographed yellow crown, red robe over a yellow suit, and the hair is red. The arms are extended from the sides and the legs are practically nonexistent. The dolls were widely advertised in newspapers and on coupons given at the restaurant.

The 1973 doll is very similar, the main difference is the earlier doll has a circle on the chest above the buckle. The 1973 doll's circle is a medallion marked Burger King. The 1972 doll is unmarked; the 1973 is marked with the date and name on the back of each foot.

The 1972 *Burger King,* hamburger restaurant's trademark figure. $3.00.

The colors vary a bit with the 1973 doll having a more orange than yellow suit.

In some localities these dolls were offered in 1974 and 1975. No **Burger King** dolls were offered in 1976 or 1978.

The 1977 **Burger King** doll is unlike the two previous dolls. It is a 15-inch doll that represents a person dressed as a king, as seen in Burger King television commercials. The doll wears yellow and red lithographed attire and has a red beard. It was free with the purchase of a $5.00 booklet of gift coupons.

Plastic hand puppets of this **King** were given free at some restaurants.

The Burger King Restaurant's premium doll was completely changed in 1977. The new *Burger King* doll, 15-inches, resembles a real king, with red beard and mustache and a red and yellow suit. Marks: "Burger King", on belt buckle. $3.00.

Burpee Seeds. This seed company not only sells seeds to grow delicious garden treats, it sells the scarecrow to keep the birds away. In 1978 the W. Atlas Burpee Company offered a six-foot inflatable scarecrow. To facilitate the job of blowing it up, each leg was a self-contained unit. The scarecrow originally cost $4.95, but was increased to almost $10.00 within one year. Some stores selling Burpee Seeds had a scarecrow on display.

Buster Brown Hosiery Mills, a division of Skyland International Corp. This company has had a close and complicated association with Buster Brown. A quote from a letter written by Frances L. Charman, curator of the Buster Brown Historical Museum in New York City explains: "Mr. Frank Miller, who operated a hosiery mill in Chattanooga, was one who bought the name." (From Mr. Outcault, the creator, at the St. Louis World's Fair in 1904. See Buster Brown Shoes for more information.) "He then changed his mill to Buster Brown Hosiery Mills. Sometime later his son dropped the name and changed the entire operation to United Hosiery Mills. Then in the 40's he had a change of heart and applied for the name again, and luckily it had not been snapped up by someone else."

She goes on to say that Miller's grandson encouraged the company's identity with Buster Brown. A widely used logo of the company has been Buster and Tige having a tug-of-war with a stocking.

An announcement in the quarterly Buster Brown Stocking Magazine tells of a cloth doll offered:

BUSTER BROWN DOLLS FOR GIRLS

'Cause Boys Don't Want 'Em

The Art Fabric Man has made a Doll that looks like me and a dog just like Tige. He gets 25¢ for 'em both, but he has to sell 'em to me for 15 cents, 'cause he couldn't make 'em if I didn't say so. The Doll and Dog are made of cloth, all dressed just like my clothes and the same colors. Tige has a big blue bow on, and looks awful nice. If he would only shut his mouth he would look better, but, you see, the man made him laughing, and he looks like he was going to swallow his head. When you get one of these Dolls ask your Ma to sew the two sides together, and then you stuff it with cotton, and you will have a dandy Doll all right. My Sister's got one, and when she gets mad she says, I'll slap your face, Buster,' and then she whacks the Doll a few times. If you want one of these Dolls, send me one of my stocking tickets and 15¢, an I'll send you the Doll and the Dog."

To Miss Charman's knowledge a cloth **Tige** doll with a blue bow as described here has never been found.

In 1921, when the company was operating as United Hosiery Mills they used a **Dixie Doll** trademark symbol rather than Buster Brown. At this time they also made a doll to represent the figure. (See United Hosiery Mills listing for description.)

October 5, 1948 a patent was registered by United Hosiery Mills for **Buster Brown** dolls. This may be the cloth doll printed by Knickerbocker.

We were unable to locate either of these cloth dolls, but found one manufactured by Buster Brown Textiles in 1974. It was printed on a flat sheet of cloth to be assembled by the owner. No further information is known about this recent doll.

Fabric *Buster Brown* doll manufactured by Buster Brown Textiles of New York City in 1974. It is not known if this doll was made to sell as a premium or retail. M. Kolterman collection. $10.00.

Buster Brown Shoes. The name Buster Brown has been used for many products and is a story in itself. Richard F. Outcault's comic strip, Buster Brown, began May 4, 1902 in the New York Herald. Buster was a well-dressed 10-year old son of well-to-do parents. He plagued his parents, teachers, and friends; terrorized deliverymen, maids, and pets with his elaborate pranks. Outcault seemed to come up with an inexhaustable supply of mischief for Buster and his bulldog Tige.

Every Sunday fans opened the paper to read one of Buster's tongue-in-cheek resolutions, which reflected temporary contriteness for having been punished for another prank.

To capitalize on the instant popularity of his comic strip, Mr. Outcault took a booth at the St. Louis World's Fair in 1904. He hired a midget dressed in a Buster Brown costume, hired a trained dog that looked like Tige, and proceeded to sell the name Buster Brown to anyone interested. Apparently Mr. Outcault was as talented a salesman as he was a cartoonist because 45 companies agreed to use the name Buster Brown, products from bread to cameras. To our knowledge only two of the 45 companies ever sold a **Buster Brown** doll: Buster Brown Shoes and Buster Brown Hosiery Mills.

Mr. Outcault formed the Outcault Advertising Company of Chicago to merchandise his Buster Brown character. During this time many items were manufactured with Buster Brown on it in some way: spoons, whistles, mirrors, buttons, shoe horns, and of course dolls. These items were sold at the retail level, not as premiums

A September, 1905, advertisement in Ladies World offered a Buster Brown scarf pin for a 2¢ stamp.

In 1920 his advertising company was relinquished to his son and the comic strip was discontinued so Outcault could pursue his hobby of painting.

Buster Brown Shoes have consistently used the Buster Brown figure in their advertising. The company has not changed one eyelash from the original drawing, which is contrary to most trademark figures such as Campbell Kids, Cracker Jack Boy, and

Burger King, who have departed from the original artist's conception.

At least two **Buster Brown Shoe** dolls were issued. One, a 13-inch cloth doll, is marked Buster Brown Shoes across his jacket. The other is a small all-bisque doll also marked Buster Brown Shoes.

Cloth *Buster Brown* doll, 13-inches, was based on a cartoon character created by Robert F. Outcault in 1902. The mischievous *Buster* wears a red hat and suit, white collar and cuffs, with a blue bow and matching blue stockings. Marks: "Buster Brown/ Shoes", in yellow across front of jacket. A. Wolfe collection, David Nelson and James Giokas photographers. $50.00.

At one time the shoe store had a rather novel way of enticing children to coax their mothers for a pair of Buster Brown Shoes. With each pair of shoes, the customer was given a "Buster Brown Buck." This was worth $1.00 toward the purchase of a number of premiums including an ordinary bed doll. Most of the items were stamped Buster Brown Shoes.

Through the years various Buster Brown figures have been available to managers for window and store display. Early ones are made of plaster, later ones of plastic. All are marked and most resemble the old-fashioned character, although some attributed to Buster Brown Shoes are modernized.

Butterick Publishing Company. Butterick has been selling patterns for over a century. During this time they have offered several dolls, usually with patterns to encourage young seamstresses to sew. We could only locate two of the dolls.

The November 1907, Delineator Magazine advertised an 18-inch "Butterick Rag Doll" plus an illustrated pattern sheet for 25¢. The doll wore lithographed underclothes and black high-top shoes. Her face resembles the photograph of a sweet blond-haired child about five-years old. The ad says it is "printed flat in eight colors, on durable cloth." It comes with two patterns: #313 Girl Dolls' Dress, with separate Guimpe and Coat; #312 Girl Dolls' Kimona Wrapper or Dressing Sack.

In the 1940's a 12-inch **Butterick Mannequin** doll with patterns were available from retail markets. The doll was rather crudely finished with mold seams still obvious. The doll was made of pulp. It has molded/painted hair, eyes, and mouth, and has removable arms to aid in fitting clothes. It has holes in the feet to fit over dowels on the base. The paint did not adhere well on most **Butterick Mannequin** dolls and most are found today with the paint flaked off.

Bring Your Babies Back to Dollies

To Teach the Future Mother to Dress the Future Child

313—Girl Dolls' Dress, with Separate Guimpe and Coat.

312—Girl Dolls' Kimono Wrapper or Dressing Sack.

we have prepared THE BUTTERICK RAG DOLL and a series of patterns of attractive Dolls' Dresses, etc. This doll is about 18 inches high, printed flat in eight colors, on durable cloth; quickly and easily made up. Remember it is but a step for the little ones from the making of pretty clothes for their dollies to the more useful accomplishment of making dainty garments for themselves and others. For this reason we make the doll.

Special Offer: For 25c in stamps or coin we will mail you The Butterick Rag Doll, and the two attractive Dolls' Patterns shown above. Send at once to

THE BUTTERICK PUBLISHING CO., Ltd.,

Butterick Building, New York.

Butterick Rag Doll, 18-inches tall, was advertised in the November 1907, Delineator Magazine. $40.00.

The 1940's *Butterick Mannequin*. The 12-inch doll is a rather crudely molded and painted doll. Unmarked. M. Kolterman collection. $25.00.

Another magazine ad showing the cloth *Butterick Rag Doll*. The ads says it was printed flat in eight colors on durable cloth and could be made quickly and easily.

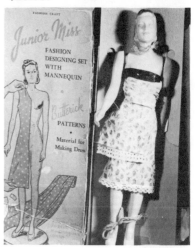

Another *Butterick* mannequin doll in original box. Could be quite nice except the painting is very poorly done. Eyes are all blue, lips red. B. Welch collection. $25.00.

Butternut Coffee. This product offered a Living Barbie doll in 1971.

82

C

Cal-Neva Club. This club in Nevada is known for its Wild Indian slot machines and sells a 6½-inch rubber doll to advertise them. The doll was sold in 1951; how long the promotion lasted is unknown. Members of the American Indian Movement (AIM) probably cringe at the sight of the grinning caricature with a scalp in one hand and a stone axe in the other.

C & H Sugar Twins were introduced in 1971 for $1.00. The 15-inch boy doll wears a blue print sarong and a flower lei. $6.00.

Cal-Neva Club's 6½-inch rubber doll was used in the 1950's to promote their Wild Indian slot machines. Marks: "Rempel Mfg./ Fred G. Reinert © Pat. N. 2459,892. K. Lansdowne collection. $8.00.

California and Hawaiian Sugar Company. In 1971 a cloth boy and girl doll were offered by the C & H Sugar Company. The dolls were advertised in magazines with full-page color ads. Each doll sold for $1.00 plus the oval from a package of brown sugar. The first ad appeared with an October 31, 1971 expiration date. In subsequent ads the date was extended to October 1972 and again to October 1973.

The C & H Sugar girl doll, also 15-inches, wears a green grass skirt, red print blouse, flower bracelets on wrist and ankle and matching flower lei. The eyes are solid black with no white showing, hair is also black. $6.00.

The 15-inch dolls have lithographed bodies the shade of the molasses-flavored brown sugar they advertise. The unmarked pair are obviously Hawaiian, with their black eyes and hair, smiling faces, tropical attire and bare feet.

The dolls were manufactured by a division of the Bemiss Bag Company of California to a design developed by an advertising agency hired by C & H.

Camel Cigarettes used a cloth car as a means of advertising. How this was distributed is not known.

Campbell Soup Company. "Mmm, Mm good!" are Campbell Soups and their dolls. The Campbell Kids are perhaps the most endearing and enduring of all the advertising dolls. Those chubby little Children with their rosy apple cheeks, side-glance eyes, and "H" mouths were perfect to duplicate in three-dimensional doll form. Doll manufacturers realized this and in 1909, four years after the first Campbell Kid illustrations were used, the doll craze began. According to the company, the first dolls were a line of stuffed velvet dolls, resembling the Grace Drayton drawings. They were manufactured by Sackman Bros. Co. (To our knowledge none of these have been found.)

A year later, 1910, the first official **Campbell Soup Kid** doll was manufactured by the E.I. Horsman Company. It had a "Can't Break 'Em" head and a sturdy cloth body filled with cork and jointed at the shoulder and hip. The dolls are marked E.I. Horsman © 1910, on the back of the head and the same information on a cloth label sewn in a seam of the body. The dolls came in four sizes: 9, 11, 12, and 15½-inches.

The first official *Campbell Kid* doll was manufactured by Horsman in 1910. This 9-inch example wears a one-piece red and white romper that is original. The head is made of the Can't Break 'Em composition. The firmly stuffed body is made of white muslin with peach-colored fabric for arms and legs. They are attached so they can be positioned. Marks: "Copyright 1910/by E.I. Horsman Co.," on label under arm; "The Campbell Kid/Trademark/Lic'd by Joseph Campbell Co./M'F'G'D' by E.I. Horsman Co.," printed on cloth label sewn on sleeve of romper. M. Meisinger collection.

From here the **Campbell Kid** doll record becomes a bit confusing and contradictory. The 1910 Horsman Campbell doll was not patented under that name by Horsman, even though the mark on the head shows the copyright mark.

A **Bobby** doll was patented in December, 1910, by Horsman and it is probably this doll that we know as the **Campbell Kid** doll. Perhaps there is an explanation that somewhat justifies Horsman using the **Bobby** doll for the **Campbell Kids** doll, too.

The originator of the Campbell Kid illustrations, Grace G. Wiederseim, first created a series for the Sunday Philadelphia Press called Bobby Blake and Dolly Drake, using two children resembling the figures she later drew as the Campbell Kids. Another twist in the story: although Mrs. Wiederseim created the Campbell Kid illustrations, Helen Trowbridge designed the dolls.

The plot thickens--Louis Amberg patented a **Bobby** and a **Dolly** doll, November 26, 1910 with the permission of Grace G. Wiederseim. It was copyrighted, trademark registered, and protected by the International Copyright.

Advertising by Amberg in 1911 included a NOTE TO THE TRADE: "We are the unquestioned originators of the Bobby Blake and Dolly Drake models, all heads copied after them are imitations. Do not be misled by inferior ones of these or of others of our numerous original dolls. We are protecting ourselves and our customers against infringers of our copyright and trademark rights."

Patricia Schoonmaker in an article on Grace Drayton in the November 1968, issue of Toy Trader gives a possible explanation of the multiple **Campbell Kid** and **Bobby** and **Dolly** dolls. She explains that Soloman Hoffman held the patent for the "Can't Break 'Em" mixture. This mixture of glue, glycerine, white zinc oxide, and Japanese wax was used to make many doll heads at his factory. The heads were sold to other doll manufacturers, who could apparently patent them as their own, upon completion. Since the paint of the dolls varies considerably, one may suspect that the second company did their own painting on the heads in addition to providing bodies and costuming.

Records show Mr. Hoffman was incorporated in 1865 as the American Doll and Toy Manufacturing Company. In 1909 his company was purchased by Aetna Doll and Toy Company; it was this company that produced the Campbell "Can't Break 'Em" heads. It seems he provided both Horsman and Amberg with heads that were interchangeably called **Bobby**, **Dolly**, or **Campbell Kids**.

Whether sold as an Amberg doll or a Horsman doll probably mattered little to customers, as long as they had one of the " . . . clever little bright-eyed youngsters," as the advertisement in Playthings read when describing the "Campbell Kid" dolls in 1911.

Another of Horsman's 1910 *Campbell Kid* dolls is this 15½-inch doll. This outfit is probably original because it has a cloth label sewn on the sleeves. The jacket is red with a plaid tie at the neck; white skirt and brown felt shoes complete the outfit. Marks: "E.I.H ©1910", on neck; "The Campbell Kids/Trademark/Lic'd by Joseph Campbell Company/Reg'd by E.I. Horsman Co."; "Gesetzlich Geschutzt in Deutschland", on cloth label on sleeve of jacket. Photo courtesy of The Smithsonian Institution.

Another Horsman *Campbell Kid* doll, 11-inches, this one has hands made of the same material as the head. Doll is in excellent condition but probably does not wear original clothing. Campbell Kid spoons tied around neck supposedly came with the doll. K. Miller collection.

This could be the rare *Campbell Baby* doll. It has Can't Break 'Em head and gauntlet hands. The cloth body is muslin with blue and white striped fabric for the legs and feet. Legs are slightly bowed. Marks: "E.I.H. © 1910," on back of neck; "Copyright 1910/By Horsman," on cloth tag sewn in dart on body. M. Meisinger collection.

Illustrations of the Campbell Kids were a success from the day they were first added to the street car posters in 1905. Grace G. Drayton had a knack for drawing the little figures. In a 1926 newspaper interview, she explains: "I was my own model because I began young. I was interested in my looks. I knew I was funny. I used to look in the mirror, and then with a pencil in my chubby fingers, I would sketch my image as I remembered it. My playmates were always delighted with the results--they always recognized me. They, too, thought I looked funny. And I kept on making rolypolys, consulting the mirror from time to time. Eventually I created a type that was as much a part of me as myself. And it grew with me though, it never grew up. When I thought of a career, I found I had one in just keeping alive these youngsters I had created in and from my own childhood."

In 1904 Grace Gebbie, at age 28, married Theodore E. Weiderseim, Jr., an employee of a lithographic company that wanted the advertising account of the Joseph Campbell Company. At her husband's request, Grace added some sketches to his advertising layout.

Timing was perfect, Charles Snyder, the creator of the jingles that Campbell had been using on street car posters for the past five years, had recommended a character be added to the advertising cards. Campbell officials like the Kids and soon they were seen wherever there was an advertisement for the quality soup in the red and white can.

The Kid's national debut was made in a black and white single column ad found in the Ladies Home Journal, September, 1905. That same year the first company publication using the Kids was printed, a booklet, Just as Easy.

From 1905 to 1912 consumers were bombarded with the Kids. Harvest, the company magazine, for Spring 1975 says: "People sent Campbell Kid postcards, kept score on Campbell Kid bridge tallies, set out Campbell Kid place cards, sported Kid lapel buttons, and painted in Campbell Kid Paint books. The roly-polys smiled from grocery store windows, and the Company's mailing envelopes proclaimed, 'From the Home of the Campbell Kids.''

Black Horsman doll, is all composition except for cloth body. Unmistakenly a Drayton doll, whether it sold as a Campbell Kid is unknown. Not original dress. Marks: "E.I.H. CO. INC.,'' on back of neck. $125.00.

In 1911 Grace Gebbie Wiederseim was divorced and remarried. Thereafter her work was signed Grace G. Drayton.

In 1912 Horsman registered a patent for Campbell Kid clothes. The boy's romper suit and the girl's dress had a deep yoke made from a cotton fabric printed with doll figures. The rest of the material used in the outfits was white with a small print and a band of solid red around the sleeve and skirt of the dress and belt of the rompers.

Many **Campbell Kid** dolls were made and sold during the teen years. Sears sold **Dutch Campbell Kids**. They were: "The cutest little dolls imaginable. Dresses are charming in bright contrasting colors. Girl with red blouse and blue skirt, white apron and striped stockings. Boy with striped waist, khaki pants and striped stockings. Cloth slippers are made in shape of wooden shoes. Both dolls 12-inches high. 89¢ each."

Sears also sold the **Campbell College Kid** doll. It was sold in their catalog with this description: "Very plump well stuffed silesia body, jointed at hips, knees and shoulders. Charming character face. Natural looking, unbreakable head. Latest style blazer jacket in college colors. Full plaited white lawn skirt, half hose and felt slippers. Height, 13-inches. Price $1.19."

Montgomery Ward, Butler Bros., and Belles Hess catalogs also advertised composition or composition and cloth **Campbell Kid** dolls. All had the look of a Grace Drayton child. The dolls ranged in size from 8½-inches to 16-inches, some had wigs or brightly painted hair. Most were costumed in rompers or dresses with cloth shoes; a few wore molded boots.

It was at this time that the **Campbell Baby** doll was advertised. (To my knowledge one has never been positively identified as being this doll.) The baby was a Horsman doll and was advertised in the McDonald Bros., 1919 Christmas catalog.

Many Campbell Kid look-alike dolls in bisque and composition were sold from 1925, all with the look that Drayton made popular. The Campbell company did not mention giving any of these companies a license in our correspondence. Many of these manufacturers designed and marketed dolls similar to the Drayton figures, but they made no reference to either her or Campbell Kids. Germany produced small all-bisque dolls with the Drayton look that are often sold as **Campbell Kid** dolls in today's antique shops.

Other dolls that Grace G. Drayton designed are sometimes mistaken for Campbell Kids because most of her figures have such a distinctive look. Drayton's **Gee Gee, Peek-a-boo**, and **September Morn** are certainly close cousins to the Kids.

The **Campbell Kid** dolls manufactured during this time span (1910 to 1925) often had sateen bodies with horizontal striped sateen legs that doubled as stockings. Most marked dolls had a cloth label sewn in the seam with identification although some had a sticker on the chest. The exact words vary, but most give credit to the Joseph Campbell Company. That is, the ones that are marked. Many, many were unmarked.

In the 1920's Grace gave up her job as illustrator for the company and Ray Williams took over. The Kids did not change noticeably under his pen, as they did under later illustrators.

In 1925 Horsman manufactured a rather lean "Campbell Kid" type doll with a cloth body and composition head and limbs. Some of the dolls were painted brown and dressed in an Indian costume. The dolls were not as popular as the earlier Can't Break 'Em Kids.

In 1929 an especially adorable **Campbell Kid** doll, 13-inches tall, known as the Petite, was manufactured by American Character with rights purchased from Horsman. The doll's limbs and head were strung with elastic so they could be posed (a first for the Kids). The cost of the doll varied according to the costume, from a low of $1.00 for a simple dress to $100.00 for the doll in the fur coat outfit. Shoes on the Petite doll were removable.

With the **Petite** doll the soup company began an extensive nationwide advertising campaign. The opening announcement of the doll was a large color ad in the Comic sections of the *American Weekly,* which reached 10,000,000 readers June 9, 1929. January Playthings that year said: "Take a ride anywhere in the street cars, subway, elevator--pick up almost any important national magazine and the first full-page advertisement--usually in color features the famous red and white messages of the Campbell Soup Company and one or more of the hundreds of clever little color illustrations and poems that tell you of the adventures, the hopes, and the longings of the Campbell Kids that children everywhere know and delight in. Millions of people, old and young, have seen these rollicking happy-go-lucky little figures--and now they come to life in a charming new doll--the **Petite Campbell Kid**. This new creation of the American Character Doll is one of the many new 1920 innovations in Petite dolls that make this more interesting than ever before in its history. The Campbell Kids will be dressed in many of the interesting costumes featured in Campbell advertisements and is so made that it assumes any pose pictured in national advertising. Added to the appeal of its national reputation is the appealing character of the doll itself. It is distinctly new in many features, and so attractive that mothers are certain to buy them all year round."

The role and emphasis on the Kids in the Campbell Company

advertising has varied from time to time as they perceived the Kids popularity with the public. Until 1922 nearly 100% of the Campbell ads used the Kids. Radio advertising was began by Campbell in 1931, and the Kids did not lend themselves to this type of media. In 1934, with the depression still gripping the nation, the Kids were out. Realism was in--drawings of life-like children and Carolyn Campbell, a fictional mother figure, replaced the Kids. Then World War II struck and the Kids were back in making patriotic appearances in magazines with such slogans as: "Buy War Stamps," "Better Soups for Victory," and "Be Glad You Can Share."

By the mid-forties the Kids had sunk to an all-time low with the company. They were nixed by editoral policy as shown by company records that state: "In editorial pages, the Kids cannot be used," and "The Kids are not realistic-(and) would be a serious impediment . . "

Television saved the Kids in the 50's and they were revitalized to entice a new generation of children to eat their Campbell Soup. A few years before their revitalization, another fine quality **Campbell Kid** doll was placed on the market. Horsman manufactured a composition doll in 1947. It came in four outfits: as a chef with a tall white hat and an apron worn over rompers, the companion doll wears a short full-skirted dress with rick-rack trim and has a ribbon stapled to the molded hair, the other pair are in blue and white outfits with horizontal-striped tops and blue pants for the boy and a blue skirt for the girl.

The 1947 Horsman Kids came with a card pinned on the front with identification and the picture of a can of Campbell's Tomato Soup. They wore painted stockings and painted Mary Jane shoes.

In 1947 Horsman manufactured a 12½-inch composition *Campbell Kid* doll that closely resembled the adorable children Grace G. Drayton created to advertise Campbell Soup. This particular doll was manufactured in 1948, when a few modifications were in effect: the shoes did not have a strap painted over the instep and the clothing was different. This doll still has her original cardboard tag and clothing. Marks: "Campbell Soup Co.," on neck; "Campbell's KID/A HORSMAN DOLL/Permission of Campbell Soup Company," on paper tag. Margaret Woodbury Strong Museum, B. Jendrick photographer. $125.00.

Campbell dolls seemed to sell in pairs, thus doubling the usual number sold. Perhaps this is a carry-over from their beginning when they were confused with Bobby Blake and Dolly Drake.

Horsman changed the dolls slightly a year later, in 1948. The painted shoes had no strap; they were painted slip-on shoes. The blue outfits were a modified a bit. The rompers were shorter and had straps over the shoulder and the hat had a visor.

Occasionally collectors confuse the 1929 **Petite** with the 1947 Horsman doll. Although similar, there are differences. The Horsman Kids are 12½-inches tall, the Petite Kids are 13-inches. Horsman dolls wear molded Mary Jane shoes in 1947 and slippers in 1948. The Petite dolls wear removable shoes. Horsman dolls have ringlets molded to stand out from the head with a hollow look to the ringlet near the face. Petite doll's hair shows comb marks, but the hair lies close to the head in flat curls. The Horsman dolls have chubby legs, dimpled knees, and toes that point in. Petite Kids legs are more slender with less detail. Petite Kids have painted nostrils, few lashes painted and the iris of the eye is rimmed in color. The Horsman eye is white with a black heart lying on its side for the pupil and iris. The actual dolls are easy to identify because both are marked. The Petite is marked on the back of the neck: A PETITE-/DOLL. The Horsman has a tag pinned on and is also incised on the neck: Campbell Soup Co.

In 1951 the Campbell Kids were up-dated and standardized. Two years later (1953) the Ideal Toy Company was licensed to manufacture **Campbell Kids** dolls, 17½-inches tall, with vinyl heads and cloth bodies. The girl wears a checkered dress; the boy a checkered romper suit. Both wear white chef hats and aprons. The dolls sold in retail outlets for $4.98 each.

In 1954 to further the Kids, the company authorized 34 manufacturers to produce Campbell Kid items. Plaques of the Kids were popular to hold hot pads, note paper, or a thermometer. Children could make mudpies in Campbell Kid dishes, read their Campbell Kid books, cut out Campbell Kid paper dolls, push a Campbell Kid doll buggy, or wear clothes made of fabric printed with the Kids.

During the mid-fifties several squeeze dolls were made to represent the Kids. They did not follow the new specifications and some came in colors not usually associated with Campbell--green and also yellow.

The early 50's marked the time of a disastrous doll innovation called Magic Skin. Bodies were made from a soft latex and stuffed with cotton, much like a rag doll. The feel of the new material inspired the name--Magic Skin. Unfortunately it had two other magic qualities. It changed color, one day the doll would be flesh colored, the next it would be spotted, and in no time at all, it would turn black. Magic Skin was also known to do a disappearing act; sometimes the bodies would deteriorate right on the merchant's shelves.

Ideal manufactured **Campbell Kid** dolls made with Magic Skin bodies. The bodies of many disappeared leaving only vinyl heads, which appear regularly at flea markets. The Magic Skin **Campbell Kid** dolls sold at stores and Sears catalogs in 1955 for $2.99 each. They were 9½-inches tall, some had glassene eyes, although most of the eyes were painted. Some dolls had molded shoes and stockings others had removable shoes and stockings.

The following year Ideal offered a smaller doll with a durable vinyl body. Both these dolls and the 1955 dolls were advertised as twin dolls and came dressed in his or her chef outfits of red and white.

About this time the Reliable Manufacturing Company of Canada produced a 9½-inch vinyl **Campbell Kid** doll that is like the Ideal doll.

Climax to the Campbell Kid revitalization of the 50's was the Campbell Kid Birthday Celebration that began in 1956, which seems a year late, since the Kid's debut was 1905. Fifty-one years after this debut Campbell Soup offered their first premium doll. To quote the company: "The "Kid," a baby-type doll with plastic head and soft rubber body, was offered to consumers for a Campbell Soup label and $1.00. It pulled in 560,000 requests."

To celebrate the 50th birthday of the Kids, the Campbell Soup Company offered, for the first time, a premium doll. The first ones in 1955 came out on Magic Skin bodies that discolored (note photo) and often disintegrated. The bodies were changed to vinyl and as a result grew a half-inch, to 8-inches in height. The dolls were manufactured by Ideal and were also sold in other costumes at the retail level. Doll wears original clothes and stands beside folder that came with the doll. Marks: "Campbell Kid/Made by/Ideal Toy Corp.," on back of neck. M. Rice collection. $15.00.

The doll was manufactured by Ideal and had a Magic Skin body. This premium may have also had the more permanent vinyl body on later dolls. The doll wore a white pinafore apron over a red and white checked blouse with a solid red skirt. It had removable shoes.

The offer was so successful Campbell offered a **Cheerleader** doll the fall of 1957. Ideal manufactured the **Cheerleader**. It is 8-inches tall, of good quality vinyl, and has molded shoes and stockings. The cheerleading outfit consists of a white knit top with a script "C" on the front and a gathered red skirt. It cost $1.00 plus one label and was offered for four years, from 1957 to August, 1961. Only 270,000 of these dolls were dispersed.

From 1957 to 1961, Campbell Soup offered the *Campbell Cheerleader* doll. It is 9½-inches tall and wears a knit top with a red cotton skirt. The shoes and stockings are molded/painted. Marks: "Campbell Kid/Made by/Ideal Toy Corp.," on back of neck; "C" on front of dress. B. Beisecker collection. $15.00.

In addition to the doll, extra costumes could be ordered: night gown and lounging robe, school dress and pajamas, rainy day attire, party dress, and a red vinyl carrying case with pink lining divided in two compartments for doll and clothing. The cost was $1.00 for each outfit or the case.

This undressed Kid looks like the previous doll, except it was made by a Canadian firm. B. Welch collection. $15.00.

To measure the success of the Kid's revitalization and to determine their popularity in relation to other trade characters, two surveys were conducted.

Before the 1951 promotional campaign, a survey showed only 37% of the people could identify the Kids. They rated a low fourth behind Aunt Jemima, the Birds Eye Kids, and Borden's Elsie. The first three trademarks were recognized by 80% of the people surveyed.

After the promotion and after the 1956 birthday celebration with its premium doll, the Campbell Kids improved their percent from 37% to 72%. They were still in

fourth place, but a much higher fourth. That year only two trademark characters showed gains in recognition, Speedy Alka Seltzer and the Campbell Kids.

After the **Cheerleader** doll premium expired in 1961 the company waited two years, until 1963 to bring out the third premium doll. It was a noticable change from the early Drayton looking Kids and the previous vinyl premium dolls. Apparently it met company approval because the three successive premiums offered used this doll, wearing different outfits.

The third offer was the **Scotch Highlander** doll, 10-inches tall, jointed at neck, shoulder, and hips. According to the company, they chose the predominant clan Campbell tartan to make the Scottish

The third Campbell premium doll is totally different from the previous premium dolls. It is 10-inches tall and jointed at the shoulder, hip, and neck. It was offered in 1963 to promote Campbell's bean products. The tartan chosen for the *Scotch Highlanders* is the most well known from the Campbell clan. Unmarked. M. Rice collection. $20.00.

kilt. And yes, the Kid does wear something under the kilt, red knit pants. The costume is complete with hat, shoes, stockings, spats, and belt.

The **Scotch Highlander** doll was offered from March 1963 to January 1964. The price was $1.50 plus two bean product labels. About 93,000 were mailed to consumers.

In 1966 the same doll dressed as a chef was introduced. It wears a shirt, neckerchief, pants, apron, and a chef hat with a script "C" on the wide brim. Only 20,000 of these dolls were ordered, the least of all the Campbell premium dolls. The offer expired February 1968.

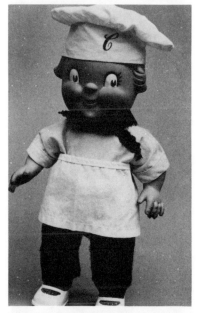

The 10-inch *Chef* doll was offered from 1966 to 1968, and received the least requests of any Campbell Soup Company premium doll. Unmarked. Sally Esser collection, B. Esser photographer. $10.00.

The same basic doll as the **Scotch Highlander** and the **Chef** was used for a pair of **Campbell Kid** dolls. The boy and girl were offered from August 1971 to May 1972 for $2.00 each plus two chicken soup labels. The boy wears red pants and a striped shirt. Both have removable shoes and stockings.

The 10-inch boy and girl dolls offered by Campbell in 1971. Both wear complete original outfits. Unmarked. S. Ricklefs $10.00.

The *Campbell Girl* wearing the afternoon dress that could be ordered separatly. Unmarked. S. Esser Collection, B. Esser photographer. $10.00.

Upon receiving the dolls a folder was enclosed offering four sets of clothing for $1.00 each. The four outfits were: a tennis suit consisting of pants, shirt, and racket; an afternoon dress set with dress, underpants, and hatbox; a party dress set with dress, underpants, and purse; sleepy time with pajamas, comb, brush, and mirror. These dolls were popular--129,575 were sold.

In 1973 three cloth **Campbell Kid** dolls were available at the retail level. Sears and Montgomery Ward sold similar cloth dolls with yarn hair dressed as a chef. An especially good quality pair of Kids was made in Japan. The girl wore a removable red dress and the boy a pair of blue overalls. Both had patent leather looking shoes made from black oilcloth.

A Japanese company manufactured these quality cloth *Campbell Kid* dolls in 1973. The 16½-inch girl wears a red dress with eyelet trim on the neck and sleeves. A small waist apron is also trimmed with the eyelet. The black oilcloth shoes are sewn on. Yellow yarn is used for the girl's hair. Marks: "Campbell Kids," on cloth labels. S. Russell collection. $10.00.

In 1973 both Sears and Montgomery Ward sold pairs of the Kids in their catalogs. The dolls were manufactured by Knickerbocker and were 12-inches tall. They were exactly the same, except the Ward's dolls have a "C" on the brim of the of the chef hat. Marks: "The/Campbell/Kids," plus a list of materials used is printed on a tag sewn in the seam of the leg. $5.00.

Campbell Kid boy doll has blue pants and a blue and white checked shirt. S. Russell collection. $10.00.

During the 1950's many Campbell items appeared on the market. This 7-inch squeak toy is probably of that decade. He wears green pants and neckerchief; one hand holds a spoon and the other arm has a molded/painted towel folded over it. Marks: "C", on brim of chef hat. $7.50

To commemorate the nation's Bicentennial, Campbell offered a set of **Colonial Campbell Kid** dolls. They were offered from January 1976 to well into 1977. The impact of inflation can be realized in the rising cost of the **Campbell Kid** dolls. The Bicentennial pair cost $4.95 each plus four soup labels. The cost of the same doll dressed as a **Scotch Highlander** cost $1.25 only ten years ago.

The costumes on the Colonial pair are especially attractive. The girl wears a long red-checked dress, white apron, and mop cap. The boy wears a blue felt three-cornered hat, white ruffled shirt, blue vest, and knee pants. Both dolls wear white stockings and black slip-on shoes.

During the recent promotions, the Kids were mailed in a very sturdy cardboard box with a tight fitting flap lid.

A firm vinyl *Campbell Kid* squeaker doll has molded/painted clothes and features. The dress and stockings are red, shoes are white, and the hair is yellow. Unmarked. $5.00.

The 10-inch vinyl Bicentennial premium dolls are the same dolls used in the past three premium promotions. The dolls are nicely costumed in colonial style outfits. The boy has molded/painted brown hair; the girl's is yellow. Each doll cost $4.95. Unmarked. $25.00-35.00 pair.

Backtracking to the mid-1960's to follow the Kids relationship to the company's advertising, at this time they were considered old-fashioned. One company official said, "I watch hours of children TV and 'teen television and 'adult' television, and I am absolutely convinced that the medium has few places for the 'Kid' commercials. I have read the history of 'the Kids' and recognize the identification people once enjoyed with them, but I cannot help thinking we must kindle a strong feeling that Campbell's Soups are made for today--today's people homes, today's tastes, today's life, 'The Kids' say yesterday."

The company wondered, was the opinion valid? They wanted to know, so a study was made. The results were not encouraging for the Kids. The children participating guessed the Kids age anywhere from 10 to 90. The prevailing idea was that a Campbell Kid was probably a woman or girl dressed up like a woman. The conclusion was the Kid was not boyish enough to be recognized definitely as a boy, nor girlish enough to be recognized as a girl, nor childish enough to be viewed as a child. Perhaps looking back, a study could be made of the study. Remember the sixties, it was indeed difficult to distinguish girls from boys and the young from the old trying to appear young.

The favorable part of the research was the Campbell Kids were definitely identified with the product they had represented for sixty years. As a result of the study the Kids were less visible during the next few years.

Then the seventies hit, and what was old-fashioned before, was suddenly--in. Nostalgia brought back the Kids. Children and adults clamored for any premium with the Campbell Kids on it.

These *Campbell Kid* dolls were made in bisque by the late Goodie Bennett. G. Cannon collection, G. Cannon photographer. $150.00 each.

In 1978 Norcross brought out an extensive line of Campbell Kid products, mugs, stationery, and cards to name a few items.

The price of the old Campbell Kid related items has soared, especially the dolls. In 1978 a pair of 1947 Horsman composition dolls in top condition sold for $300.00. Even the vinyl dolls of the 60's became expensive. The **Scotch Highlander** doll in original costume brought $30.00. Dolls in good condition and original costumes brought good prices, but even an old 1910 Horsman with Can't Break 'Em head and not a fleck of paint still on the head brought $35.00.

The Campbell Kids have gone through cycles of popularity and disfavor. They seem to endure. It is difficult to imagine a store with no Campbell Soup or Campbell Soup with no Kids.

CHRONOLOGY OF CAMPBELL SOUP COMPANY

1869 Company began with Abram Anderson and Joseph Campbell in New Jersey. Sold only peas and asparagus.

1873 Joseph Campbell takes over company; sells canned vegetables and fruit butters.

1892 Joseph Campbell & Company established, became the Joseph Campbell Preserve Company.

1897 Dr. J.T. Dorrance develops condensed soup for the company.

1898 Five varieties of condensed soup available.

1899 Company begins advertising on posters in street cars with jingles created by Charles N. Snyder.

1900 Won coveted gold medal in Paris Exposition (label today has a facsimile).

1904 Campbell Kids, as sketched by Grace Gebbie Wieder-seim, are accepted as characters to accompany jingles.

1904 Birth of Campbell's Pork and Beans.

1905 Company becomes Joseph Campbell Company.

1905 Company's first publication, Just as Easy, uses Kids for illustrations.

1905 Kids make debut in September Ladies Home Journal.

1909 Campbell Kid doll boom begins with a line of stuffed velvet dolls, resembling Grace G. Wieerseim's drawings.

1910 First official Campbell Kid doll is manufactured by E.I. Horsman, cost $1.00 at retail stores. Can't Break 'Em material used for head, body of sturdy muslin firmly filled with cork. We found three sizes: 11, 12, and 15½--inches. All dolls are marked EIH© 1910, on back of neck and also had the same information on a cloth label.

1910 - 40 F. Wallace Armstrong Co. produced Kid artwork.

1911 Grace signs work Grace G. Drayton after divorce and remarriage.

1911 Campbell Kid dolls patented and sold in England in three sizes: 10½, 13, and 15½--inches tall.

1912 Horsman secures patents for clothes for Campbell boy and girl with doll motif on striped romper; girl's dress made of same material, felt shoes. Dolls wearing these clothes pink sateen bodies, same heads as the 1910 dolls.

1912 Butler Bros. advertise 9½ and 12-inch Kids.

1913 Montgomery Ward catalog offers pair of 11-inch Kids for 98¢.

1913 Rare 10-inch Campbell Baby with ribbon in hair, curved baby legs on doll with long dress, straight legs on same doll with short dress.

1914 ca. Small all-bisque dolls resembling Kids manufactured in Germany.

1914 Kids wear wigs.

1914 Campbell Kid look-alike, Peek-a-boo doll, becomes popular. Composition with upper torso cloth, barefoot, assorted costumes, only 7-inches high.

1914 E.I. Horsman registers patent for 16-inch German Kid.

1914 "The Great Campbell Kids" dolls, 14-inches tall, cork body, unbreakable composition head, arms, and legs. Boy wore checked pants, girl striped dress, cost 98¢ each.

1914 Junior Campbell Kids available, copy of the 14-inch Kids, except smaller, cost 48¢.

1915 Butler Bros. wholesale catalog "Our Drummer" lists a 12-inch Kid dressed either as a boy in rompers or a girl in a dress.

1916 Campbell Kid College dolls sold in Sears Catalog for $1.19. Dressed in a striped blazer with initial on front with a white pleated skirt. Same catalog offers Dutch Campbell Kids for 89¢, 12-inches.

1916 Roy Williams takes over drawing the Campbell Kids from Drayton.

1916 Belles Hess catalog, 12-inch Kids, with composition head and hands, jointed cloth body, and dressed in a floral dress sells at 59¢.

1922 Company changes name to Campbell Soup Company.

1925 Soup cost 12¢ a can and came in 21 varieties.

1925 Horsman manufactures dolls with composition head and limbs, cloth body, has a lean look, eyes not to side. These dolls are often brown and may not have been sold as Campbell dolls although they have the Drayton look.

1926 Corrine Pauli is artist for Campbell Soup Company.

1929 Campbell Kid, 13-inch, Petite Doll is manufactured by American Character Company. First all composition Campbell Kid doll.

1931 Radio advertising for Campbell Soup begins.

1933 Campbell Kid Town offer for 10¢.

1940 - 50 Ward Wheelock Company of Philadelphia produces Kid artwork.

1947 Horsman makes jointed 12-inch composition Kids, five styles of clothing.

1948 ca. Horsman modifies Kids, by painting shoes without strap over instep and changing costumes.

1950s Paul Fennel in Hollywood produced Kid art work and television ads.

1951 Campbell Kids are updated and standardized by Johnstone & Cushing Studios.

1953 Campbell Kid wall plaques manufactured by Miller Studio. Heads with hook to hold hotpads, full figure with thermometer, figure with note pad, and two decorative placques of Kids dressed as farmers.

1954 Thirty-four manufacturers licensed to produce Campbell Kids items: cookware for children, books, paper dolls, doll furniture, buggy, bicycle, fabric, clothing, and many more items.

1955 ca. Squeeze-toy dolls in un-Campbell colors such as blue, yellow, and green.

1954 Boy and Girl Campbell Kid chef squeeze toys manufactured by Oak Rubber company for retail stores.

1955 Twin Kids chef dolls, advertised in Sears catalog for $2.99, 9½-inches tall, vinyl heads, Magic Skin latex bodies filled with cotton that disintegrated in a short time. Made by Ideal.

1955 Reliable Company in Canada manufacturers a marked doll like the one by Ideal.

1956 Official birthday promotion Campbell Kid doll offered for the first time by the company 7½-inch doll was manufactured by Ideal.

1957 - 61 Second Campbell premium doll, Cheerleader; made by Ideal.

1960 Mel Richman Studio of Philadelphia producers of Kid artwork.

1963 Scotch Highlander, third Campbell premium doll is offered, totally different from Ideal dolls.

1966

- **68** Chef, fourth doll offered by Campbell, same as the Scotch doll.

1971 Boy and girl Kids offered, same as the Scotch and Chef dolls.

1973 Montgomery Ward's catalog advertises 12-inch Campbell pair made of cloth for $1.49 per pair; dressed as chefs; made by Knickerbocker.

1973 Sear's catalog advertises a 12-inch Campbell pair made of cloth for $1.49 per pair; dolls made by Knickerbocker and appear to be the same as the Ward's dolls, except the Ward's dolls have a "C" on the apron.

1973 Japanese make a 15½-inch cloth Campbell pair of excellent quality. Girl has yellow yarn hair and a red dress. Boy has brown yarn hair and wears blue overalls and a gingham checked shirt. Each cost $1.49.

1974 Campbell Kid dolls sold in Mexico.

1976 To celebrate the Bicentennial Campbell offers Kids dressed in nice quality Colonial costumes. Same as the four previous dolls. Designed and produced by M & S Shillman Co. of N.Y.; all are 10-inches tall.

Canadian Club Whiskey, imported in bottle by Hiram Walker Importers. This Canadian whiskey used an interesting felt doll for display. The **French Grenadier**, 19-inches tall, wears a blue uniform with a long cape and hat with a chin strap. It was made to fit a fiberboard background showing the Eiffel Tower.

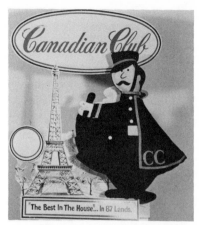

Canadian Club's *French Grenadier*, 19-inches, is made of royal blue felt with lavender pink edging monogram. Marks: "Canadian Club/86.8 Proof. Blended Canadian Whiskey". A. Wolfe collection. $12.00.

Caravelle Candy Bar, a product of Peter-Paul Company. A 10-inch doll made from a plastic replica of the Caravelle Candy Bar has vinyl covered wire limbs that can be posed. The nose, eyes, and

Caravelle Candy Bar doll is marked: "Made in Hong Kong/Pat. pending, on hat. M. Hiter collection. $5.00.

mouth are hard plastic glued to the bar. Gloves, boots, and hat are yellow vinyl. Date and method of distribution are unknown.

Carey Salt. In 1979 a hand puppet named **Bath Buddy** was offered for 50¢. The washcloth puppet is made of white terry cloth with facial features and the Carey Salt logo on the front.

Carnation Malted Milk. In 1965 a Barbie doll was offered for $1.75 with the label from either natural or chocolate flavor malted milk. Three costumes were also available: Bride's Dream, Career Girl, or Sophisticated Lady. The outfits range in price from $1.75 to $2.75.

Carnation Milk Co. The Horsman Doll Company manufactured an 18-inch vinyl doll labeled the **Carnation Cry Baby** in 1962. The Carnation Milk Company has no record of the doll so presumably it sold from retail stores. The doll has a jointed body, sleep eyes and a synthetic wig.

Carrols. This hamburger restaurant, known as "Home of the Club-Burger," gave free plastic hand puppets in 1977.

Hand puppet given free at Carrols, a hamburger restaurant. A. Pfister collection. $1.00.

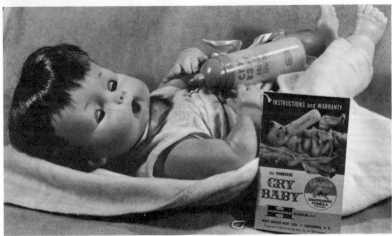

The *Carnation Milk Cry Baby* was manufactured by Horsman in 1962. It is an 18-inch jointed vinyl baby doll with sleep eyes and synthetic wig. The doll is wearing original clothing and has original bottle and tags. Marks: "Horsman Doll, Inc./1962/No. 2000." N. Ricklefs collection. $20.00.

Central Flour Company.
(See Istrouma Flour.)

Ceresota and Heckers Flour, products of Standard Mills Company. Two cloth dolls were found that represent the trademark used by these two brands of flour, one doll was made in 1912, the other in 1972.

Today both Heckers and Ceresota use the trademark of a little boy in a wide-brimmed hat sitting on a stool slicing a huge loaf of bread. In 1912, probably only Ceresota used the trademark because the doll is known as the **Ceresota Boy** and it is only marked Ceresota Flour, not Heckers.

The doll is one of the finest early cloth dolls. It is 16-inches tall and printed in rich oil-based paints. **Ceresota Boy** wears trousers, short-sleeved shirt, suspenders and boots, his hat has a brim that is cut from a separate piece of fabric, making it three-dimensional. The doll is well-marked; cost and method of distribution are unknown.

The more recent doll, 1972, is a prestuffed cloth doll made by Chase Bag Company. It was advertised on packages of flour for $1.00. The 15-inch doll is lithographed totally in purple. In Chicago, Milwaukee, and Philadelphia the doll is known as the Ceresota doll. In the area around New York state it is called the Heckers doll. Both brands of flour advertised the doll on the packages of their flour.

Today Heckers and Ceresota are manufactured by the same milling company, Standard Mills Company of Kansas City, Missouri. Heckers was first milled by the Heckers family in 1843 in New York City. Ceresota was milled about that time in the Chicago area. Both brands have changed hands many times.

Lovely oil-painted cloth doll, 1912, representing the *Ceresota Flour Boy*. The 16-inch doll wears dark red pants, white short-sleeved shirt, blue suspenders and black boots. The brown hat has a brim cut from a separate piece of fabric, making it three-dimensional. Marks: "Ceresota Flour," across shirt front; "The Northwestern Consolidated Milling Co. Flour," going around a disk on the back suspenders; "Ceresota," across the middle of the disk. Courtesy of Ralph's Antique Dolls. $125.00-225.00.

According to company literature, there is a legend connected with Ceresota that explains both the name and the little boy trademark. Back in the days of mythology there was a beautiful goddess of harvest named **Ceres**. Her brother Jupiter announced that her little son should be given a name. He announced to the child: "Part of thy name shall be 'Ota,' in our language 'Son'; the rest is thy mother's and these two shall represent honor, integrity, and devotion."

The boy, Ceresota, had many adventures and met many

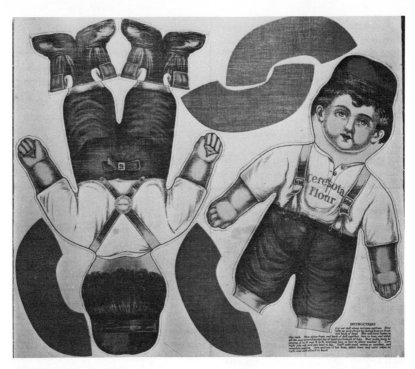

Uncut old *Ceresota Flour Boy* shows back view and hat and boot construction. **<u>Playthings by the Yard</u>, 1973. $125.00-225.00.**

fascinating people. One of his friends was a flour miller whose ambition was to make the finest flour in the world. Ceresota decided to help him, so he taught the miller how to select the choicest wheat; how to build machines that would screen and sift and polish each perfect grain; and how to mill it into beautiful white flour.

In time the miller's ambition was realized and his flour became the finest in the world. Out of his gratitude to his friend the miller named his flour Ceresota and put a picture of the little boy on every bag.

The trademark was an easily recognized symbol for foreigners desiring the unbleached flour milled by Heckers and Ceresota. It closely resembled the flour they used before coming to America. The little boy is stamped in purple on packages of flour today

The 1972 unmarked *Ceresota/ Heckers Flour Boy* is stamped in purple ink on flour packaging since the late 1800's. The 15-inch doll was advertised on packages of flour. $5.00.

Cheer Detergent, a product of Procter and Gamble Co. In the early 1960's Procter and Gamble were anxious to obtain consumers for their detergent that was being touted as able to clean in cold water. What better way to tempt customers than with a visible premium. Ten-inch vinyl dolls with rooted wigs were attached to king-sized boxes of All-Temperature Cheer. Both Black and Caucasion dolls were offered. They wore a shirt, pants, and boots.

Ten-inch vinyl dolls were attached to king-sized boxes of Cheer detergent in the early 1960's. The dolls had rooted synthetic wigs, closed mouth, jointed body, and painted eyes. Marks: "Made in Hong Kong." W. Dingman collection. $2.00.

Chee.tos, a product of Frito-Lay, Inc. In 1974 this cheese flavored snack food offered a 12-inch cloth **Chee.tos Mouse Man** doll for $1.00. The doll has large felt ears and wears a lithographed business suit.

The mouse originated in 1967 for television commercials. To keep up with the times the mouse, on television, has undergone many changes in the past decade. He went through the "Astronaut", "Genie" and "Cheesy Rider" stages. The company thinks another doll will be tried again in the future.

The 12-inch *Chee.tos Mouse* doll was offered in 1974 by Frito Lay's cheese snack. The mouse is gray with a blue business suit, orange neck tie; it has large felt ears. Also on the photo are small pink, orange, and blue erasers that were included free in packages of Chee.tos. $5.00.

Chef Boy-ar-dee. This product offered a Barbie Doll with two outfits for $3.98 plus 3 proofs-of-purchase in 1972.

Chesapeake and Ohio Railway. Chessie, the little kitten asleep on a pillow with covers tucked warmly around the neck, has been the symbol of this railway line for many years.

Chessie's original name was "The Sleeping Cat." It was under that heading that an etching appeared in a New York newspaper

CHESSIE KITTENS

ABY DIAPER CHESSIE
inches, white with
olored diaper.
rder No. 620 . . . $4.00 ea.

CHESSIE CARDS
Double/Deck Set.
Order No. 616...$2.50

ENGINEER KITTEN
11 inches, grey color.
Order No. 617 . . . $5.00 ea.

LARGE CHESSIE
15 inches, blue or pink
Order No. 618 . . . $6.50 ea

MUSICAL CHESSIE
11 inches, pink or grey
Order No. 619 . . . $6.50 ea

Order by Number, Description and Price—see order blanks in back of booklet

A page from the Chesapeake and Ohio Railway's museum and sales room catalog. Their trademark, Chessie, is available in many forms, this page shows a baby *Chessie* in a diaper, playring cards, *Engineer Chessie*, and a musical plush *Chessie*.

in 1933. An official of the railway clipped the picture and presented it as a possible illustration for ads announcing the company's new air-conditioned sleepers. The company approved the idea and ads went out with the slogan: "Sleep Like a Kitten in Air-Conditioned Comfort."

The company noticed that everyone seemed to adore the little kitten. A year later, 1934, the railway purchased exclusive rights to the sketch from its creator, Viennese artist G. Gruenewald and **Chessie** became an integral part of the Chesapeake and Ohio Railway.

Today several **Chessie** kittens are sold by the company at their museum in Baltimore, Maryland. Included are a 9-inch white plush kitten wearing a colored diaper; and 11-inch gray plush kitten wearing an engineer hat and a scarf; a 15-inch sleeping kitten that comes either in blue or pink plush; and the fourth kitten is an 11-inch musical **Chessie**.

Chesty Potato Chip Company. A **Chesty** squeak doll was offered by this Indiana company. The 8-inch boy doll may have been a promotion of the 1950's judging from the style of haircut. Pants, shirt, and features are molded/painted. The distinguishing feature of **Chesty** is his May West chest.

Chesty Boy was a premium of the Chesty Potato Chip Company ca. 1950. The 8-inch squeak toy has an almost bosomy-sized chest. Marks: "C", on shirt. R. Keelen collection. $10.00.

104

Chicken of the Sea, a product of Ralston Purina Company. Two dolls have been made to represent the mermaid trademark of this canned tuna fish. The first was made in the mid-1960's and is vinyl from the waist up; the lower body and fish tail are stuffed cloth. The 20-inch doll has a blonde rooted wig, blue sleep eyes with heavy make-up as was popular at the time, and a closed mouth.

The second **Chicken of the Sea Mermaid** is all prestuffed cloth with lithographed details. The 15-inch mermaid is one of the Shoppin' Pal series made in 1976 by Mattel for sale in retail stores. Other dolls in the series are **Morton Salt Girl** and the **Crackerjack Boy**.

The *Chicken of the Sea Mermaid* doll was manufactured by Mattel in 1974 to sell in retail stores for about $5.00. The 15-inch mermaid is all cloth with lithographed details and yarn hair. Of course, it has human torso and a fish tail. Marks: "Quality Originals by Mattel Shoppin' Pal/Mattel, Inc. 1974," plus a list of the material used in the doll is included on a sewn-on label. $10.00.

Chiquita Brand, Inc., a subsidiary of United Brands Company. Three **Chiquita** banana dolls have been sold. The first doll came out in 1944, the year the trademark symbol was designed. It was offered to consumers via Kellogg's Corn Flakes for 10¢ and the top from the package. The 10-inch doll was stamped on a sheet of fabric that would be mailed from New York or Ontario depending on whether you lived in the United States or Canada. The fabric was loosely woven and filled with sizing; therefore, when washed the doll lost much of its appeal. The Kellogg's Chiquita doll was a brief one-time offer.

The first *Chiquita Banana Doll* was offered in 1944 to consumers on packages of Kellogg's Corn Flakes. It is stamped on rather poor quality fabric. (The second was a squeak toy that we were unable to find.) Marks: "Chiquita Banana," on lower edge of skirt. K. Lyons collection. $12.00.

The second **Chiquita** banana doll was a rubber squeak toy that was considered by the company as a bath tub toy. It was sold as a premium in the early 1950's. Consumers were informed of the offer through coupons at the banana display in the grocery store. We were unable to find this doll and learned of it from correspondence with the company.

The third **Chiquita** doll, of fabric, has been sold as a mail-in premium since 1974. The doll was introduced in women's magazines and in the Sunday comics. It cost $1.75 plus two seals from Chiquita bananas. A kit, shirt, record, and cookbook were also offered. Sales for this doll continue to be brisk, even though it has received almost no advertising the past few years. The lithographed colors on this doll are bright and colorful.

The company is aware of other **Chiquita** dolls, but says, "They are illegal ventures, as the Chiquita figurine is indeed a registered trademark."

The Chiquita symbol was designed by an advertising agency in 1944, the same year two songsmiths wrote the jingle "Chiquita (little one) Banana" for the United Fruit Company.

From the song came the trademark--a banana dressed like a senorita with side-glance eyes, a smiling open mouth, arms, and legs. The figure wears a south-of-the-border style costume of a sombrero adorned with fruits and flowers and a dress with ruffles at the sleeves and hem.

From the trademark came fantastic success--so impressive the subsidiary's name was changed to Chiquita Brands, Inc.

Chocks, a multiple vitamin of Miles Labratories, Inc. To encourage children to take Chocks Vitamins, the company offered a

The third *Chiquita Banana Doll* offered by this banana company was offered in 1974 and sales continue to be brisk even though it has received no recent advertising. The 16-inch cloth doll is wearing a red dress, hat, and ballerina shoes, all lithograped. Marks: "Chiquita," on blue trademark on front of dress.

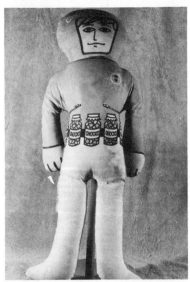

Charlie Chocks, a 20-inch cloth doll, was offered by Chocks Vitamins in 1970 and 1971 for $1.00. Marks: "Charlie Chocks" on helmet; bottles around waist all have a "Chocks" label. $6.00.

20-inch **Charlie Chocks** doll in 1970-71. The cloth-stuffed doll was $1.00 with no purchase necessary. Charlie's lithographed space suit is bright pink with white pants. Bottles of Chocks Vitamins encircle Charlie's waist, like bullets in a belt.

Chore Girl, a product of Metal Textiles Company. A 16-inch cloth stuffed doll was offered in the early 1970's by Chore Girl, the copper pan scrubbers. A company spokesman says that contrary to rumors there has never been a Chore Boy doll offered by this company.

The *Chore Girl* doll was a premium of the copper pan scrubbers of the same name. The 16-inch doll was sold in the early 1970's. Marks: "Chore Girl", on front of apron. S. Ricklefs collection. $6.00.

Chrysler Corporation. In 1973 some Chrysler car dealers gave a plastic bank in the shape of a man to their customers. **Mr. Fleet**, as he is called, is 10-inches high and holds a large wrench.

Mr. Fleet, a 10-inch plastic bank, was given to customers by some Chrysler car dealers. Marks: "Mr. Fleet", over front pocket; "Chrysler Corporation/1973 Made in U.S.A.," on bottom. $5.00.

Church's Fried Chicken. In 1973-74 children could receive a free plastic hand puppet on their birthday from Church's Fried Chicken Restaurant.

Church's Fried Chicken Restaurant gave free hand puppets to children on their birthday. Marks: "Churchie/Happy Birthday from Churchie," on front. $1.00.

Cinderella Frocks. In the early 1940's stores, which sold this line of children's dresses, were given a 22-inch mannequin for display. The mannequin is made of very firm rubber that has been painted. To aid in dressing the figure, the arms are removable. When a new style dress became available, often a small one to fit the mannequin was also sent. That way the display was always up with the current fashion. The mannequin has molded blonde hair with a molded bow and molded shoes with a strap over the instep. The shoes fit on a dowel on the pedestal.

This 22-inch mannequin doll was used for display in stores selling Cinderella Frocks. The doll is molded and painted with either faded or pale colored paint. As new fashions became available, the mannequin was sent a new dress from the company. The dress this mannequin is wearing is made of silk organza, white with purple design on the bodice and the reverse colors on the skirt. Marks: "Cinderella Frocks," on pedestal. M. Edinger collection. $25.00.

Clairol Hair Products. "Glamour Misty-the Miss Clairol doll with hair you can color," the ads read in 1965. Ideal Toy Corporation designed and manufactured a 12-inch vinyl doll for Clairol. The dolls sold from retail outlets for about two years.

Glamour Misty came with a kit, which consisted of a robe, comb, and three washable non-toxic coloring crayons, so the blonde doll could become a redhead or brunette. She wore a rather unbecoming navy blue dress with a deep V-neckline and blue boots.

Glamour Misty, the doll made by Ideal Toy Corporation for Clairol Hair Products, had a rooted blonde wig that could be colored by a child with three washable coloring crayons included in the kit. The 12-inch doll sold in retail stores in 1965 and 1966. This doll is in original box. Marks: "Ideal Toy Corp./W12-3," on head; "© 1965 Ideal/2 M-12," on hip. N. Ricklefs collection. $10.00.

In the late 1950's **Clairol Bear Twins** were used for display in beauty shops using Clairol products. One brown bear, with a blue ribbon to match his mood, was crying; she didn't use Clairol. The Honey Blonde bear with a red ribbon, to match her happy mood, is all smiles because she uses Clairol.

Another *Glamour Misty* doll showing a different outfit, also original. K. Lyons collection. $8.00.

The 15-inch bears are plush with vinyl masks faces. A fringe of blond hair forms bangs on the smiling bear. The crying bear has molded bangs.

Clark Candy Bar. A molded/painted doll about 7-inches tall holding a Clark Can-

The soft vinyl *Clark Candy Bar* doll is about 7-inches tall and holds a replica of the candy bar he advertises. $10.00.

The *Clairol Bears*, 15-inches, were a beauty shop display available in 1958 to hairdressers using Clairol Hair Products. Supposedly the brown crying bear with a blue ribbon didn't use Clairol. The honey blonde bear with a red ribbon is all smiles because it used Clairol. T. Baxter collection, David Nelson, James Giokas photographers. $10.00 each.

dy bar was found. Date and method of dispersal are unknown. The soft vinyl doll has yellow hair, red and blue striped shirt, and blue pants. One hand holds a Clark bar (all molded) and the other hand is pointing to the candy.

Cliquot Club Ginger Ale.
In the 1920's Effanbee manufactured a **Cliquot Eskimo** (pronounced Klee-Ko) doll with composition head, cloth body and limbs. The doll wore a furry Eskimo suit with only the face showing. The skin is light brown with a black painted forelock, and squinty eyes. The doll may have been intended for managers to use in display.

The company did extensive advertising in magazines in the twenties and thirties. In the forties they advertised via a clever song on the radio. The company continues to be in business.

Close-up Toothpaste, a
product of Lever Brothers. This red toothpaste "with real mouthwash" has had four major

The 8-inch *Dumbo* was one of six Walt Disney characters offered by Close-up Toothpaste in 1974. The gray plastic toy is well made, tail, legs, and head are moveable. He wears a yellow plastic hat and a cloth collar. Marks: "Walt Disney/Productions/Dakin & Co./ Product of Hong Kong," under body. $4.00.

known promotions, the first was for Disney character dolls, the second for a pair of monkeys, the third for a pair of bears, and the fourth for a pair of puppies.

In 1974 the Disney characters, **Mickey Mouse, Minnie Mouse, Donald Duck, Pinocchio, Pluto**, and **Dumbo** were available for $1.00 each plus an empty carton of Close-up Toothpaste. The vinyl characters had moveable limbs and were from 6 to 8-inches high. They were well made with careful detail and quality plastic. Some wore cloth costumes.

Mickey Mouse with his droopy-drawers was one of the Walt Disney characters offered by Close-up Toothpaste. Other characters besides *Dumbo* and *Mickey* were: *Minnie Mouse, Donald Duck, Pinocchio,* and *Pluto*. $4.00.

In 1976 the **Close-up Cuddleups** were introduced. This pair of 9-inch plush acrylic monkeys are in a close embrace via a piece of Velcro inside each paw. One monkey is caramel colored with a ribbon on top of its head, the other is dark brown plush. Both have beige faces and closed eyes made of felt. The pair cost $3.95 plus the back panel from a carton of toothpaste, which is 1/3 the price toothpaste, which is 1/3 the price they were selling for at retail stores.

Close-up Toothpaste's *Cuddle-up Monkeys* have been extremely popular. The 9-inch pair were made by Fun Fair from plush acrylic in shades of brown with Velcro on the paws so they can be joined together. They were available until June 1977 for $3.95 retail. $6.00.

The monkeys were so successful, Close-up Toothpaste introduced *Cuddle-up Bears* the following year, late 1977. They are also made of brown acrylic plush and have Velcro on the paws. The bears cost $3.95 and were available until June 1978. $6.00.

The fall of 1977, a new pair of plush animals were introduced, the **Close-up Bears**. The 10-inch pair are designed similar to the monkeys, with Velcro to hold them in a close embrace. They are made from dark brown plush with beige noses, paws, and ear linings. One bear wears a tiny blue felt baseball cap, the other a pink ribbon. This pair also cost $3.95, and the offer expired June 30, 1978.

The *Close-up Puppies* were the most recent Close-up Toothpaste promotion. The pair are brown and tan plush and jointed in an embrace via Velcro. One has ribbons on the ears. Amee Jo DeMello Collection. Still available.

The next year the **Close-up Puppies** were introduced. They are 10-inches tall, made of brown and tan plush, and they are also joined in an embrace via Velcro. With their eyes closed in bliss they have an especially sweet expression.

Club Aluminum Cookware, a division of Standard International. The Horsman Company made an 11-inch vinyl and plastic **Cooky** doll for this cookware company in 1968. The doll was used in full page color advertisement with this statement: (If you'd like Cooky, our walking cover doll, send $3.00.)

After you cook does your husband still think you're a doll?

Club Aluminum Cookware used the doll *Cooky* in their magazine ads in 1968 and later. The bottom of the ad mentions that she is available for $3.00. The 11-inch doll is plastic and vinyl with rooted wig. Marks: "H/14". $10.00.

Coast-to-Coast Hardware Stores. This chain of hardware stores used a 20-inch inflatable **Elfy** doll at some time. No one at the local store recalls the doll.

EL FY

The inflatable *Elfy* is a premium offered by Coast to Coast Stores. K. Miller Collection. $3.00.

Coca-Cola Company. According to the director of archives for this world-famous beverage company, five or six dolls have been used as promotional items. An old coupon indicated that the first Coca-Cola premium doll was **Tickletoes the Wonder Doll.** "The only doll in the world with rubber legs and rubber arms and those rolling-sleeping eyes. Squeeze either leg or turn the doll over and it cries. She can clasp her hands, turn her head, suck her thumb, enjoy her pacifier. Wears beautiful baby clothes, stockings, moccasins, rubber panties. Regular price of this doll is $7.50. One coupon is given with a case of bottled Coca-Cola. Our offer-- present 20 of these coupons and $2.75 cash at our office and receive one Tickletoes Wonder Doll. Offer expires Dec. 31, 1930." This ad was undoubtedly written before the truth-in-advertising laws. Only doll in the world with rubber arms and legs? The coupon was presented by the St. Louis, Missouri, office.

Another doll, **Buddy Lee**, was available in the early 1950's. It was dressed in the uniform of a route salesman and was more accurately an advertising doll for the H.D. Lee Company, which made the uniform. (See H.D. Lee.)

In July 1958 a **Santa Claus** doll was produced for Bottlers of Coca-Cola for the Christmas season. Santa Claus had been associated with "Coke" since the depression, when the company began a yearly promotion featuring Santa Claus.

Artist Haddon Sundblom was given the job of drawing a Santa to use in the Coca-Cola advertisements that Christmas season of 1931. This was no easy job. There was much confusion as to what Santa Claus should look like. For 200 years in America the Saint

Coupon for *Tickletoes* doll offered by Coca-Cola Bottling Company of St. Louis in 1930. "The wonder doll, rubber legs and rubber arms." Courtesy Coca-Cola Company.

Nicholas concept prevailed. Judging from old Christmas card illustrations Saint Nicholas was a thin elderly man with a solemn kind face. He wore any color or style attire, often a long robe tied with a rope.

Coca-Cola produced a magazine advertisement featuring a realistic version of Santa that was well received. So when Haddon Sundblom was hired to draw Santa, he looked for a person to use as a model. He found the perfect person, a retired salesman named Lou Prentice. Mr. Prentice was enthusiastic with a twinkle in his eye like a grandfather with a surprise tucked in a pocket. Smile wrinkles folded often at the corners of his eyes and mouth.

For many years Sundblom drew a holiday portrait of Mr. Prentice in a fur-trimmed red suit with big black boots. Coca-Cola made sure their Santa appeared on posters, cardboard cutouts, Christmas cards, billboards, and in magazines. After Mr. Prentice died Mr. Sundblom used his own face as a model for Santa Claus.

Largely as a result of Coca-Cola's advertisements, America's visual image of Santa Claus became Sundblom's drawing of Mr. Prentice in a red suit. How difficult it is to visualize any other type of Santa Claus.

The 1958 Coca-Cola Santa doll was manufactured by the Ruston Company of Atlanta. It has a vinyl face, hands, and boots, with polyfoam-filled plush body and legs. A miniature bottle of "Coke" is held in one hand. It is reminiscent of the wonderful ads showing Santa sneaking the "pause that refreshes" while delivering a bagful of toys.

Another doll some collectors consider a Coca-Cola advertising doll is Remco's **Mimi** doll. This doll sang the very popular "Coke Song" that begins, "I'd like to teach the world to sing in perfect harmony." In keeping with the world brotherhood emphasis of the song the doll sang the song in several languages by means of a battery-operated record player in the body. Four two-sided records provided the songs.

The "Santa Claus" doll was used as a promotion item for bottlers of Coca-Cola during the 1958 Christmas season. The 15-inch doll has a vinyl face, hands, and boots with a red plush body filled with polyfoam. It is holding a miniature bottle of "Coke" in one hand. K. Miller collection. $20.00.

For some reason, perhaps poor advertising, the doll was unsuccessful and by 1974 Remco was no longer in business.

The attractive doll is 19-inches tall, vinyl and hard plastic, long rooted blonde hair, painted eyes, full lips open/closed. Several costumes were available for "Mimi," each representing one of the languages sung on the records.

Coca-Cola is probably the most widely recognized trademark in the world. The cola beverage, in its distinct bottle, is sipped in the Patagonia Desert, villages in the Himalayas, on micro-islands in the Pacific, and points in between.

The origin of this carbonated drink is credited to a pharmacist from Georgia, J.S. Pemberton. The idea for the concoction came in about 1880, but it was six years later that it became a reality. Most likely it was intended as a headache remedy. The first year was not exactly successful, Pemberton earned $50.00 from sales and spent $73.96 on advertising. Pemberton died at the age of fifty-five, never having the pleasure of seeing his caffeine beverage a popular soft drink.

In 1888 business improved and Asa Chandler owned Coca-Cola in addition to several other products: Botanic Blood Balm, Delectalave (a liquid dentifrice), and Everlasting Cologne.

Ten years later, 1898, the first building built specifically for the Coca-Cola Company was opened in Atlanta, Georgia, and Coca-Cola was on its way to becoming the most popular soft drink in the world.

Coco Wheats Cereal, see Little Crow Foods.

Colgate Company. Long before Colgate teamed up with Palmolive there was a **Colgate Baby Bunting** doll that sold in retail stores. The 1917 doll had composition head and hands with a cloth body and legs. The wig is mohair, the eyes and mouth are painted. Each doll held a container of Cashmere Bouquet talcum powder. (See Irish Spring.)

Collingbourne Cotton Company. The only information found about this company comes from a sheet of cloth cutouts they offered. The cutouts are titled **Collingbourne's Happy Family**, and consist of a girl doll labeled Flossie, a tiny doll labeled Baby, a cat, and a bear labeled Mascot. A logo printed on the fabric says "Collingbourne's America's Best Cotton/ABC".

Collingbourne's *Flossie* and a tiny doll labeled *Baby*. Included in the Happy Family are also a teddy bear labeled *Mascot* and a cat. Playthings by the Yard, 1973. $35.00-50.00.

The two dolls have printed undies, shoes and ankle length stockings. The small teddy bear is in a sitting position. The cat has a ribbon around its neck with Collingbourne's printed on it both in front and back.

Concorde Confections.

The London Times Newspaper used the cartoon character Andy Capp in their cartoon section and for their advertising for many years. Today Andy is popular in America as well as Britain. Andy is also reported to have been used to advertise this confection company. The **Andy Capp** doll is 6½-inches tall and made of foam rubber. It is a careful copy of the surly comic strip character, even down to the drooping cigarette. Clothing is molded/colored.

Andy Capp was offered by Concorde Confections about 1972. The 6½-inch doll wears a black plaid cap. Marks: "Bindy O Daily Mirror/Made in England." A. Wolfe collection, David Nelson, James Giokas photographers. $5.00.

Continental Bus Line.
See Trailways, Inc.

Cook's Flaked Rice and Malto Rice. (See American Rice Foods Manufacturing Company)

Corn Products Refining Company now **Best Foods,** a division of CPC International Inc. This company's products: Argo Starch, Mazola, and Karo Syrup all widely used an Indian maiden trademark figure prior to 1930 in their ads and on their labels. Today's Argo Starch box continues to carry this trademark.

The *Indian Princess* is a chubby rendition of the trademark widely used through the 30's by Corn Products Refining Company. The company's products using this trademark include: Argo Starch, Mazola Corn Oil, and Karo Syrup. The Argo Starch box uses the trademark today. The 10-inch doll wears a molded/painted corn husk gown. Unfortunately this dear doll was decapitated and needs mending. R. Coons collection. $50.00-75.00.

In 1919 the figure was offered as a frozen charlette type doll 10-inches tall. The **Indian Princess**, as she was called, was manufactured by the American Ocarina & Toy Company. It was advertised as being made of Lignum fiber and unbreakable. As the example photographed shows, the doll is breakable and we would class the material as composition.

The princess doll is a chubby child rendition of the trademark figure, wearing a green husk gown with kernals of corn down the front. The cost was 25¢, which was expensive in that day.

Coronet Brandy. A 19-inch waiter with a tray in one hand and a towel folded over the other arm was used as a display item for this drink. The head of the figure is shaped like a brandy snifter.

The Coronet Brandy figural is 19-inches tall and is probably made of composition on a wood base. The metal stand held a bottle of brandy. $20.00.

Coty Cosmetics. The Arranbee Company manufactured a doll they called **Miss Coty** after Coty cosmetics. The 10½-inch vinyl doll is much like **Little Miss Revlon**. It has rooted hair, closed mouth and is jointed at the waist. The doll is marked on the back "X" and also a "P". A tag reads "Miss Coty"/R & B Doll Co.

Country Kitchen Restaurants. This restaurant chain has used several promotional items since it began business in the mid-1960's. The items offered were introduced to managers via advertising agencies. The managers could order the premiums they desired, if any.

A large, 24-inch, cloth doll was sold at Country Kitchen Restaurants in 1975. The face has a pom-pom nose, plastic eyes with movable black pupils, and lithographed mouth and freckles. The clothing is removable and includes a floppy gold felt hat, red knit shirt, and blue pants. The hair is brown yarn. The doll is loosely stuffed, but well designed and constructed. Marks: "Country Boy", across front of shirt. K. Lyons collection. $10.00.

Therefore, one restaurant might have a particular doll where the one in the next city would not. As different advertising agencies were employed to handle the account the emphasis and premiums were changed.

At first the premiums were sold at the cash register. Later the premiums were obtained free by saving coupons. The coupons were given to children under twelve when they ate at the restaurant. Extra coupons were given at birthdays, one for every year of age. This plan proved unsatisfactory because often by the time the child had saved the required coupons (120 for a doll) the item would no longer be available. Many managers started deducting 10¢ from the cost of the premium for each coupon. Today most premiums are sold and displayed at the cash register.

The Country Kitchen Restaurant chain made available to managers two cloth dolls with yarn hair and removable clothes. The boy, 13-inches tall, has a lithographed face with closed eyes. He is barefoot. Marks: "Country/Boy", in script on front of shirt. I. Mather collection. $10.00.

In 1975 a 24-inch cloth doll was sold. It had a lithographed face, yarn hair, pom-pom nose and represented a country boy. The clothes were removable and included overalls, shirt, and floppy hat.

A few months later a 13-inch boy and girl doll were available through the coupon plan. These were also nice quality dolls, with removable clothes and yarn hair. The girl wears a dress and apron, in one hand she carries a flower, the other holds a basket.

The boy wears a felt hat, shirt and pants. The lithographed eyes are closed. Both girl and boy go barefoot.

Cox Gelatine Company.

The only information I could find about this company comes from the cloth doll given to their customers. The lithographed cloth doll is a sweet looking child dressed in the native costume of Scotland. The background fabric

This cloth doll dressed in native Scottish costume is copied from the trademark used on boxes of Cox Gelatine. Date unknown. Directions printed on background fabric include suggestions of what to stuff the completed doll with: sawdust, bran, or cotton. These products are quite different from the dacron batting used to fill dolls today. Marks: "Cox's Gelatine", on hat band. Playthings by the Yard, 1973. $30.00-50.00.

that would be cut away if the doll were assembled says: "Duplicates may be obtained from the Cox Gelatine Company representing (J. & G. Cox, Ltd., Edingburgh.) 100 Hudson Street/New York. Sent with compliments in the belief that every woman is interested in some child and will make up the doll to please some little one."

Cracker Jack, a product of Borden Company. As far as I can learn, two Cracker Jack dolls have been manufactured to resemble the sailor boy trademark of this popular popcorn confection. The first was sold in 1917, the second in 1976. Both dolls were produced by toy companies for the retail market.

The 1917 doll, manufactured by Ideal, has composition head and hands with cloth body, arms, and legs. The hair and eyes are molded/painted. He wears a white sailor suit and hat and carries a miniature package of Cracker Jack.

The 1976 version is 15-inches tall and all cloth. Mattel Toy Company manufactured this doll and two other advertising dolls in their Shoppin' Pal series. (See Chicken of the Sea and Morton Salt.)

Sailor Jack as Mattel named him, has lithographed facial features; orange hair and wears a navy blue sailor suit and hat. He also carries a tiny box of Cracker Jack.

The confection Cracker Jack was first concocted in 1890 by F.W. Rueckhein in his popcorn company. One day he dipped a batch of popcorn and a handful of peanuts in a molasses syrup. One company taster sampled it and exclaimed: "That's a crackerjack!" Thus a new product and a new name were born.

The sailor-boy symbol came years later, prior to World War I when the country was proudly displaying patriotism. Through the years the sailor boy and his dog, Bingo, have been modernized to look up-to-date.

In 1974 Mattel Toy Company manufactured a cloth version of the Cracker Jack trademark to sell in retail stores. The 15-inch *Sailor Jack* doll carries a miniature box of Cracker Jack, the caramel candy coated popcorn confection. The navy blue suit is also the body, therefore, not removable. No need to worry about losing the hat, it is sewn onto the head. Marks: A cloth tag listing the materials used and giving the name of the series, "Shoppin' Pal". Box is well marked. $10.00.

Cracker Jack has had other claims to fame besides its trademark symbol and delicious flavor. Cracker Jack used the first wax-sealed moistureproof package, which has been used since 1904, marking the advent of waxed paper.

The other distinction is their introduction of toy surprises hidden amidst the popcorn. What child hasn't reached his hand down the small box trying to find the little treasure without spilling any of the tasty popcorn? Cracker Jack continues to be one of America's favorite treats.

Cranston Print Works. In 1975 this fabric company of Cranston, Rhode Island issued a cloth boy and girl doll to commemorate their 150 year anniversary. The boy, 14-inches tall, is dressed like a sailor 150 years ago. The girl doll, also 14-inches tall, is wearing a long dress of the 1820 period.

Doll collectors who sew are probably familiar with this company's quality printed fabric, the name is often printed on a selvage.

A 14-inch cloth couple dressed in 1825 costumes was used to commemorate the 150th anniversary of Cranston Print Works, a fabric company. The sailor boy wears faded blue pants, red shirt, blue jacket, and a blue tie. The girl is holding a bouquet of red flowers and is dressed in a long blue dress, her brown hair is held back from her face by a white bandeau. Marks: "Cranston Print Works 1825-1975," on back of boy doll; both have handtags that say "I'm 150 years old." P. Coghlan collection, Harry Sykora photographer. $10.00 pair.

119

Cream of Wheat Corporation, a product of Nabisco since 1960. The Cream of Wheat chef has been smiling from packages of hot cereal since 1899. Dolls representing the affable chef came much later, when is difficult to pin-point. Johana Anderton's book Twentieth Century Dolls says the dolls were made from 1922-52. Searching patent registrations provided no listing for a Cream of Wheat doll. Nor is one mentioned in the Colemans' Encyclopedia of Dolls, which covers dolls made up to 1925. I was unable to obtain dates or information about the chef dolls, as Nabisco said in response to my inquiry, "Information regarding its (Cream of Wheat's) early promotions has been lost in the annals of time." What a shame!

The 1930 *Chef* doll without apron and hat, shows unusual one-piece legs. This doll is occasionally called Rastus by doll collectors, no place could I find any company literature using that name. $30.00-$35.00.

The doll information comes from old ads and the dolls themselves. We found three sizes: 16, 18, and 20-inches high. The dolls were all printed on a flat sheet of fabric, to be cut, stitched, and filled by the owner. The faces on the dolls resemble a photograph of the chef found on the cereal package. Clothing consists of striped pants, a white shirt, detachable chef hat and apron. The dolls all hold a lithographed bowl marked Cream of Wheat.

The oldest edition of the doll is printed in drab colors, beige, maroon, brown, and black on muslin. It is 16-inches tall.

The next doll sold in 1930 for 10¢ and was advertised primarily in women's magazines. It is the largest, 20-inches tall.

The most recent doll is dated November 30, 1949 and is 18-inches tall. The last two dolls use bright colors: red, yellow, and blue on white fabric. The third doll is unusual because the two legs are one piece of fabric with no cut line to separate them.

The doll is often referred to as Rastus by doll collectors. No research verified that name was ever used by the company. Where the name originated is unknown.

It is possible that chef dolls other than those listed, were issued by Cream of Wheat. It is a symbol that lends itself well to doll promotions.

More information is available about the cereal than the dolls, as one would expect. Cream of Wheat was perfected in 1898 by a miller named Tom Amidon, who lived in the little railroad town of Grand Forks, North Dakota. Amidon took some purified wheat middlings home to his wife to cook for cereal. The white particles of the wheat softened in the boiling water and became a nourishing breakfast food that the Scotsman and his family enjoyed often. Soon other employees tried the creamy wheat breakfast food and they also found it appetizing. Amidon was certain the cereal would also be popular with the public, but the company, like many small milling companies was still suffering from the depression in 1893, and it could afford no finances for a new adventure. They did agree to allow Amidon to include a few boxes of the cereal along with their flour shipment to New York.

Amidon painstakingly cut out cardboard cartons by hand for the new cereal and a co-worker Mapes, who had once been a printer, found an old printing block of a black chef holding a saucepan over his shoulder to stamp on the front of the box. At this time the descriptive name Cream of Wheat was chosen to finish off the box.

The largest *Chef* doll is 20-inches tall and sold in 1930 for 10¢. It wears red and white striped pants, white shirt, black shoes with red bows. It is missing the hat and apron. Marks: "Cream of/Wheat," on bowl. $30.00-35.00.

In 1949 an 18-inch *Cream of Wheat Chef* doll was sold. It is unusual because the red and white striped legs have no cut line to separate the legs. The apron and hat were cut from white material and attached to the doll. The photographic face is a good likeness to the chef on the cereal label. K. Lyons collection. $30.00-35.00.

An early Cream of Wheat *Chef* doll, probably sold in 1920. The muslin doll is printed in browns and blacks with a touch of red. The doll's face is a photographic copy of the face used on their cereal box since 1899. It is probably missing a hat and apron. Marks: "Cream of/Wheat," on bowl. Courtesy Ralph's Antique Dolls. $30.00-35.00.

In time their brokers were telegraphing: "Forget the flour, send us Cream of Wheat." Amidon and his partner continued to sell their hot cereal in the poorly-fashioned cartons for about a year. One day while at Kohlsaat's Restaurant in Chicago Mr. Mapes was attracted to a congenial black waiter and asked to take his photograph posing as a chef. The waiter obliged and was paid $5.00. From that day neither Mr. Mapes nor anyone else in the company ever saw the waiter again. Many people presented themselves as the original chef, but supposedly Mr. Mapes was in possession of certain information which made it possible to detect imposters. Since 1899 the likeness of that waiter has been printed on cartons of Cream of Wheat cereal.

To satisfy the public's desire for the new cereal it became necessary to enlarge, so a large mill was built in Minneapolis in 1900, and another in 1928. Cream of Wheat continued to adjust to the desires of the consumer by producing a five-minute cereal in 1939 and an instant Mix 'n Eat cereal in 1966.

From 1908 through the thirties Cream of Wheat used some of the finest full-page magazine ads ever done. All of them used the wonderful black chef. Ed W.V. Brewer was one of the most popular artists who painted ads for Cream of Wheat. Other artists were James Montgomery Flagg and Denman Kilbert. These ads have become popular with today's collectors.

In 1961 Cream of Wheat was sold to Nabisco, who was trying to establish greater diversity from the cracker industry they'd made famous. Since Nabisco has owned the cereal, no dolls have been offered.

Crescent Flour, a product of Voight's Flour Products. An ad was found that advertised a "charming sleeping doll" for only $1.00 by saving coupons from Voight's Flour Products.

Save the Coupons from "VOIGT'S FLOUR PRODUCTS"

A WONDERFUL OFFER!

A CHARMING SLEEPING DOLL

Regular Price $2.50

ONLY $1.00

A SPECIAL PLAN TO

Make Children Happy

Save the Coupons from "VOIGT'S FLOUR PRODUCTS"

An advertisement for a doll offered by Crescent Flour, a product of Voight's Flour Products. Date unknown. Ad is printed in red and blue and measures 21½ x 17 inches. A. Wolfe collection, David Nelson, James Giokas photographers. $8.00-10.00.

Crest Toothpaste, a product of Procter & Gamble. A 15-inch cloth **Raggedy Ann** and **Andy** were premiums of this toothpaste in the early 1970's. These are the same dolls manufactured by Knickerbocher Toy Company and sold through thousands of retail outlets.

Crete Flour Mills. See Victor Flour.

Cricket Cigarette Lighter, a product of the Gillette Company. In 1972 a 24-inch inflatable green cricket, which resembled the cricket seen in TV commercials, was used in store displays where the lighters were sold. The inflatable plastic toy may also have been offered as a premium in some areas.

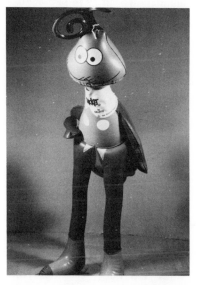

Cricket Lighters were advertised by a 24-inch inflatable green cricket wearing an orange vest and shoes. The *Cricket* was used for store displays in 1972 and may have been offered as a premium at that time on a limited basis. Marks: "Cricket by Gillette/The Gillette Co. 1972, 1973," on collar. K. Lyons collection. $4.00.

Crown-Zellerbach. See Zee's Toilet Tissue.

Crunchberries. See Quaker Oats Company.

Curad, a product of the Kendall Company. The **Curad Taped Crusader** bank was offered in early 1977 for $1.50 plus a bandage wrapper. The 8-inch plastic **Crusader** is an accident-prone boy with bandages on his head and arms.

The *Curad Taped Crusader* is an 8-inch plastic bank offered in 1977 on boxes of Curad bandages. The *Crusader* wears molded/painted clothing and several bandages. Marks: "Curad," across chest. K. Lyons collection. $3.00.

Curity, a product of Kendall Corporation. Five nurse dolls have been produced for the retail market and named **Miss Curity** after the line of first-aid supplies it represents. One store display figure was also found.

The most well-known **Miss Curity** doll was manufactured by the Ideal toy Company in 1949. Ideal's "First Lady of First Aid" is a 14-inch hard plastic doll with a swivel neck, and joints at the shoulders and hips. The body is the P 90 size used on the Elizabeth Hubbard Ayers, Toni, and Betsy McCall dolls.

The 14-inch *Miss Curity* doll was manufactured by the Ideal Toy Company in 1949 for the retail market. The doll is dressed in a white nurse uniform and cap with a blue cape, lined in red. This "Miss Curity" has lost her first-aid book and kit, but is photographed with the MISS CURITY FUN BOOK, a 16 page coloring book that was used as a promotion by the Kendall Company for their Curity line in 1951. Marks: "Ideal Doll/Made in U.S.A.," on back of head; "Ideal Doll/P-90," on back of body; "Miss Curity," label on uniform pocket; "Miss Curity," in black letters on cap. A. Wolfe collection, James Giokas photographer. $40.00-50.00.

Ideal's **Miss Curity** has a blonde wig made of Saran, and blue sleep eyes with upper lashes and heavily shadowed upper and lower lids. She wears a blue cape and a long-sleeved nurse uniform and cap marked with her name. Included in the doll box is a play nurse kit, with bandages, tape, and scissors. Ideal's **Miss Curity** is the same doll as their **Toni** except it has heavy eye shadow and a Saran wig rather than the lux- uriant nylon wig the **Toni** doll is famous for.

In 1953 Sears offered a **Miss Curity** doll that was listed as plastic and vinyl. It appears to be the same doll as the Ideal, except a vinyl material was used to make the head. The ad says it is a 14½-inch doll with platinum blonde glued-on wig, sleep eyes, and it came with a first-aid book and kit. The doll and accessories retailed at $11.39, a fairly expen- sive doll for the 1950's.

The oldest and largest **Miss Curity** doll has occasionally been referred to as a Bauer and Black doll because of the Bauer and Black booklet sold with the doll. Bauer and Black, like Curity, is a division of the Kendall Corpora- tion. This 21-inch doll was manufactured in 1946 of composi- tion. It has blue sleep eyes, a syn- thetic wig, and wears a white uniform marked **Miss Curity**. The manufacturer is unknown.

In 1953 an unknown company manufactured a tiny 7-inch **Miss Curity**. This doll is hard plastic with a one-piece body and legs. The head and arms are moveable. It is much better quality than many hard plastic advertising dolls this same size. The doll has a glued-on wig of blonde hair, sleep eyes, long painted lashes, and a painted cupid bow mouth. The uniform is made of thick white plastic that has a texture to make it resemble cloth. The cap is firm plastic mark- ed Curity. Molded-painted white shoes and knee stockings com- plete the outfit.

The fifth **Miss Curity** is 20-inches tall and was on the market in the late fifties and early sixties. It is marked AE, and it has high heel feet, closed mouth, open/shut eyes, and rooted hair. The vinyl doll wears a white dress and a cap marked **Miss Curity**.

A lovely hard plastic display doll of **Miss Curity** was offered to stores selling the Curity line. The figure is 19½-inches tall molded in one piece with feet that fit onto a wood base. The figure is dressed in white nurse attire: uniform. stockings, shoes, and cap. The face is bright and well painted.

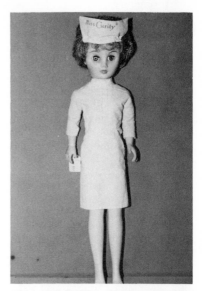

A magazine ad showing the advertising for the *Miss Curity* doll.

The fifth *Miss Curity* doll was available at retail stores in the late fifties. It is 20-inches tall and made of vinyl. Marks: "AE, 2006-2" on back of neck; "Miss Curity," on cap. $15.00-20.00.

A small, 7-inch *Miss Curity* doll wears original plastic uniform and cap. Date, manufacturer, and dispersal method unknown. M. Meisinger collection. $10.00.

A well-made 19½-inch display doll used at stores selling Curity products. Marks: "Miss Curity," across top of pocket. A. Pfister collection. $15.00-25.00.

D

Dairy Queen. This restaurant chain used Dennis the Menace in their advertising since 1972. Several cloth dolls from this cartoon series have been found, but the company says the dolls were never promotional items for their company. Dennis and his group have appeared on other promotional items such as kites, iron-on patches, rings, balloons, and coloring books, but no dolls.

Since 1972, Dennis has been slowly phased out because the company believes the character appeals primarily to the under 15-year old child, and that is not who is buying the most hamburgers.

See listing under Texas Dairy Queen.

Dak Meat Company. A copy of their trademark, **Thor**, has been made into two dolls, one

Thor is a premium of the Dak Meat Company. The 14-inch cloth doll represents the Viking trademark used on tins and packages of this meat, a product of Denmark. Marks: "Thor," on front and back of hat. $6.00.

cloth and one vinyl. The 14-inch cloth doll is prestuffed with lithographed viking outfit and flowing red beard.

The later doll is made of heavy gauge vinyl and has the same viking outfit and red beard. It is inflatable to 28-inches tall, and was available until December 1974 for $2.50 plus the trademark from Dak sliced meat.

Thor was reissued in 1974 as a 28 inch inflatable Viking. Marks: "DAK/Danish Ham". $4.00.

Dan River. This fabric company offered an adorable cloth doll, **Buttons**, in 1947. The head has a seam down the middle of the face to give contour to the nose, button painted eyes and nose, removable red and white dress, and yarn hair. The 12-inch doll carries a leaflet shaped like a pocket book that tells her story. The doll was advertised in magazines and newspapers for $4.95.

This *Buttons* doll, 12-inches, has a mask face, cloth body, and yarn hair. The dress is original, but is not the one seen in most the ads. The identification tag resembles a pocket book. Steward collection. $20.00.

Dash Dog Food. Animal Fair manufactured a basset dog premium for this brand dog food.

According to a label on the hind foot, this plush dog was: "Created Exclusively for Dash Dog Food by Animal Fair, Chanhassen, Minn." It is 19-inches long and 11-inches high. The open mouth is lined with red fabric. $6.00.

De Met Candy Company. (See Mr. Turtle Candy.)

Denny's Restaurants.

The *Deputy Dan* hand puppet was given free in 1976 at Denny restaurants. $1.00.

Derby Oil Company. In the late 1960's a 17-inch cloth doll, made to resemble a serious look-

The *Derby Man*, 17-inches tall, was a $1.00 premium used in the late 1960's by the Derby Oil Company. $6.00.

127

ing gas station attendant was offered to gasoline customers. The red jacket over blue pants, white shirt, and bow tie were lithographed on the prestuffed cotton doll.

Dodge Automobiles. Only one doll has been used by this company, as far as I can learn. **Little Profit** is a six-inch nodder doll dressed to resemble a fortune teller (prophet?). A turban covers tha paper mache head; body and base are made of heavy plaster. The doll was given to Dodge car dealers in the 1960's. The same doll has been used by other companies for a small gift to conventioneers.

Little Profit was given to Dodge Automobile dealers in the 1960's. The 6-inch nodder doll has a paper mache head and a plaster body and base. Marks: "Little Profit" on disk on front of turban. K. Landsdowne collection. $8.00.

Dole Bananas. In 1972 Dole offered a 2-foot long plush pillow in the shape of a banana with the Dole sticker. It cost $2.95 plus two Dole labels and was available until December 31, 1972.

The *Dole Banana* pillow was advertised with this magazine ad in 1972.

Dolly Madison Bakery Products. This company uses the characters in Peanuts cartoons to advertise their products. Several doll collectors have written

Plastic hand puppets given by Dolly Madison Bakery Products. S. Esser collection, B. Esser photographer. $1.00.

to say they think the company has sold dolls representing the characters. We have been unable to locate the dolls or information. The cartoon characaters have been made in cloth and vinyl by various manufacturers to sell in retail stores, but they have no connection with the Dolly Madison products.

Dolly Madison has given free plastic hand puppets of the Peanuts crowd. The puppets are marked with the company name.

Domino Sugar. A 15-inch plush bear was offered by this sugar company in 1975. The $2.98 bear is a replica of the **Domino Bear** who entertains at the Six Flags Recreation Parks.

Domino Bear, 15-inches, was a premium of Domino Sugar Company in 1975. $7.00.

Dots Candy, a product of Sweets Candy, Inc. The Dots Candy doll is one of a set of four the Hasbro Toy Company manufactured to represent a candy product. The doll wears a green suit with a bib and mop hat. The body

of the doll, which is also the suit, is filled with styrofoam pellets. The dolls sold at retail stores in 1973.

Dots was one of four bean-bag type dolls manufactured by Hasbro to represent candy products. They were sold at retail stores in 1975. Marks: "DOTS", on bib. K. Lyons collection. $8.00.

Downey's Honey-Butter. A 10-inch yellow plush bee wtih pom-pom nose, felt wings,

Downey's *Honey-Butter Bee* is 10½-inches tall and is made of a plush fabric. Marks: "Downey's Honey-Butter,"on ribbon around neck; and a tag that says it's a tubbable toy. R. Keelen collection. $7.00.

129

and feet, and plastic eyes was offered in the mid-1970's. The bee sold for $3.95 plus two carton lids and was also available at retail stores.

Drake Brother's Company. As far as I can determine this company is no longer in business. In 1917 the Reliance Novelty Company of New York manufactured a doll named **Dolly Drake** (Takes the Cake) to advertise Drake Pound Cake. The doll was made to sell for $1.00 at retail stores. It is 19-inches tall; made with composition head and limbs and a cloth stuffed body. The doll has a blonde wig, painted eyes, closed mouth and wears a yellow dress with "Drakes" printed on it, a baker's hat, pantelettes, shoes, and stockings.

Dr. Pepper. This soft drink company in 1972, offered a 12-inch Miss Teenage America.

Duncan Hines Double Fudge Brownie Mix. To promote this mix a 26-inch Brownie doll in costume was offered in limited locations, in 1970 for

Brownie, 26-inches, was offered in limited areas to advertise Duncan Hines' Double Fudge Brownie Mix. The jacket is brown with separate white collar, orange belt with silver cardboard buckle. Legs are orange with bown felt elf shoes. Hat is orange. Entire costume is made from felt. A. Wolfe collection, David Nelson, James Giokas photographers. $12.00.

$3.95. The head is vinyl with large pointed ears, little bulb nose, line smile with tongue in yum yum position. Felt clothes are also the body.

Dunkin Donuts. Shops located in the east and mid-west sold a 24-inch plastic inflatable **Munchkin** doll in 1976. The doll cost 99¢ with the purchase of a box of donut holes, or Munchkins as they are called at this donut franchise. In some areas this doll was still available in 1977.

The inflatable *Munchkin* doll was offered in 1976 at Dunkin Donut shops. The 24-inch doll advertised the famous donut hole treat also named Munchkin. $3.00.

Duquesne Beer. A plaster figural, intended for display on bars, features a 9½-inch **Duke**, the mascot figure for the beer with the same nickname. **Duke** wears a painted outfit with gold buttons and epaulets. A mug of beer is held up in a toast.

Duke is the mascot for Duquesne Beer as featured on this display item. Marks: "Have a 'Duke'/DUQUESNE/Pilsener/The Finest Beer in Town." L. Yagatich collection, Donald G. Vilsack photographer. $25.00.

Dutch Boy Paint.

In 1891, 25 makers of white lead consolidated to form the National Lead Company. It became apparent that a trademark symbol was necessary to bind these diverse companies together. Since 1778 when the first white lead company began operation, the Dutch process was used to refine their product. This thought, along with the Dutch people's reputation for whitewashing everything spic and span, led to the idea of the Dutch Boy symbol.

Consumers were first introduced to the Dutch boy line of paint in 1899. The young boy with hair to the bottom of his ear lobes seems more in style now than when he was sketched by Dutch artist, Yook. Unbelievable as it seems, an Irish lad, Michael Brady posed for

the final painting that was executed by Lawrence Carmichael Earle. So beneath that Dutch cap lurks a soul as Irish as a leprechaun. The Dutch Boy always carries a paint brush and a bucket of paint. He wears bib overalls and wooden clog shoes.

A paper mache display figure, 30-inches tall, was used at stores selling Dutch Boy Paints. Date is unknown, but it closely resembles the 1913 magazine ad. Marks: "Old King Cole Inc./Canton, Ohio, U.S.A.," on sticker on base. Arlene Wolfe collection, David Nelson, James Giokas photographers. $30.00-50.00.

Many premiums, such as dolls and wooden shoes have been used during the Dutch Boy's 79 years of existence. These items, along with many display figures are on display at the office in Baltimore, Maryland.

One of the earliest dolls is a 4-foot tall stuffed doll of the Dutch Boy. In about 1948 key dealers were given one of these dolls. (We were unable to locate one of these.)

A 10-inch kneeling **Dutch Boy** was located that was probably used for display. It is made of unknown composition.

This figure of the *Dutch Boy* was probably used by dealers in their stores. It is 11-inches tall and made of a hard substance that appears to be rubber. Courtesy Libals Antiques. $35.00.

Dutch Boy doll wears a blue flannel hat with a visor and bib overalls over a white shirt. The clog-shaped feet are yellow. Marks: "Dutch Boy," stenciled across overall bib. $15.00.

In 1953 a 15-inch stuffed doll with mask face was used by dealers. The doll has yellow yarn hair, closed mouth, painted eyes, and wears blue overalls and cap.

In 1956 a 12-inch puppet with vinyl head and cloth body made to fit over the hand, was free with the purchase of a gallon of paint. It was used to introduce a new line of paint manufactured by Dutch Boy Paints.

A 12-inch hand puppet with a vinyl head and cloth body was given free with the purchase of a gallon of paint in 1956. The molded/painted head has a blue cap, yellow hair and a smiling mouth. Marks: "Dutch Boy", across bib of overalls. $8.00.

Dutch Maid Egg Noodles. In 1976 a 12-inch prestuffed cloth doll was offered for $1.00 by this brand of noodles. The doll is one of the most simple, much like a child might draw. The fabric is closely woven white cotton with a minimum of lithographed detail.

The offer expired September 30, 1976. A needlepoint kit of the Dutch Maid could also be ordered.

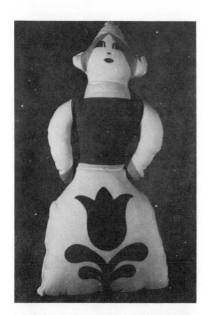

In 1976 a 12-inch cloth *Dutch Maid* doll was offered by Dutch Maid Egg Noodles. The doll is made from a coarse closely woven fabric with what looks more like stencil than lithograph details. The bodice is aqua, the skirt is white with a big red tulip. The face has simple features. Unmarked. $4.00.

Dy-o-la Dye. This old Burlington, Vermont Company offered at least three little cloth dolls in the 1910 to 1930 period, luckily all are well marked. They are produced by a photographic process that gives delicate shading and detail to the face and the clothing. Judging from the nunber of old Dy-o-la dye cabinets that turn up, it must have been a widely used commodity in its time.

One doll wears her hair in the Mary Pickford style with long blonde ringlets and a bow on top of the head. Her printed dress has a square neckline with a tie, the short sleeves are cuffed and held in place with buttons. Shoes point to the side and have considerable detail. The 10½-inch doll holds a 10¢ package of Scarlet Dy-O-la dye.

This Dy-o-la dye doll has a Mary Pickford hair style and wears a neck tie. Marks: "MY NAME IS" on front of the belt (There is no continuation of what the name is.); "My mother uses Dy-o-la" is on the back of the dress; she also holds a package of Scarlet dye. P. Coghlan collection, Harry Sykora photographer.$50.00.

This little Dy-o-la doll is only 8-inches tall. A green sash rides low on her red dress. The colorful outfit includes blue socks, gold shoes, and a red hair bow in her brown hair. Marks: "My name is Dy-o-la" on front of sash; "Dy-o-la" on back sash. P. Coghlan collection, Harry Sykora photographer. $40.00.

The short dress indicates a 1930 vintage doll offered by Dy-o-la dye. The doll wears a baby blue dress, white socks, black Mary Jane shoes, and carries a little black haired doll in her arms. Marks: "Dy-o-la", on binding around neck of dress; "Dy-o-la Dye Dolly", on back of dress. P. Coghlan collection, Harry Sykora photographer. $40.00.

The next doll is tiny, only 8-inches tall. Her skirt is a bit shorter and it has a low-slung belt that was popular in the teens. Her hair is bobbed with a part to one side and a ribbon.

The third doll, 10½-inches, is probably early 30's. The dress has climbed shorter and the hair is also short. This doll holds a wee doll in her arms. From a coupon we learned the doll cost 5¢ plus an envelope of Dy-o-la dye.

All three were advertised on little cards that were inserted in boxes of dye. A card was found for the third doll. It read, "four colors on linen." It is possible that there were more than these three dolls from this company.

E

Eastman Kodak Miracode System. In 1971 a cloth **Champion Retriever** dog was given to Kodak representatives at a convention. The 17-inch long dog is made of yellow fabric with black lithographed detail. The intention of the idea was to express a champion at retrieving information stored on microfilm.

In 1971, Eastman Kodak's yellow and black cloth *Champion Retreiver* dog was given to representatives to introduce a new data retrieval system of the same name. Marks: "Kodak, Miracode Systems, The Champion Retriever," on one side of a plastic disk hung around the neck; "Are File Documents Lost, Strayed or Stolen? Call your KODAK representatives," on the other side; "C. Eastman Kodak Company, 1971," on the underside of the dog. $10.00.

Until 1962, this company used only the trademark name Kodak. It was a name George Eastman personally selected for the camera he invented. Eastman is quoted as explaining the selection, "The letter 'K' had been a favorite with me--it seemed a strong, incisive sort of letter. Therefore, the word I wanted had to start with 'K.' then it became a question of trying out a great number of combinations of letters that made words starting and ending with 'K.' The word 'Kodak' is the result . . . It became the distinctive word for our products."

The name was extended to include Eastman when the company began marketing textiles.

(See Palmer Cox Brownies for Brownie Camera advertising dolls.)

Elgin Nut Margarine and Everbest Nut Margarine, products of B.S. Pearsall Butter Company. In 1920 this Elgin, Illinois company offered a free "Koko Kid" doll to promote their two brands of margarine. At

KoKo Kid Marks: "KOKO KID", across back of neck; "ELGIN Nut Margarine/The Finest Table Quality/Unexcelled for Cooking and Baking/Awarded Grand Prize and Gold Medal, Paris and Liege for/Superior Quality in Competition with the World; the Good Housekeeping Seal; Save the valuable coupons for/high grade household articles/given free." A. Wolfe collection, David Nelson, James Giokas photographers. $35.00.

the beginning of the promotion the doll was given free by the grocer upon a receipt of a **Koko Kid** jingle written by the child desiring the doll. Later in the promotion it was necessary to mail the jingle to the company and they would mail the free doll. The doll was also called "Kid Kokonut".

The cloth doll is 4½-inches tall and lithographed in brown and yellow on white fabric. The doll is a copy of their trademark figure: a child with large eyes that roll, as the doll ad says. The doll has side-glance eyes, a circle nose, and a dot for a mouth, giving the doll a fearful expression. Perhaps the **Koko Kid** is sneaking its snack of bread spread with margarine. The front of the dress has a checked border, like the boxes of margarine. In the back the border has no checks on the doll, instead prizes are printed.

Eskimo Pie Corporation. This manufacturer of ice cream treats has used a figure attired in Eskimo Clothing since the 1930's. In order to obtain additional value from the popular trademark, a cloth Eskimo doll was developed. According to the company, in 1964 a 15-inch **Eskimo Pie Boy** was introduced as a consumer premium on the back of ice cream wrappers for $1.00. The doll was clothed predominantly in brown.

The color combination and facial design was modified in 1975. The later doll is attired in a red parka with white hood, brown pants, and white boots. The line smile shows the tip of a tongue in one corner, yum-yum style. This doll is marked, the other one is not. Both dolls were manufactured by Chase Bag Company.

A 37-inch inflatable **Eskimo Pie Boy** was used in store displays, but was never offered as a consumer item.

The Eskimo Pie Corporation introduced the *Eskimo Pie Boy* doll in 1964. The doll wears a lithographed brown parka with a white hood and a red diamond design across the bottom, brown pants, red boots and gloves. Unmarked. Elizabeth Wright collection, Keith Studios photographer. $6.00.

A 37-inch inflatable *Eskimo Pie Boy* was used in displays by stores selling the Eskimo Pie brand of ice cream treats. $7.00.

Esskay Meats, a product of Schuderberg-Kurdle Company. **Baron Von Esskay** is an 11-inch

In 1975 the *Eskimo Pie Boy* doll was modified. The plastic bag the doll arrives in reads: "For best results: open and protect it immediately in the warm arms of a loving child." Marks: "Eskimo Pie" across jacket. Elizabeth Wright collection, Keith Studios photographer. $2.00.

Baron Von Esskay was offered by Esskay Meats, a company in Baltimore, Maryland. The World War I flying ace wears a red jacket, blue pants, blue scarf, and white helmet. Marks: "Baron Von Esskay" on front of jacket; "ESSKAY," on back. A. Pfister collection. $6.00.

cloth doll. He wears a long scarf tossed over one shoulder, goggles, a jacket unzipped to mid-chest, and with zippers at the end of each sleeve. A dapper mustache, smiling mouth, and round nose complete this doll, all lithographed of course.

Esso. A rotund little 5-inch bank was offered in the late 1950's to advertise the service station of Russillo & Colucci according to printing on the back. The **Esso Attendant** doll is made of hard plastic with molded/painted uniform, hat, and features. Much hand work has been done to outline the belt on the uniform and the features of the face. This may have been done by one of the owners, rather than from the distributor.

This 5-inch bank was used to advertise an Esso Service Station. It is a copy of the uniformed Esso Attendant, wearing a gray uniform and hat. It is possible that the hand-painted detail on the face and the outlines around the belt were done by one of the owners rather than by the manufacturers. Marks: "Esso," on front of the uniform and hat; "Rusillo and Colucci/Ft. Hill Ser. Sta./Central Ave.," on the back. A. Pfister collection. $4.00.

Exxon (formerly Humble Oil Company). In 1959 the "Put a Tiger in Your Tank" advertising promotion was introduced to Chicago motorists by the Oklahoma Oil Company, which was a division of Humble Oil. To further the successful campaign a year later, prior to the holiday season, a plush toy tiger was available at service stations for $1.59 plus the purchase of at least seven gallons of gasoline.

The 16-inch tiger was manufactured by Columbia Toy Company, and over 100,000 were sold to Oklahoma Oil Company customers during the six-week period of the promotion.

In 1973 the tiger campaign was promoted nationwide by the Humble Oil Company. During this period a variety of tiger dolls, banks, and tiger tails were used in service station promotional programs. These were initiated by

Plush Exxon (then Humble) tiger, 16-inches tall, was the first tiger premium used to introduce the "Put a tiger in your tank" promotion. The plush toy was offered to customers prior to the holiday season in 1959. $8.00.

local, district, and regional people using a number of suppliers, depending upon availablility.

In addition to the plush tiger used in 1960 we have found, a fabric tiger, two tiger pillows, and a plastic bank. Undoubtedly there are others.

During Humble Oil's (now Exxon) "Put a tiger in your tank" promotion, many tiger premiums were sold at stations selling that brand gasoline. This tiger head is an 11 x 12-inch pillow with lithographed orange, black, gray, white, and yellow features. Marks: "Friends-of-the-tiger." $4.00.

A 17-inch cloth rendition of the Exxon (then Humble) tiger. $8.00.

Another tiger pillow, 11 x 11, used by Humble Oil (now Exxon) during the late 1960's. $4.00.

Exxon's Tiger was also manufactured as an 8½-inch hard plastic bank. Marks: "Humble Oil/Refining Co./Made in U.S.A.," incised on bottom. $5.00.

F

Fab, a product of Colgate-Palmolive Company. In 1954 this washday detergent offered an "American Doll in an Album," the album being a box that opens like a book. The doll is 7-inches high, open/shut eyes, synthetic wig and dressed in a long rayon dress to represent some famous American woman. Eight dolls were offered: Martha Washington, Dolly Madison, Betsy Ross, and Pricilla Alden, Barbara Fritchie, Molly Pitcher, Clara Barton, and Mary Todd Lincoln. Similar dolls have been offered by other products. (See Blue Bonnet Margarine, Atlantic Richfield, and Reddi Whip.)

Prior to that time Fab advertised the same doll as a $1.29 value, free. The date was cut from the cliping found, but judging from the price it preceeded the $1.00 doll.

In 1956 a 9-inch walking doll with washable hair was available for $1.00 plus boxtops. Coupons were enclosed in the detergent and shows a doll that resembles Vogue's Ginny doll dressed in a dress with a blue bodice and a white skirt with various sized and colored dots.

A year later a similar doll was offered for the same price, but it was smaller, 7¾-inches, and it wore a pink taffeta dress with blue braid trim, hat, shoes, and stockings. This doll is much like the Ginny doll. It came with a brochure advertising the availability of three extra costumes: bride for $1.00, lounge set for 50¢, and daytime for 50¢.

In 1958, Fab returned to the 9-inch doll offer, except the doll came dressed in a dress similar to the smaller doll, a salmon to pink cotton fabric dress and no hat.

Near Christmas, 1954, Fab detergent again offered the Americana Doll in an album-like box, this time for $1.00. M. Meisinger collection.

The smaller 7¾-inch doll was available from Fab detergent in 1957. She wears a pink dress with blue trim and a pink straw-like plastic hat. The larger doll, 9-inches, wears a pink cotton dress trimmed in white and has no hat. Both wear plastic shoes, the small, pink and the larger, white. These dolls were also offered by Lustre Creme Shampoo. M. Kolterman collection. $5.00-7.50.

Facit-Addo, Inc. This Swedish company sold many adding machines in America prior to computers. Two dolls were manufactured to represent their trademark figure, a bright looking fellow with a high-pointed hat.

The larger doll, 15-inches with a 10-inch hat, was manufactured in Germany of heavy vinyl. It has molded/painted side-glance eyes, a line smile, and came in either yellow or gray vinyl. The doll is jointed at the neck, shoulder, wrists, ankles so it can easily be positioned to stand. This **Facit Man** was designed with magnets to hang upside down in a window for display.

The smaller **Facit Man** doll, 4-inches, is a miniature copy of the larger doll.

Facit Man, 25-inches tall with hat, was used for display in stores selling Facit Business Machines. The vinyl suit came in either yellow or gray. Smaller versions were also used. Marks: "West Germany", on bottom of one foot of suit; "Facit", across hat; "Facit" on disk on front of suit; also numbers randomly placed on pointed hat. $20.00.

Fairy Soap, a product of N.K. Fairbank's Soap Company. Ads for this 5¢ oval bar of soap that "purifies the pores" were found in magazines up to about the 1930's. Then the company must have merged or gone out of business. The usual ads showed a sweet child in a big hat sitting on a large bar of Fairy Soap, her legs dangling over the side with the slogan, "Have You a Little Fairy in Your Home?"

Horsman made a doll to represent the **Fairy** and it was described in Playthings, 1912. The doll has Can't Break 'Em head, composition hands, cloth body and limbs. The hair is molded/painted and features are painted. The mouth is closed. She wears a costume patterned after the child in the ads.

Fanny Farmer Candy.

The *Fanny Farmer* doll is cloth with a plastic mask and painted features and hair. The fabric body is pale pink with yellow and green flowers. A removable lace and fabric skirt has a ribbon belt marked "Fanny Farmer." The ties on the hat are also marked "Fanny Farmer." $4.00.

Farmer's Brand. Except for what is printed on the doll, nothing is known about either the doll or the company. The doll, 15-inches tall, is cloth and represents a young farmer boy. The boy wears a lithographed straw hat, overalls, and an open neck shirt. A label on the back of the suspenders says: "J. LeRoy/Farmer/Cedar Rapids/Iowa." A can of Farmer's Brand Sweet Corn sticks out of a back pocket.

J. Le Roy Farmer is a 14-inch cloth doll with a red shirt and blue pants. Marks: "J. LeRoy/Farmer/Cedar Rapids/Iowa," on back of suspender; a can of corn sticking out from the back pocket is lithographed to represent the real product and has a label of "Farmer's/Brand/Sweet Corn." J. Varsalona collection. $35.00.

Fashion Two-Twenty Cosmetics. In 1969 a sales incentive award was **Carol the Color Me Doll**. It is a 12-inch doll made of white plastic, except the face, arms, and legs, which are flesh tone. Five color-on wipe-off crayons are included for the owner to color the hair, eyes, and

clothing to her own preference. The doll was manufactured by Multiple Toymakers of New York City.

Carol the Color-Me Doll was a sales incentive for Fashion Two-Twenty Cosmetics. It is white, except for the arms, legs, and face which are flesh color. Five crayons came with the doll to color to please the owner. The colors wiped off if the effect was not satisfactory. A. Wolfe collection, David Nelson, James Giokas photographers. $8.00.

Faultless Starch. This old Kansas City, Missouri company has been selling starch since 1887. In about 1910 when starch came in small envelopes that had to be emptied and carefully stirred lest the starch become lumpy, two dolls were offered. **Miss Lilly White** and **Miss Phoebe Primm** were stamped on flat sheets of fabric, to be cut, stitched, and stuffed by the owner. Two dolls cost either 5¢ or 10¢ depending on whether you sent in 6 or 12 fronts from a package of starch. The dolls were printed by the Saalfield Publishing Co.

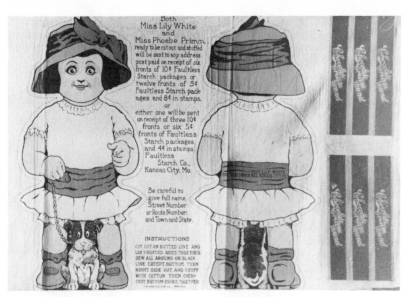

Bright-eyed *Miss Lily White* wears a snow-white dress, a big hat, sash, and shoes. A little dog sits between her legs. Marks: "Miss Lily White/Faultless Starch Doll, Kansas City, Mo.," on back of sash; cost and instructions are printed on the background fabric; one end has strips printed with Chocolate Cream Brand. V. Rasberry collection. $40.00.

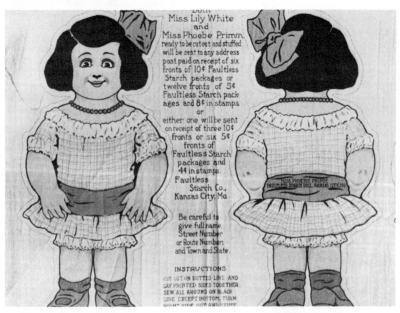

Miss Phoebe Primm was probably offered about 1910 according to a company spokesman. Marks: "Miss Phoebe Primm/Faultless Starch Doll, Kansas City, Mo.," on back of sash. V. Rasberry collection. $40.00.

Miss Lizabeth Ann is another cloth Faultless Starch doll that was offered prior to 1920. The exact dates are unknown because all the company's records were destroyed in the 1952 flood. **Lizabeth Ann** is 19½-inches high, wears a white dress with red and blue lines and has brown hair.

Nowadays Faultless starch comes in a spray can with no fuss no muss. Remember having to wash the strainer when the starch had to strained for lumps? Thank heavens for spray starch and even better for wash and wear clothing.

Near the turn of the century *Lizabeth Ann* was offered by the Faultless Starch Company. The 19½-inch cloth doll came on a sheet of fabric, to be completed by the owner. Marks: "Miss Lizabeth Ann/Faultless Starch Co./Kansas City, Mo.," on back of belt. E. Rogers collection. $35.00.

Federal Savings and Loan, New England. Chase Bag Company manufactured a **General Greene** for this company. No further information is known.

Fels-Naptha Soap, a product of the Fels Company. Ads in 1925 magazines proclaim, "Fels Naptha--the Golden Bar with the Clean Naptha Odor." As a child that isn't quite how I remember the smell. It was so strong it was rubbed on places where wood ticks burrowed under the skin; they would crawl out, probably to avoid the smell.

In the 1920's the company used a cloth Ragsy Kewpie named "Arabella" in all their magazine ads. To our knowledge the doll was never sold as a premium by the company.

In the thirties the advertisements changed, a cleaning lady in a long dress named **Anty Drudge** became the trademark. In 1933 the company offered an 11-inch

The *Anty Drudge* doll was offered by Fels and Company in 1933 to advertise Fels Napta Soap. The doll is 11-inches tall, wears a dress with the words "Fels Naptha Soap" printed all over in red, like the wrapper on a bar of soap. Marks: "Anty Drudge," across green apron. Playthings by the Yard, 1973. $55.00.

cloth **Anty Drudge** doll printed on a sheet of fabric to be assembled by the owner. Her dress is pale yellow like the soap, with the words, "Fels-Naptha Soap" written all over it in red, to resemble the wrapper on a bar of soap. She wears spectacles, a cap and apron, and holds a bar of soap in one hand.

Final Touch. This fabric softener has had three promotional offers that we were able to find. In 1974 Looney Tune cartoon characters were available for $1.00 plus a label. **Porky Pig, Yosemite Sam,** and **Sylvester** could be ordered. These and other Looney Tune characters were also offered by Aim Toothpaste.

In 1975 a fluffy stuffed snowman was offered for $1.75 plus two labels. The plush snowman was manufactured by A & L Novelty Company and the offer expired June 30, 1975.

In 1977 **Lovie Lamb** was available for $2.99 plus a label. The plush lamb was made by Fun Farm©.

Fisk Tires, a product of Uniroyal. At 3 o'clock one morning Burr E. Griffin, a fledgling ad artist, received the inspiration for what later became the Fisk Tire trademark. Four years later, 1910, the "Fisk Boy" was copyrighted and he made his first appearance in the March 7, 1914 issue of The Saturday Evening Post. Along with the pajama clad child holding a large tire with one arm and a candle in the other Griffin coined one of the most widely promoted puns, "Time to Retire."

The *Final Touch Snowman* was available in 1975. The 11-inch snowman is white plush with black plush and felt hat, black pom-pom eyes and nose, red felt mouth and a red print scarf. Marks: "From the Animal Playland of A. & L. Novelty Co., Inc.," on a cloth label. A. Wolfe collection, David Nelson, James Giokas photographers. $8.00.

A 4-inch bisque *Fisk Boy* is missing his tire and candle. The two-piece pajamas are sewn on to the doll, making it difficult to check for marks. $125.00.

Two dolls were found that resemble the Fisk trademark. One is a 21-inch composition doll, head, legs, and body in one piece with jointed arms. The doll has molded/painted hair, droopy eyes, and a yawning open/closed mouth. The doll is unmarked.

A small bisque doll of the **Fisk Boy** was also manufactured. It is 5-inches tall. One arm is bent to hold the tire, the other straight to hold the candle. Pajamas are sewn on.

The 21-inch composition *Fisk Boy* doll has painted yellow hair and sleepy blue eyes. Pajamas and tire are not original. Unmarked. B. Welch collection. $80.00.

Flaked Rice. See American Rice Foods Manufacturing Company.

Fletcher's Castoria, a product of the Glenbrook Laboratories. A colorful cloth "Mammy Castoria" doll was offered. The 11-inch doll is probably mid-1930's vintage, judging from the Fletcher's Castoria box she holds in the crook of her arm. Prior to 1932 the Castoria bottle was packaged in a wrapper.

Mammy Castoria resembles the cloth Aunt Jemima doll. **Mammy's** hands are clasped in front of her apron.

Mammy Castoria, 11-inches tall was offered by Fletcher's Castoria in the 1930's. Her brightly colored attire includes a skirt with green, red, and blue stripes; a yellow and white polka dot apron, yellow shawl, and yellow bandana. Marks: "Mammy Castoria," bottom of skirt; holds a black and white box of the laxative. P. Coghlan collection, Harry Sykora photographer. $60.00.

In by-gone days it seemed Castoria was the remedy for most any childhood complaint from too many green apples to an aching head. Many brands of Castoria have come on the market, but none have had the success of Fletcher's.

The Castoria name and formula was patented by Dr. Samuel Pitcher, a physician in Hyannis, Massachusetts. In 1868 the mild laxative, which he had been prescribing to his patients, was placed on the market.

Aware of Pitcher's success, Charles H. Fletcher obtained the purchasing rights to the product. He realized the patent was valid for only 17 years, so he decided to use his name and distinctive

145

signature as a trademark. The association of the name and the product proved so successful it was almost impossible for any other company to enter the market with another brand of the formula after the 17 years.

The company claims, "Today's Fletcher's Castoria leads its market as the only leading laxative for children, and is given by more mothers than any other laxative."

Flintstones Vitamins, a product of Miles Laboratory. In 1971 an inflatable **Fred Flintstone** doll with removable clothes was offered for $2.00 plus a label. The heavy vinyl doll was a replica of the popular prehistoric cartoon character.

In 1971, *Fred Flintstone*, the cartoon character, was given free to dealers carrying Flintstones Vitamins. The large inflatable is unusual because the plastic clothes are removable. The figure is well marked. K. Miller collection. $6.00.

Florida Department of Citrus. To promote Florida citrus products, of any brand, this organization has offered three **Orange Bird** premiums. The figure is a Walt Disney trademark.

In the early 1970's a 5-inch plastic bank was used by this organization. The head of this **Orange Bird** resembles an orange, and the bird is sitting.

Florida Department of Citrus used the *Orange Bird* in bank form for one of its promotions to sell Florida orange juice. The 5-inch bank is hard plastic with touches of green and yellow on the beak and body. Marks: "Florida/Orange Bird ® Walt Disney." $3.00.

The 16-inch inflatable *Orange Bird* with yellow beak, green feet and wings. Marks: "Drink/Florida/ Orange Juice," on back of head; "The Orange Bird. © Walt Disney Productions," on back. $3.00.

A 16-inch inflatable **Orange Bird** was also offered.

In 1975 a 13-inch plush and felt **Orange Bird** was offered for $3.00 plus proof-of-purchase from frozen concentrate, chilled, or canned orange juice from Florida. The original expiration date was June 30, 1975. It was extended to March 31, 1976 or until supply was exhausted.

The 15-inch *Sunny Jim* doll was purchased in 1978 in England. This cereal and trademark figure were popular in the United States sixty years ago. They are sold now only in England. The doll wears a red jacket, black and white hat, white trousers, and black and yellow shoes. Marks: "Sunny Jim," across hat; carries a replica of the Force Cereal package. M. Hiter collection. $4.00.

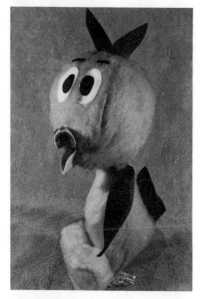

The plush *Orange Bird*, 13-inches tall, was offered in 1975. The bird is orange plush with green felt topknot and wings. The beak and eyes are also felt. $4.00.

Force Cereal. This breakfast food was advertised in the early 1900's in America. Between 1905 and 1915 a character named **Sunny Jim** was used in their advertising. Using humorous jingles written by Minnie Hanff, **Sunny Jim** was transformed from a pessimist to an optimist upon eating his Force cereal.

Sunny Jim is a colonial fellow with white hair tied at the nape of his neck and a sprig of hair protruding from the top of his bald head.

About 1905 an 18-inch muslin doll, purportably designed by W.W. Denslow, the illustrator of the Wizard of Oz, was manufactured and could be purchased with Force boxtops.

In 1909 a **Sunny Jim** doll was manufactured by Hahn and Amberg. This 12-inch doll had a composition head with painted features and a white or blue fur stuffed body and limbs. The promotion said: "Bright as the Sun, Cute as can be, I'm yours--'for Fun,' as you can see."

A year later Butler Bros. added another **Sunny Jim** doll, this one also had a composition head, but when the doll was pressed the mouth would open and a bellows sounded a voice.

In 1914 Ideal Novelty and Toy Company manufactured a **Sunny Jim** doll. Description is unavailable.

Information of **Sunny Jim** and

Force breakfast food has been minimal. In about 1915 magazine ads for this cereal ceased in America. Whether the cereal was discontinued or whether it merged with one of the large cereal producers and was given a new name is unknown.

An earlier cloth *Sunny Jim* is two inches larger and has some highlights lithographed on the shoes, and some color on his cheeks. Marks: "Sunny Jim," across hat; carries a replica of the Force Cereal package. J. Varsalona collection. $12.00.

From 1920 to the present, Force has been sold in England. Recently a cloth **Sunny Jim** was purchased by a friend. The doll is 15-inches tall, and printed in profile, the same on each side. **Sunny Jim** is a humorous looking fellow with wrinkles, long ears, white hair, squinty eyes, and rather lean. He carries a lithographed box of Force Wheat Flakes.

Franklin Ice Cream. This brand of ice cream was popular during the 1920's when full page ads appeared regularly.

A 14-inch cloth doll was found that is marked with this company's name on the skirt. It appears to be circa 1920.

An old 14-inch cloth doll marked: "Always buy/FRANKLIN'S DOUBLE XX/Ice Cream/From Parkview/ Finest Ice Cream possible to Make." K. Lyon collection. $25.00.

Franco-American Spaghetti Company. In 1966 an 8-inch **King Sauce** or Dragon hand puppet was offered for 50¢ plus two labels from their Franco-American King Sauce.

See Spaghettios for **Wizard of O's** doll.

Franklin Life Insurance Co. Benjamin Franklin, the namesake of this insurance company is represented by a 12-inch cloth doll, **Uncle Ben.** The doll has lithographed features and lithographed clothing that includes the famous pince-nez, a coat, pants, and vest. The doll has been available throughout the 50 states during the 1970's. Ads state the doll is free. "The only thing we ask in return is a few minutes of your time to tell you the Franklin story."

The *Benjamin Franklin* doll, 12-inches tall. The lithographed outfit includes a yellow vest, black coat, red knee pants, and white stockings. Dolls with other color combinations have been issued. Marks: "Franklin Life/Insurance Co.," on back. $8.00.

Fresca, a product of the Coca-Cola Company. This diet drink offered a **March Hare** in 1970 for $6.95 plus a proof-of-purchase from a carton of Fresca.

The 28-inch plush *Fresca Dog* offered in the Denver area. Dog is reddish-brown with white markings. $7.00.

In about 1975 the formula for Fresca had to be changed to conform to the regulations to discontinue the use of cyclamates. It has been a slow climb to reach the success it enjoyed prior to the modification of Fresca's original recipe.

A 28-inch brown plush St. Bernard-type dog with a Fresca can fastened to his collar was offered in the Denver area in the mid-70's.

Fresca's *March Hare* was offered in 1970. The large, 28-inches tall, plush rabbit wears a bow tie and an orange and purple vest marked: "Fresca". $12.00.

Frito-lay Corn Chips. In the early 1970's 8-inch plastic International Dolls were advertised on packages of Frito-lay Corn Chips. The same type doll has been offered by many other products.

At the same time 24 small "Dolls of the World" were offered on the same packages. The advertisement for these dolls read: "Get the complete collection of 24 beautifully detailed dolls for only

$1.00 and two top name panels from large bags of FRITOS corn chips. Use the convenient order form below."

In the 1960's erasers were offered in packages of corn chips. The erasers were about one-inch high and represented the "Frito Bandito" and other characters from Frito-lay TV commercials.

Cheetos, another product of Frito-lay offered a cloth mouse in 1974.

Frostie Root Beer. A 16-inch prestuffed cloth doll with a lithographed brown suit and long white beard was offered by this beverage in the early 1970's. The arms and legs are cut free from the body and it is well marked.

A *Frostie Man* doll, 16-inches tall was offered in 1972. The doll wears root beer colored clothing and has a long white beard. Marks: "Drink/Frostie ® /Root Beer," on pointed cap; "Frostie/Root Beer ® /Frostie Man, Frostie!, on back of doll. $8.00.

Funny Face, a product of Pillsbury Company. This powdered beverage that is so popular with young children has offered three sets of promotional items. All are patterned after the faces on the flavors of drink mix: **Goofy Grape, Choo Choo Cherry, Lefty Lemon,** and **Freckle-faced Strawberry**.

In the mid-70's cotton pillows, 14-inches, were offered for $1.50 plus 5 empty packages of Funny Face.

"Funny Face Pals" were similar, but were made of plush fabric and only 10-inches. In 1975 they cost $2.00 plus 3 empty packages of Funny Face.

The third offer was for 3½-inch plastic walking toys. By hanging a string weighted with a disk over the edge of a flat surface, such as a table, the toys would walk.

Many other promotional items have been offered by this product such as: mugs, tee shirts, kites, and frisbees.

Pillsbury's Funny Face drink mix offered four cotton fabric pillows, each representing a flavor of their beverage. *Goofy Grape* is purple with a green hat. Four large protruding teeth and cross eyes indeed give him a goofy-looking appearance. Unmarked. $3.00.

Choo Choo Cherry is red and wears an engineer's hat of blue and white striped cotton. $3.00.

Lefty Lemon has locks of yarn hair dangling from the baseball cap. $4.00.

"Freckle-faced Strawberry" is red with one lone tooth showing from the line smile. $3.00.

Choo-choo Cherry wears an wide felt smile, and felt eyes and feet. $4.00.

Pillsbury's 3½-inch plastic Funny Face walking toys. From left to right are: Goofy Grape, Choo-Choo Cherry, Lefty Lemon and Freckle-faced Strawberry. S. Esser collection, Bruce Esser photographer. $2.00 each.

G

Gas Service of Kansas City, Missouri. An excellent quality plush **Genie** doll was given free to customers with the purchase of a gas appliance by this company. Gas companies in other cities also used the **Genie** promotion in the early 1970's.

The 18-inch doll is made of plush fabric with a molded painted mask face. The animated face has a smiling open/closed mouth, wide-open eyes, and large pointed ears. The flame-shaped head is made of three colors of plush to resemble the gas pilot light.

Hand puppet given free to children at Gasho Restaurant. $1.00.

General Electric Company. In 1929 an excellent quality wood-jointed doll with composition head was manufactured by Cameo Product, Inc. to advertise General Electric Radios. It is not

An 18-inch plush and vinyl *Genie* doll was given free to customers purchasing a gas appliance in the early 1970's. The Gas Service of Kansas City, Missouri gave this particular doll. Marks: "Genie/Gene Hazelton," on label. $12.00.

Gasho Restaurant. A plastic hand puppet was given free to children eating at this Japanese food restaurant.

Bandy. Marks: "General Electric/Radio," on hat; "Art Quality/Manu. by Cameo Prod., Inc./Port Allegany, Pa./Des. & by JLK," on foot.

known whether this doll was given to customers purchasing a radio, used by dealers for display, or dispersed some other way. The 18-inch **Bandy** doll represents a bandmaster. He wears a tall hat, a band jacket with epaulets on the shoulders, and carries a baton. The doll has joints at the knees, wrists, elbows, ankles, and neck. It is well-marked.

See Hotpoint.

General Foods. See dolls listed under the following General Foods products: Birds Eye Frozen Foods, Jello, Baker's Chocolate, Post's Cereals, and Maxwell House Coffee.

General Mills. In 1971 the 6½-inch **Dawn** doll, manufactured by Topper Corporation, was

Sippin Sam and his companion *Sippin' Sue* were offered in 1972 by a General Mills cereal. The dolls have open/closed mouths to accomodate a tiny straw. Both dolls have molded painted hair and eyes. The suede-like jacket and pants are original. $3.00.

offered free with three Cheerios package seals or for 75¢ plus one seal. The doll offered has blonde hair and is dressed in a blue and white party dress. An accessory package with three dresses, hangers, mannequins, black poodle, hand bag, and comb and brush set was available for one seal plus $1.00.

In 1972 two 6-inch vinyl dolls, manufactured by the Kenner Toy Company, were offered. **Sippin' Sam** and **Sippin' Sue** have molded hair, painted eyes, dimples, and open mouths to accomodate a tiny straw. Which cereal offered these dolls is unknown.

Sippin' Sue wears her original western outfit. $3.00.

In 1974 the **Heather** doll, manufactured by Mattel, was offered for 75¢ plus one Frosty O's box bottom. Also included in the offer was a 33 1/3 R.P.M. record and stand.

In 1975 General Mills offered four carefully detailed monster dolls to represent their line of presweetened cereals given monster names. The 7 to 8-inch molded vinyl dolls were manufac-

153

tured by Product People of Minnesota and were also sold at retail stores. The dolls, and sugar-sweetened cereals of the same name are: **Fruit Brute**, a brown wolfish creature with molded striped bib overalls; **Frankenberry**, a purple monster with a twistable waist; **Boo Berry**, a white ghost; and **Count Chocula**, a brown Dracula-looking fellow. Each was available for $1.00 plus the corresponding box top.

Mattell's *Heather* doll was offered by General Mills. The 1974 offer included a record and stand. $3.00.

Boo Berry is 7½-inches high. $4.00.

Fruit Brute a brown wolfish toy, is 8-inches tall and is dressed in molded bib overalls. Marks: "Fruit Brute/General Mills, Inc. REG. TM," on back. $4.00.

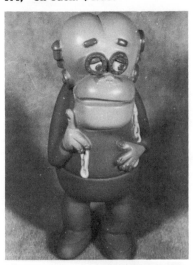

Frankenberry and the others in the series cost $1.00 plus the corresponding cereal box top. This purple and pink monster has a twistable waist and is 7½-inches tall. $4.00.

The latest known offer is the **Trix Playmate** offered in 1977 on boxes of Trix cereal. The **Playmate** is a 9-inch vinyl rabbit with a squeaker. It is all white with tinted facial features. It cost $1.00 plus one proof-of-purchase seal.

See also Hamburger Helper.

Fearsome *Count Chocula* wears a brown outfit. $4.00.

The *Trix Playmate* was offered for a short time in 1977 on boxes of Trix cereal. The rabbit is white with tinted cheeks. Marks: "Trix," on heel of one foot; "General Mills, Inc. REG. TM," around back of other foot. $4.00.

Georgia-Pacific. See MD Toilet Tissue.

Gerber Products Company. To settle the many stories concerning the adorable Gerber baby trademark, let me quote Mrs. Sylvia T. Fogg, Company Publications and Company Historian (now retired):

"We are often asked the origin of our well-known trademark. There have been many theories about it, and some people have claimed to be the model for the Gerber Baby. It has even been said that the late Humphrey Bogart was the model for the Gerber Baby, but this is not true. Actually the picture used by Gerber Products Company is an unfinished charcoal sketch submitted by the late Dorothy Hope Smith in 1928. She indicated that she would complete the sketch if the age and size of the baby were approved. The sketch was so appealing that the artist's unfinished rendering became the world-famous Gerber Baby."

In 1936 the first *Gerber Baby* dolls were introduced. They were 8-inches tall. Either a girl in pink or a boy in blue could be ordered for 10¢ . The girl (shown) wears a long dress, booties, bonnet, and sweater with a sewn-on satin ribbon. In one hand is a can of Gerber Baby Food, the other hand holds a blue toy dog. Unmarked. Photos furnished by Gerber Products Company. Very Rare.

In 1954, a 12-inch rubber *Gerber Baby* doll was available. The doll originally wore a flannel sleeper with a bib that was stitched to read Gerber Baby in script. Marks: "Gerber Baby/© Gerber Products Co.," on head; "Mfd. by/The Sun Rubber Co. Barbertson, O. U.S.A./ Pat. 21188882/Pat. 2160739," on back. $12.00.

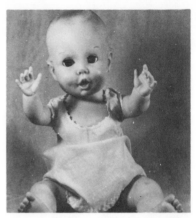

The largest of the *Gerber Baby* dolls, 18-inches, was manufactured by The Sun Rubber Company and sold at retail outlets. It was offered in Sears Catalog in 1955. Marks: "GERBER BABY/© GERBER PRODUCTS CO.," on back of head; "MFG By/THE SUN RUBBER CO./Barbert Ohio U.S.A./ Under One or more U.S. Pat./ 2118682, 2160739, 2552216/ PAT. PEND.," on back. $12.00.

The 1966 *Gerber Baby* doll was not Gerber's usual high quality doll. The doll illustrated does not wear original clothing. Marks: "Gerber Baby/© Gerber Products Co." on head. $12.00.

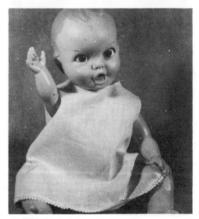

A Gerber mystery doll, this doll was not mentioned in the material provided by the company. It is 14-inches tall, made from firm vinyl with a pink cast. The painted hair is yellow and the eyes are painted. It has the nurse/wet feature. Marks: "The Gerber Baby/ ?er Prod. Co./19 © 72," on back of neck. (The vinyl has been marred destroying the letters of what probably read Gerber.) $10.00.

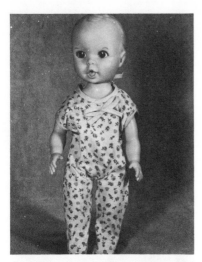

In 1972 a *Gerber Baby* doll was offered that had yellow hair, rather than the brown hair that all the previous *Gerber Baby* dolls had. The 11-inch vinyl doll, manufactured by Uneeda, has painted eyes and wears a one-piece sleeper outfit. Marks: "The Gerber Baby/ Gerber Prod. Co." on back of neck; label on suit says, "Gerber/Made in the British Colony/of Hong Kong."$7.00.

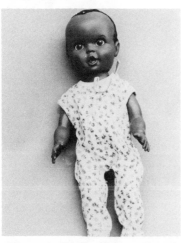

The black *Gerber Baby* doll is the same mold as the white 1972 doll. Uneeda manufactured these dolls. Marks: "The Gerber Baby/Gerber Products Co./19 © 72. S. Esser collection, Bruce Esser photographer. $12.00.

Since the Gerber Baby was "Born" in 1928, millions of mothers have requested reprints of the trademark, possibly because they were able to see their own child in that very special face.

To capitalize on their successful trademark, five Gerber Baby premium dolls have been offered. According to the company they are as follows:

1936-39 - an 8-inch stuffed cloth doll of quality sateen, for 10¢ and three Gerber baby food labels. The boy doll came dressed in a blue pram suit; the girl wore a long dress and a sweater in pink. Approximately 27,000 were sold in the three year span they were offered.

1954 - a 12-inch rubber Gerber baby doll, for $2.00 ($3.95 value) and 12 product labels was offered. The doll was manufactured by Sun Rubber Company and had movable legs, nurse/wet feature, and a cry box. It came with a nurser bottle, cereal boxes, cereal dish and spoon all scaled to the doll's size. The offer expired in 1955 and was the best seller of all the Gerber premium dolls. The doll was sculpted by Bernard Lipfert.

1955 - a 12-inch Gerber baby doll was offered to the Canadian market through media advertising and Miss Frances and the Ding Dong School. The offer expired the following year.

1966 - 14-inch soft vinyl Gerber doll was offered for $2.00 ($3.75 value) and 12 product labels. The doll was manufactured by Arrow Industries and was considered by the company the same as the 1954 doll sans dimples. It had one dimple and a lop-sided smile. This doll was not well received. The offer expired June 1967.

1972 - A 10-inch firm-vinyl Gerber doll sold for $2.50 and 4 product labels. Uneeda Company manufactured these dolls. They had painted eyes. The 1972 doll marked two firsts: first with yellow hair, all other in the series had brown hair. Also first time a black doll was available. In some areas the black doll was promoted at a later date.

We found one doll that is marked Gerber and the date 1972, which has become a mystery. The company made no reference to a 14-inch doll manufactured in 1972. Perhaps it was sold at the retail level.

In 1955 Sun Rubber Company manufactured two Gerber baby dolls for the retail market. They were pictured in Sears Toy Catalog in 14-inch and 18-inch sizes complete with layette.

The growth of the Gerber line of baby foods is noted in the information found on the magazine advertisements for their premium dolls. When the little cloth doll in 1936 was offered only nine Gerber products were listed as available to obtain the necessary food labels: Strained Vegetable Soup, Carrots, Spinach, Beets, Green Beans, Prunes, Peas, Tomatoes, and Cereal. By the expiration of that offer in 1939 three more products had been added: Apricot, Apple Sauce, and Liver Soup.

In 1978, Gerber's Golden Anniversary Year, 150 foods were marketed for babies. In July 1978, Gerber Company opened a display in Fremont, Michigan showing all the Gerber dolls used for advertising. To celebrate Gerber's 50th Anniversary an anniversary doll has been made by the Gerber Company. The doll is a careful copy of the Smith sketch. It is 16-inches tall, made of heavy vinyl with a cloth body. The doll is being offered through retail outlets for $18.50.

Gillette Company. To commemorate the Bicentennial, this company offered **George and Martha Washington** dolls. The lithographed dolls are made from a fabric that is more coarse than most recent cloth dolls.

George, 15-inches, has thin legs and is wearing a colorful colonial costume. **Martha**, 15-inches, wears a long dress, has gray hair, oversize hands, and a tiny waist.

The dolls were manufactured by the Chase Bag Company in 1974 and were available until March 31, 1976. They cost $2.50 each plus certain proof-of-purchase marks on any of the following Gillette products: White Rain Shampoo, Tame Creme Rinse, or Adorn Hair Spray.

George and Martha Washington dolls were offered by White Rain Shampoo to help commemorate the Bicentennial. *George* is 15-inches tall and wears a two-toned blue outfit. Marks: "The Gillete Co. 1974," on back of one foot. $5.00.

Martha wears a bright fuchsia colored dress with a tip of shoes peeking from under the long skirt. She is also prestuffed cloth and 15-inches tall. Marks: "The Gillette Company 1974," on bottom of back skirt. $5.00.

For other dolls see Cricket Lighter and Toni.

The Gillette Company sells a variety of products, but began by selling only one tiny, item--a razor blade. Mr. King C. Gillette claims he changed the face of man by changing his shaving habits.

As a young man, it was King Gillette's goal to invent something that was used often and thrown away, making it necessary to keep purchasing the item. "One morning I found my razor dull, and it was not only dull but it was beyond the point of successful stropping. It needed honing, which meant it would have to be taken to a barber or cutler. 'A razor is only a sharp edge,' I said to myself, 'and all back of it is just support. Why do they go to all the expense and trouble of fashioning a backing that has nothing to do with shaving?'" With those thoughts Gillette dreamed what was later named the Gillette razor, a thin piece of steel with a clamp in the middle of the handle.

For six years Gillette worked on his dream and tried to find financial backing. Finally in 1901, Gillette persuaded some friends to raise the sum of $5,000.00 to form a company, and start manufacturing. The first Gillette Razor was marketed in 1903, 51 razors and 168 blades were sold. But it was a start, and soon it seemed every man in the country had a smooth face. Thanks to a plucky traveling salesman.

Glenmore Distilleries.

In the 1940's this Louisville, Kentucky company provided a handsome Southern gentleman display doll to dealers selling their product.

In the 1940's the *Colonel Glenmore* doll was used for display at bars selling Glenmore Distillery products. The 22-inch dandy wears a black felt coat, tan vest, white pants, a bow tie and gold watch chain. Marks: "Colonel Glenmore/Glenmore Distilleries/Louisville, Kentucky," on ribbon worn across the chest. Ken Lansdowne collection. $80.00.

Gold Dust. A product of the N.K. Fairbank Company. Years ago this cleaning powder was widely advertised. Most women's magazines carried an ad proclaiming the virtues of doing dishes, scrubbing floors, or some other cleaning project, with Gold Dust. A prominent part of the ad and the box was their trademark, two little black children known as the "Gold Dust Twins."

One 1919 ad said in tiny print to send for your cloth Gold Dust moppets. And we talked with people who remembered playing with bisque, cloth and composition dolls they knew as the **Gold Dust Twins**. Unfortunately we could find no other information nor any dolls.

Gold Medal Flour, a product of General Mills. An old cloth doll and a recent doll kit are known to have been offered by this product. The doll was probably

The 7½-inch Gold Medal Flour doll was probably printed on flour sacks. The doll wears a red and black plaid dress and an apron copied from the Gold Medal Flour label. Marks: "Eventually/ Washborn Crosby/GOLD/MEDAL/ FLOUR/Why not now?, printed on apron. D. Braden collection. $20.00.

printed on a flour sack in the 20's or 30's. It is printed in red and black on white, plaid dress, black hair, and red open mouth. The arms and hands are printed in front of the body, giving the doll a simple outline shape. Doll is well marked.

The 1975 doll kit was advertised as an **Ozark Dough-head Doll**. The kit cost $3.95 plus the coupon found in a bag of Gold Medal Flour. Also included was a 48-page booklet on Ozark doll-making.

Gold Medal flour was originally milled by the Washburn Crosby Company. It was named from its award of the gold medal in 1880 at the Miller's International Exhibit. The company had three entries, and each one received an award--gold, silver, and bronze medals. Their top-grade flour truly earned its name--Gold Medal. In those years its slogan, "Eventually. Why not now?" was almost as famous as the flour itself.

James Bell, a miller at Washburn Crosby Mills, could see how small milling companies were at the mercy of the wheat crop in their locality.

In 1928 Bell presented to the Washburn Crosby board of directors his plan to combine reputable millers across the country into a single organization. The idea was approved and Washburn Crosby became the first to sign. In less that a year 24 companies had merged, marking the origin of the huge General Mills organization.

Good and Plenty Candy, a product of Quaker City Chocolate & Conf'y Co., Inc. This licorice-filled candy was one of four candies chosen in 1972 by Hasbro Toy Company for four of their bean-bag dolls. **Choo Choo Charlie** wears a striped engineer suit and a sewn-on hat with three locks of brown hair peeking out.

The 10-inch doll is nylon tricot fabric filled with styrofoam pellets; face and hands are vinyl.

Choo Choo Charlie, by Hasbro Toy Company. Marks: "Choo Choo Charlie" across cap. K. Lyons collection. $8.00.

Good Humor Ice Cream Company. The musical sound of the Good Humor truck laden

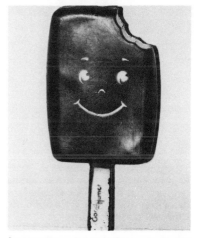

This bearer of frozen treats offered a vinyl likeness of an ice cream bar on a stick in 1975. Marks: "Good/ Humor," on stick. J. Varsolona Collection. $4.00.

with frozen goodies offered something besides edible treats in the mid-1970's. A vinyl toy in the shape of a chocolate ice cream bar on a stick was available. The toy had a face drawn on the side and one corner had been sampled, a bite is missing.

Good Value Margarine. In 1979 the common 8-inch plastic International Dolls were offered by this brand of margarine. Thirty dolls were available for the coupon found on the package and $2.25.

Gorton's Codfish. A contributor sent an interesting 7¼-inch vinyl fisherman doll that has been offered by this company.

The 7½-inch fisherman is an advertising doll from Gorton's Codfish. The vinyl doll is jointed at the head and shoulders; legs and body are one-piece. The face is especially well molded and includes brown hair, brows, and beard with a pipe in the corner of his mouth. The yellow plastic rain suit and hat are removable, as are the black overshoes. Marks: "Made in Hong Kong," on back. B. Welch collection. $8.00.

W.T. Grant Stores. The **Bucky Bradford** doll was a promotional item to advertise Bradford House Restaurants located in W.T. Grant Stores. Date unknown. The 9½-inch vinyl squeak doll has molded/painted detail that includes a pilgrim outfit.

This chain of stores has gone out of business.

Bucky Bradford **was a promotional item of W.T. Grant for their in-store Bradford House Restaurants. The 9½-inch vinyl doll wears a molded/painted blue pilgrim outfit. The hair, shoe buckles, and dish are yellow. Marks: "It's Yum Yum Time," on dish; "Bucky Bradford," on pedestal. $6.00.**

Green Giant Company.

The Jolly Green figure has become a familiar character to most Americans. The big giant's "Ho, Ho, Ho," is heard on television commercials, he is seen in magazine and newspaper ads, and he has been copied for numerous promotional dolls.

The company has offered two **Jolly Green Giant** dolls and three **Little Sprout** dolls. They are as follows:

1. 16-inch **Giant**, June 1966 expiration date, cloth 50¢ plus three labels or no labels and $2.50.

2. 28-inch **Giant**, 1973, cloth $2.75.

3. 6½-inch **Sprout**, 1971, one-piece vinyl, price ranged from free to 75¢ depending on the amount of labels sent.

4. 10-inch **Sprout**, 1973, cloth 75¢.

5. 24-inch **Sprout**, 1976, inflatable vinyl, price ranged from free to $1.50 depending on the amount of labels sent.

The first "Jolly Green Giant" doll, 16-inches tall, was offered in 1966. It was cloth with a lithographed leaf tunic and hat. The simple face has three dots and a line mouth. Unmarked. $8.00.

Product People, a toy manufacturer that was in Minnesota, also produced a **Jolly Green Giant** doll, intended only for the retail market. It was an excellent quality

9½-inch vinyl doll made to separate at the middle. The doll probably sold in the early 1970's.

The Green Giant Company has also offered two dolls with no resemblance to their trademark. **Country Girl**, an 18-inch vinyl doll with rooted wig, and open/shut eyes, was offered in 1956. The unusual feature of this doll is it makes a coo sound. The doll wore a dress, hat, waist apron, and shoes. It cost $2.50 plus 2 labels from Green Giant peas. Order coupons were available at point of sale.

A 24-inch *Sprout* made of inflatable vinyl was introduced in 1976. The tunic and hair are a darker green. It has a ring on the head for hanging. $4.00.

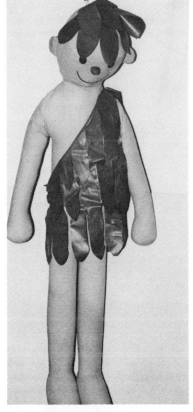

The company did not mention this doll, which is approximately five feet long, as one of their premiums, but it is unmistakenly patterned after the *Jolly Green Giant*. No further information is known. J. Varsolona collection. $12.00.

Product People, a company no longer in existence, made this top quality *Jolly Green Giant* doll. The 9½-inch doll is two shades of green vinyl. Notice the doll breaks into two parts just below the leaf tunic. Unmarked. $8.00.

H

H.W.I. Hardware Company. An inflatable vinyl man was used in 1976-77 by this company. Protruding ears and a pointed finger on one hand are the noticable features of this inflatable promotion item.

The H.W.I. Hardware stores used this vinyl inflatable man in 1976-77. Marks: "HWI/Your Link to Value ® " $6.00.

Hamburger Helper, a product of General Mills. Carrying

The 14-inch white *Helping Hand* is like a glove with three fingers and a thumb. C. Erikson collection. $4.00.

out the theme of helping the cook, this product put out a 14-inch **Helping Hand**. The white plush hand was manufactured in 1976 by Animal Fair. It has plush nose, plastic eyes, felt brows and mouth.

Hamm's Beer. Some years the black and white **Hamm's Beer Bear** is prominently seen in ads and commercials. Other years he seems to be hibernating.

A celluloid black and white bear about 8-inches tall was used for displays. Apparently one foot was attached to a pedestal so it could stand.

The **Hamm's Beer Bear** was also made in black and white plush with a small radio accessible through a zipper in the back.

The *Hamm's Beer Bear* is about 8-inches tall and was used for display. The black and white bear has been used for many years by this brand of beer. Recently he has been a prominent figure in television advertising. Unmarked. $8.00.

Hanes. The **Hanes Babies** were dolls of the 1950's. They are 21-inches long, with vinyl head and hands, cloth body and legs.

The 21-inch *Hanes Babies* were used in the 1950's. Doll on left wears pink two-piece sleepers; doll on right wears mint green sleepers. The dolls have vinyl heads and hands, and cloth bodies and legs. The open/closed mouth is yawning, eyes closed. Unmarked. Arlene Wolfe collection, David Nelson, James Giokas photographers. $25.00.

Hanover Potatoes. In 1972 a 20-inch inflatable **Elfie** doll was available for $1.00 plus proof-of-purchase.

Hardee's Restaurant. **Gilbert Giddyup** was offered in 1971 by this quick food chain.

Elfie is an inflatable doll offered by Hanover Potatoes. The elf wears a green outfit with white buttons, collar, and cuffs; hair and features are brown. Marks: "ELFIE" across front. L. Yagatich collection, Donald G. Vilsack photographer. $6.00.

In 1971 the Hardee Restaurant franchise used a *Gilbert Giddyup* doll attired in an orange cowboy outfit with a star badge marked "H". An "H" is also on the back of the neckerchief. Marks: "Gilbert". $8.00.

Hawaiian Punch, a product of RJR Foods, Inc. "Punchy" the Hawaiian Punch mascot began his career in 1961 when he was created by a Los Angeles advertising Agency. Punchy's line in TV commercials at that time was, "How would you like a nice Hawaiian punch?" Then he hauls off and gives the big guy a sock in the jaw. Of course, that was before violence on TV was a no-no. Today's **Punchy** still gives the big guy a punch, but it is more sedate.

It is interesting to note, the company replaced Punchy in 1966 with a hula girl, but reinstated the mascot when it was decided the girl attracted attention for her, but not their product.

Punchy the Hawaiian Punch mascot was created to promote this red beverage in 1961. Not until the late sixties or early seventies was a doll made to resemble the mascot. It is a 13-inch cloth doll. Unmarked. $7.00.

Apparently the company is sold on Punchy because they offer many items marked with his likeness at their souvenir shop, included are: towels, radios, shirts, frisbees, and even a raft.

Two dolls have been manufactured to resemble the mascot. One is an inflatable doll, which sells for $1.50 at the souvenir shop and is still available. The other **Punchy** doll was offered several years ago and is a 13-inch prestuffed cloth. It has so few appendages it resembles a pillow rather than a cloth doll.

The inflatable *Punchy* doll is available today along with many other items sold from the Hawaiian Punch souvenir shop. The figure is unmarked but readily recognizable by the unusual headgear. $2.00.

Heckers Flour. See Ceresota Flour.

H.J. Heinz Company. During the Christmas seasons between the years 1895 and 1900 a doll prize contest was advertised via posters. The posters pictured a lovely German bisque doll. The information at the bottom of the poster said: "I am one of the 57 Varieties. Guess my name and you can have me Christmas Day. I have light hair, blue eyes, and I am dressed in a handsome blue silk gown."

Store customers presumably guessed the name of the doll and someone in the Heinz company either selected the name that was most appealing to them, or had actually pre-selected a name in order to determine the winner from each outlet that was featuring the premium. We found the poster, but not the premium doll.

The vice-chairman of the company says their records show no other dolls ever being used as premiums or as representative of their company.

In 1977 a plush bunny and a bear were offered for $4.95 each plus 24 Heinz Baby Food labels. These 14-inch animals are replicas of the Bunny and Teddy Bear pictured on the baby food labels, and were advertised by coupons at point of sale.

The Heinz Company was formed in 1869 by H.J. Heinz and L.C. Noble and was known as Heinz and Noble. One of the first products marketed was horseradish. At that time horseradish was bottled in a dark green bottle to disguise the true content--turnips. From a three-quarter acre plot of horseradish plants the partners harvested, processed, and packed the pungent root in clear bottles. Cooks were delighted to find at the grocer's a good horseradish in a bottle they could trust.

Heinz and Noble prospered-- adding celery sauce and pickles to the line. Then the disastrous 1873 panic struck and the company went bankrupt. Heinz had hard times for a few years, but he was determined his fortune could be made in the food industry.

His family and friends supported him to the total of $3,000 to launch a new business. This company was named F & J Heinz Company, after a cousin Fredrick and a brother John, who advanced him money.

One of the new products introduced was ketchup, or catchup, or catsup--however you prefer to spell the spicy tomato sauce so commonly used by most of us. Heinz preferred the spelling Ketchup, which was nearer to the original "Kechap" spelling used in the seventeenth century when English sailors were introduced to the new sauce by natives in the port of Singapore.

In 1876 making Ketchup was a two or three day chore. It involved picking the tomatoes, washing, peeling, grinding, and cooking, cooking, and cooking until just the proper consistency was reached. Then it could be bottled and the mess cleaned up. Housewives welcomed the opportunity to purchase the sauce already bottled and be spared the work doing it themselves.

Pickles was another line Heinz had the foresight to see would be profitable. Making pickles was even more time consuming than making ketchup and the results were often unpredictable. Cucumbers had to be stored in brine for weeks before the cooking could even begin on many recipes. Many a pickle crock became a flower pot after Heinz began making such a variety and such top quality pickles.

Besides being able to recognize sellable products the little German also had the knack for advertising. In 1896 he originated the trademark '57 Varieties." Inspiration for the symbol came while Henry was riding in an elevated train in New York City. Among the advertising cards in the train was one extolling the virtues of a brand of shoes that offered "21 styles."

"It set me thinking," he said later. " 'Seven, Seven'--there are so many illustrations of the psychological influences of that figure and of its alluring significance to people of all ages. Fifty-eight or 59 Varieties did not appeal at all to me--just '57 Varieties.' When I got off the train, I immediately went down to the lighographer's where I designed a street-car ad and had it distributed throughout the United States. I did not realize then, of course, how successful it was going to be."

A few years later New York City's first electric sign, six stories high blazed with 1,200 lights, proclaiming "57 Varieties." At the top was a big Heinz pickle, brillant advertising for the Heinz Company.

Finally in 1969 the Heinz Company decided to retire the old trademark. That year Heinz, had, not 57 varieties, but at least 1,250 products in their roster, and more being added every year. The familiar old trademark was replaced with a new one, just the name Heinz, although for old times sake "57 Varieties" is still used on a few selected products.

Henderson Glove Company. This Creston, Iowa company offered an 11-inch cloth **Indian** doll. The date and other information are unknown because the business is no longer in existence. The doll was probably sold flat to be made by the owner.

The defunct Henderson Glove Company used this *Indian* doll at one time. The 11-inch doll is printed mostly in brown, with some white and other colors. M. Hiter collection. $25.00.

This same doll has been found with no mark of identification. So perhaps Henderson Glove Company purchased a small order and the other dolls were sold retail.

Herald Press. In 1971 a 16-inch cloth advertising doll with lighographed detail was manufactured for Herald Press. The old-fashioned looking doll has the features of a young girl with a scattering of freckles across her cheeks. She wears a bonnet tied closely to her head, a few stray strands protrude at the forehead. How the doll was offered is unknown.

An old-fashioned doll was used by Herald Press. The 16-inch doll has white hands and face with black eyes and red mouth. Her dress is light blue with a matching bonnet. Gray stockings with black stripes, black hightop shoes and a long white apron complete the lithograped costume. Marks: "Herald Press 1971," on back of apron. Betty McConnell collection, David Nelson, James Giokas photographers. $8.00.

Highland Mist Scotch Whiskey. A 28-inch composition fellow wearing traditional Scottish costume was used to advertise this liquor.

Holland-American Lines.

This is one of many ocean liners that sold souvenir sailor dolls from 1926 to about 1940. The 12½-inch doll is made of velvet with a composition head (some had velvet heads with glass eyes), and sideglance eyes. The navy blue sailor

This fellow from Scotland is used to advertise Highland Mist Scotch Whiskey. The composition doll is 28-inches tall and wears a yellow, black and red kilt, black jacket and molded painted stockings and shoes. $75.00.

Hires Root Beer. A delightful inflatable black cow was offered by this soft drink company in 1976.

One of many souvenir sailor dolls sold by ocean liners from their gift rooms. This is marked: "Holland-American Lines," on a ribbon around the hat. K. Landsdowne collection. $20.00.

Black Cow is a 40-inch long inflatable bovine used by Hires Root Beer. Marks: "Hires Root Beer," on logo; "Black Cow," on side. J. Ciolek collection, Visual Images photographer. $12.00.

suit is also the body, hands and feet are white cotton fabric.

The dolls were manufactured in England by Deans and are often confused with English artist Nora Welling's dolls. The sailor dolls are identified by ribbons worn on the hats stamped with the name of the liner they represent, such as SS Queen Mary.

Honey Bear Farm. In 1952 a **Honey Bear** could be ordered from this company in Wisconsin. No further information is known.

Honeywell, Inc. The cloth doll **Allergy Annie** was a promotion offered by the "Cleaner Air People." The doll is unusual because it has a sad weepy face with circles around the eyes, tears, and red nose. The prestuffed lithographed doll holds a daisy in front with one hand; the other arm hangs to the side with only the hand cut free from the body.

Allergy Annie was a promotional feature of the Honeywell Company, "The Cleaner Air People." *Annie* is obviously allergic to the flower she is holding in front of her aqua jumper. The other arm is cut free from the body. The doll is unmarked, but easily identified by her weepy nose and eyes. $12.00.

Hoover Vacuum Company. An 8-inch nodder doll named **Hoover Housewife** posed with her vacuum was undoubtedly an advertising aid created before ERA. The doll is made of a plastic like material. The hair, facial features, clothes, vacuum, and base are all molded/painted. Details of when or how this figure was used is unknown.

The 8-inch nodder doll, "Hoover Housewife" pushes her Hoover vacuum. She wears a pink and white dotted blouse, pink shirt, white apron, and red shoes, and has molded/painted yellow hair. Marks: "Brother, you're strictly from Hoover!" on front of base; "C6856 NAPCOWARE ® " on bottom. Arlene Wolfe collection, David Nelson, James Giokas photographers. $18.00.

Hostess Bakery Company. In the 1970's a 48-inch inflatable **Happy Ho Hos** was available from store outlets for $3.00. The toy is named after the chocolate cake treat named Ho-Ho.

Happy Ho Ho, is a 48-inch in-flatable toy used by Hostess Bakery Company to promote their Ho-Ho treats. Marks: "Happy/HO/HO," on front. $6.00.

Hotpoint, a division of General Electric. A **Hot Point Man** doll was used in about 1930 to promote Hotpoint cooking ranges. The 16-inch doll is composed of wooden beads and a composition head. The features and attire are molded and painted. The doll's hat is made from Hotpoint's emblem: a large H with a triangle inside.

The name Hotpoint was originated for a flat-iron perfected by Earl Robinson, an Illinois Power Company superintendent. Long, before the energy crisis, Mr. Richardson was looking for something besides home lighting to consume its overbundance of kilowatts. Around the turn of the century he came up with an electric iron. But it was unpopular because the center was too hot. His wife suggested the heat be concentrated at the point where it could be used for gathers and pleats. The new design was what the public wanted. By 1905 Hotpoint irons outsold every other brand.

The original Hotpoint Electric and Heating Company began a series of mergers. Today it is under the management of General Electric and the name is used on many appliances--not one of them a flatiron!

Hot Tamale Candies. A cloth **Hot Tamale Kid** doll has been offered on boxes of this fire-flavored candy from about 1967 through 1975. The older dolls are 18-inches high, and cost $1.25. Later dolls are 16-inches high, and cost $1.35.

Hot Tamale Kid wears a yellow sombrero, red shirt, white pants, striped serape, and is barefoot. Marks: "Hot Tamale," across brim of sombrero. $4.00.

Howard Johnson Restaurants. A doll has been manufactured to represent the waitresses who work for the biggest restaurant chain in the world. The "Howard Johnson" girl is 11½-inches tall, plastic body and legs with vinyl head and arms. It has black painted eyes and brows and wears an outfit copied from the waitress uniforms: a hounds tooth check dress with waist apron. The doll was manufactured in Hong Kong and that is the only mark.

I

IGA Stores. The Independent Grocer's Association, in limited areas, offered a 12-inch cloth doll called the **Tablerite Kid**. The doll is a cowboy with arms out, hands ready to draw a pistol. Must be a good guy; he wears a big white hat. The pattern for this doll would be more difficult to make than most of the prestuffed cloth dolls, because the tiny arms are cut free from the body and have a bend at the elbow. As any maker of rag dolls knows, it requires careful sewing, clipping, and turning to avoid puckers. This doll has no puckers at the elbow, but the curve where the hat comes in to the neck is puckered. So many cloth dolls have very simple outlines, almost making them a pillow rather than a doll.

The *Tablerite Kid* was offered by IGA stores in limited areas. The 12-inch cloth doll has many curved seams, making it difficult to assemble. The "Kid" wears blue pants, red long-sleeved shirt, white vest, and a big white hat. $8.00.

Ice Capades. At performances by this traveling ice skating company many souvenir items are sold. One is a 9-inch vinyl doll dressed to represent one of the group's skaters. The costume is gold lame with net tutu trimmed in sequins and gold skates. The doll cost $5.00 and was available in 1975.

Icee Corporation. In 1959 two young inventors developed a new taste treat--frozen carbonated soft drink. Engineers created a machine that would mix the syrup, carbon dioxide, and water under pressure in a freezing chamber. From the chamber the soft drink could be served through a faucet, in toothpaste-like fashion, into cups. It was advertised as a brand new "Frozenated" treat that "you don't drink, you slurp through a straw!" And, "it doesn't pour . . . it chuckles into the cup."

The first *Icee* plush bear was offered in 1968. This plush bear was purchased in 1977 and is still available. The 19-inch bear is white with a red shirt, black nose, black felt mouth, and droopy felt eyes. Marks: "I," on shirt front; "ICEE Bear," on back. $10.00.

172

Soon drug stores, corner markets, and other outlets were installing the dispenser for the new icy treat. Not long after, trouble began because the new owners, who had no refrigeration expertise, were unable to service the machines. By 1964 the new drink was almost abandoned, not because the public disapproved of it, but because the machines that dispensed it had become such a headache.

In 1965 the problem was solved by creating a franchised territory, leasing the machines, and providing a traveling service man who would keep the machines in working order. The drink became very popular, especially with the preteen.

The vinyl *Icee Bear* bank was free for redeemable points in 1974. The 8-inch bank is still available, but now costs $2.75 plus 3 Bear Points or 600 Bear Points. Marks: "ICEE," on cup. $3.00.

The ICEE trademark was first used in 1965. The product mascot is a white bear, probably a polar bear, with droopy eyes. At first the ICEE bear was used primarily in costume at sales promotions, contests, and business conventions.

In 1968 it was first offered as a plush toy. In 1977 the plush ICEE bear was still available. The washable white plush bear measures 19-inches sitting, the red plush shirt is part of the body. It has black nose, felt eyes and mouth and a felt block I on the shirt.

ICEE also has an 8-inch bear bank made of squeezable vinyl. The mascot is sitting with a large cup of ICEE between his legs.

Other items are also available: notebook, T-shirt, watch, beach towel, and jacket. To order any of the ICEE items one must save points (like trading stamps) from the side of each ICEE paper cup. By collecting these points 'kids redeem prizes." For example, the bank can be redeemed free for 300 points or 3 points and $2.75.

Stores provide a slotted cardboard sheet to hold the tiny points. Children often go to extremes to find cups, so they can cut out the points and increase their collection, I know.

To advise stores of the Icee advertising promotions, this ad was sent to managers.

Ideal Flour, manufactured for Plunkett-Jarrell Grocer Company. On 24-pound sacks of this flour a 14-inch **Simple Sam** doll was printed. The doll could easily be mistaken for Raggedy Andy. It has a similar face, a shirt with hearts, aqua pants, and striped legs. Only two colors are used, aqua and red. The shoes and hair appear brown because the red is printed over the aqua.

The doll itself has no marks, the sack provides the doll's identity.

Simple Sam, Raggedy Andy's look-alike, was printed on sacks of Ideal Flour. Only two colors were used, red and aqua. The 14-inch doll has no marks. The background fabric provides his name, and luckily this collector saved the entire sack, thus providing identity. A. Pfister collection. $12.00.

Imperial Granum. What is Imperial Granum?-probably a cereal. An 1897 magazine ad says, "Food for invalids and convalescents/For Dyspeptic. Delicate. Infirm and Aged Persons/Sold by Druggets."

Four dolls are known to have been offered by this product, all of them cloth. We had access to two dolls and the background fabric mentions the other two dolls.

The dolls described on the

material were: 2½-foot cloth doll that can stand alone and wear babies clothes for 50¢, and a 20-inch cloth doll for 40¢.

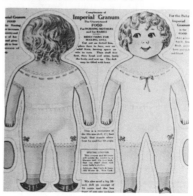

This cloth doll was offered by the Imperial Granum Company in 1918. The doll is unmarked. The background fabric provides the name of the company, date, instructions for assembling the doll, and other information. <u>Playthings by the Yard</u>, 1973. $40.00.

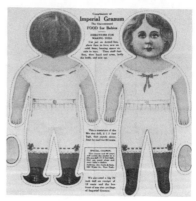

An early cloth doll given away by Imperial Granum, a company that is no longer in business. The face and hair of the two dolls are similar. Identity and other information is printed on the background fabric. $40.00.

The two dolls we have, are smaller and are very similar to each other except for the faces. Both wear dainty lace trimmed underwear, have three dimensional shoes, and blonde hair.

One, marked 1918, has little curls spilling around the face and a watermelon mouth resembling the Campbell Kids. The other doll's features and clothing are printed with a photographic or silk screen technique. The lips are closed and the hair is in a smooth style.

International House of Pancakes.

The initials of this restaurant IHOP is the name given to their kangaroo mascot. Plastic **IHOP** hand puppets have a children's menu printed on the back and are given free.

Some restaurant managers give children a small plastic **IHOP** pop-up toy. It is a kangaroo chef that fits on a spring with a suction cup on the bottom. As the suction cup releases the 2-inch kangaroo pops in the air.

International House of Pancake's *IHOP* hand puppet has a child's menu printed on the back and was given to children in some localities. $1.00.

Irish Spring, a product of Procter and Gamble. In 1976 a 19-inch leprechaun doll was offered to Canadian consumers of this hand soap. The well-made doll, manufactured by Reliable, cost $5.95 plus two side panels from a box of hand soap. The body of the doll is made of green broadcloth, it has a vinyl pixie face with white whiskers. The doll is dressed in a floppy green hat, black sleeveless jacket, and black oversize shoes. The molded/-painted eyes seem to twinkle from a little star on the pupil, the face has excellent sculpted ears and rosy cheeks.

Canadians have a difficult time obtaining United States' advertising dolls and we have a difficult obtaining theirs. Therefore, these fine quality dolls, even though recent, are bringing double their original price.

Istrouma Flour, a product of the Central Flour Company. This Little Rock, Arkansas flour company printed a 13-inch **Humpty Dumpty** doll on their sacks of Istrouma Flour. Date unknown. The doll is egg-shaped, of course, with arms and legs extending from the body. **Humpty** wears a plaid suit with a bow tie.

The 13-inch *Humpty Dumpty* doll was printed on 24-pound bags of Central Flour Company's Istrouma Flour. Marks: "Humpty Dumpty," on belt. K. Lyons collection. $10.00.

J

Jack Frost Sugar. The past decade three cloth dolls have been offered on packages of this brand of sugar. All the dolls represent a Jack Frost character and are pre-stuffed with lithographed details.

The oldest **Jack Frost** doll is 18-inches high. It is wearing a stocking cap marked **Jack Frost**, a matching suit with a diamond design on the chest, and a scarf with one end falling forward. The facial features are simple: a line smile, curve nose, and half circle eyes. A zig-zag of hair protrudes from the hat.

The earliest of three *Jack Frost* cloth dolls offered by Jack Frost Sugar is 18-inches tall. Date unknown. Marks: "Jack Frost," across hat. J. Varsalona collection. $8.00.

The next doll offered is 20-inches high. It wears coveralls marked **Jack Frost**, hat, and a striped shirt. The face is square with two dot eyes and a U smile, no nose. The hair is in a triangle with one point above the forehead and the other two where ears would be. The legs are widely separated with shoes pointing to the sides.

The next *Jack Frost* doll. Marks: "Jack/Frost," on front of suit. J. Varsalona collection. $7.00.

The latest cloth doll offered by Jack Frost Sugar was issued in 1975 and cost $1.50. The 15-inch doll wears a blue and white striped suit with a red and white striped hat. Unmarked. $6.00.

The latest doll is 15-inches tall. Wears a blue and white horizonal striped suit and a red and white striped stocking cap. The face is simple as the other two are. This doll cost $1.50 and was available until June 1975. The doll is unmarked.

Jack-in-the-Box Imperial Restaurant. During the Christmas season from 1974 through 1976 small vinyl dolls were given or sold for 25¢ to customers of this restaurant. The characters were made from vinyl that resembles rubber. They were molded over a wire armature, making the limbs easy to pose. The 4-inch dolls were carefully detailed and painted in bright colors. The names given the five dolls were: **Jack, Secret Sauce Agent, Sleepy-eyed Boy, Shake Hans,** and **Onion Ring.** They were also sold in toy stores, at a cost of 75¢.

All five of the Jack-in-the-Box dolls are quite detailed and painted in bright colors. *Secret Sauce Agent* is all purple with green eyes and teeth, and a black hat. Marks: "Jack-in-the-Box ® /Imperial/ Hong Kong"; imprint of crown following last word. $2.00.

From 1974 to 1976 Jack-in-the-Box Imperial Restaurants gave, or in some restaurants, sold for 25¢ , small vinyl dolls. The *Clown* doll was one of the 4-inch dolls. Marks: "Jack-in-the-Box ® /Imperial/ Hong Kong;" the imprint of an ornate crown is printed after the last word. $2.00.

Shake Hans can have his arms and legs posed, as the other four dolls, because of the bendable wire armature under the vinyl. Marks: "Jack-in-the-box ® /Imperial/ Hong Kong"; imprint of crown following last word. $2.00.

The sleepy-eyed boy probably has a name, perhaps Jack. These dolls were also sold in retail stores. Marks: "Jack-in-the Box ® /Imperial/Hong Kong"; imprint of crown following last word. $2.00.

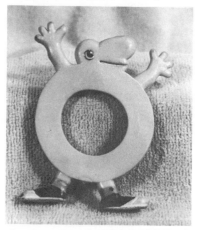

Another of the 4-inch vinyl dolls offered by Jack-in-the-Box is *Onion Ring*. A yellow ring body with arms, legs, and head makes this doll a favorite with teething babies. Marks: "Jack-in-the-Box ® /Imperial/ Hong Kong"; imprint of crown following last word. $2.00.

Jack's Restaurant. A 16-inch cloth doll presumably made to resemble Jack was found in California. No further information is known.

A 16-inch cloth doll offered by Jack's Restaurant. No further information is known. $8.00.

Jap Rose, a product of Kirk's Soap. In 1910 Horsman copyrighted the **Jap Rose Kids**, as designed by Helen Trowbridge. Jap Rose was a popular line that sold talcum powder, cold cream, and toilet water, up to about 1930's. The oriental looking dolls had Can't Break 'Em heads and hands with cloth bodies and limbs. The hair on the boy was straight, cut like he had a bowl on his head. The girl wore her hair in an oriental style with fullness at the ears. Both wore Japanese kimonas with obis around the waist.

Jell-o, a product of General Foods. This brand of flavored gelatin has had an interesting history and has been associated with two dolls.

History indicates that in spite of Jell-o's phenomenal success in this century it had many stops and starts before it soared to become the popular food we know today.

Possibly the first reference to gelatin is recorded in 1682 by a Frenchman, Denis Papin, whose experiments resulted in a method of removing glutinous material from animal bones by boiling. It has no taste, no odor, and when combined with liquid, no color, but it is pure protein. (Today's Jell-o apparently doesn't use this method of obtaining gelatin because the label lists protein with the notation it is not a source of protein.) For years the French liked gourmet foods en gelee. No one else seemed interested in the product.

The *Jell-o Girl* doll probably sold about the same time she was seen in Jell-o ads, from 1905 to 1920. The 9-inch doll is composition with a cloth torso, molded painted facial features, hair, shoes and stockings. Her hair style and costume subtly influenced later children's hair styles. The hand knitted dress is not original. The table and miniature dessert did not come with the doll. M. Lowe collection. $75.00.

It wasn't until 1845 that a patent was obtained for a gelatin dessert. Peter Cooper, inventor of the

famous locomotive "Tom Thumb" claims the gelatin patent. He did nothing with his patent. After fifty years, in 1897, a cough drop manufacturer, Pearl B. Wait, started production on an adaptation of Cooper's gelatin dessert.

The wonderful name Jell-o was coined by Wait's wife. How she became inspired is unknown. Perhaps she noticed the dessert's similarity to jelly and added the popular suffix of the day O to the prefix. Or maybe it was because the mixture had to jell before eaten and she chose the name from the phonetic sound. Whatever the reason, it is one of the most outstanding brand names in history.

Even with the great name Jell-o attached, the gelatin dessert broke no sales records. Wait sold the Jell-o business in 1899 for $450.00 to a neighbor, Francis Woodward, who had recently founded a company for a product of his own, Grain-o, a cereal drink. Woodward had no luck with the new dessert either, and tried to sell his holdings for $35.00 to a companion. Lucky for him the offer was refused, because by 1902 sales were beginning to climb and soon Woodward dropped Grain-o to concentrate on producing Jell-o.

Early magazine ads for Jell-o list it as a product of Genessee Pure Food Company. Whether this is the Woodward company is not known.

From about 1905 to 1920 Jell-o ads featured a sweet little girl about eight years old with blonde hair and delicate features. An early 9-inch composition doll with cloth body; molded/painted hair and features resembling the child in the ads was called the **Jell-o Girl**. Whether the doll was manufactured to sell under this name is unverified.

Jell-o also used the Rose O'Neil Kewpies in their advertisements.

Jensen Musical Instruments. An 8-inch cloth doll representing a happy fellow carrying a violin case was offered by this company. The prestuffed doll is well marked.

Jergens Soap. About the turn of the century the Jergens Company of Cincinnati used a 4½-inch frozen Charlotte type doll to advertise their company. It is a smiling boy child with hands together on his chest.

Jolly Joan Restaurant. This Oregon restaurant will be remembered by doll collectors for the advertising doll it sold in the 1940's. The 12-inch doll is composition, one-piece head and body, molded-painted brown hair, jointed limbs. The doll is dressed in a gingham checked dress with ruffles over the shoulder and a waist apron similar to the waitresses at the Jolly Joan Restaurant.

Jolly King Restaurant.

A 7½-inch *Jolly King* doll was sold at the Jolly King Restaurants. The doll is fabric with felt robe trimmed in white fake fur. Facial features are painted; hair is yarn. Marks: "Jolly/King," on crown; "Dream Dolls/R. Dakin & Co.," on label. R. Keelen collection. $8.00.

Jolly Roger Restaurant.

This restaurant has used the same cloth pirate premium doll as the Long John Silver restaurant.

The cloth *Jolly Roger* doll is the same pirate doll used by Long John Silver Restaurants with the exception of coloring and mark on hat. $8.00.

Junior Mints, a product of Nabisco. The cloth **Fonzie** doll was an exclusive offer of Nabisco from November 1976 to May 1977. It was first advertised in TV Guide magazine and since on over 50 million packages of candy.

The doll is unusual because it bears the face of a living person, not a cartoon or imaginary character. The **Fonz**, played by Henry Winkler, is a popular character on the weekly television show "Happy Days". The 16-inch lithographed doll is in the familiar **Fonz** pose: fists clinched in front of the body with the thumbs extended upward. If the doll talked it would be saying "Ay-Ay!"

A 16-inch cloth *Fonz* doll was offered on packages of Junior Mints in 1976. The doll bears the face of a character played by Henry Winkler in the popular TV show "Happy Days." "THE/FONZ TM," on back of jacket. $4.00.

Just Rite Restaurant. The **Li'l Miss Just Rite** doll was dispersed in several ways. In some Indiana restaurants a look-alike contest was held for girls between three and nine years of age. Every contestant received a **Li'l Miss Just Rite** doll. At other restaurants the doll was sold to customers for $1.00. The dolls were also sold as **Pigtail Annie** from retail markets.

Li'l Miss Just Rite is an 8-inch vinyl, fully jointed doll with rooted saran pigtails, and a closed mouth. The doll is dressed in denim overalls, white cotton shirt, and shoes. It was manufactured in 1965 by R. Dakin & Company.

Li'l Miss Just Rite, 8-inches tall, was dispersed in several ways by the Just Rite restaurant chain. The jointed vinyl doll was sold as *Pigtail Annie* in retail stores. Marks: "1965 R. Dakin & Co./ Product of Hong Kong," on back of head; "Made in Hong Kong" on body; "Li'l Miss/Just Rite," stamped on bib of overalls; "R. Dakin & Co./Pigtail Annie Special/Dream Dolls," on tag on wrist. R. Keelen collection. $8.00.

K

Karo Syrup, a product of Corn Products Refining Co., now Best Foods, a division of CPC International Inc. Prior to 1930 at least three products manufactured by the old Corn Products Refining Company of Argo, Illinois used the trademark figure of an Indian girl sheathed in a corn husk gown. A doll was manufactured to resemble this trademark and it was often referred to as the Karo Syrup doll. (See Corn Products Refining Company for the illustration of the doll.)

Keebler Company. This cookie company offered a 6½-inch molded/painted vinyl doll of the **Keebler Elf** in 1974. The doll was made by Chase Bag Company. The figure has been used extensively in television commercials and on packages of cookies. The elf has one arm extended, the other is bent holding the jacket lapel. It cost $1.00 plus two proof-of-purchase seals.

A dragon was also offered by this company in 1968. The pink and purple inflatable monster was 18-inches tall and cost $1.00 plus Keebler shield from a package of cookies.

The 6½-inch *Keebler Elf* doll offered in 1974 on packages of Keebler cookies. It is dressed in a green jacket, yellow pants, shoes, and a red hat. Marks: "1974/ Keebler Co.," on bottom of feet. $5.00.

Kellogg Company. Strange as it seems, many of today's dry cereals that are being condemned as void of nutrition were originally produced as a health food for patients at the famous Seventh-day Adventist Sanitarium in Battle Creek, Michigan.

In about 1880, John H. Kellogg, physician-in-chief at the "San," set up an experimental kitchen to investigate the effects of cooking upon various foods. Because the Adventists abstained from meat, Dr. Kellogg was especially eager to find a product that was vegetarian, tasted good, and provided good nutrition for his patients. Several food products were developed, one a grain mixture that was precooked, called "granola." The products were served to the patients and often when the patients left the institution they would write back requesting foods they'd enjoyed. Seeing an opportunity, Doctor Kellogg decided to go into business selling sanitarium foods. He established the Sanitos Food Company.

For many years Dr. Kellogg's younger brother, William Keith, had competently fulfilled the duties of business manager at the "San." Now his duties were being expanded to include managing the new food company. W.K. probably resented the extra responsiblity, as he was already putting in a 15-hour day. The brother was used to obeying his elder brothers' demands, so he took over the new food business. William referred to himself as "J.H.'s flunky" and admitted to doing such menial tasks as shaving his brother and shining his shoes.

Even though William managed both the sanitarium and the food establishment, J.H. was reluctant to give his little brother either status with a title or a respectable salary. Dr. Kellogg offered William what in the beginning seemed very little, one-fourth of the profits from the food company, in lieu of salary.

With clever advertising and a lot of work, William surprised his brother and himself by building the little company into a rather substantial mail-order food enterprise.

William was looking for ways to enlarge the company and felt he needed a new product. For weeks he'd been working with cooked wheat. As so often happens, the new product he'd been hoping for came as a result of an accident. One night he made a batch of cooked wheat that he intended to test later on. An interruption delayed the test, and by the time he returned the wheat was overcooked and moldy. Nevertheless, he put it through the rollers and this time instead of a messy glob, each wheat berry yielded a flake. The flakes were baked, and even though moldy, W.K. could see they had possibilities. When the Doctor tried the perfected flakes he suggested it would be best to crumble them up; Will insisted they be allowed to remain whole and be served that way--thus the flaked cereal was born.

Patented May 31, 1894, the first wheat flakes were handled by mail. Later a few food jobbers, restaurants, and department stores purchased the new foods.

Suddenly 42 companies sprang up near Battle Creek, all manufacturing the new dry cereal. The reputation of the sanitarium had made Battle Creek synonomous with healthful food, and everyone wanted to cash in on the name.

William believed the best flake came from corn and he concentrated on developing and improving this "horse food" as skeptics called the flakes. From 1898 to 1903 the product remained in the development stage. In 1906 William began making the corn flakes from corn grits, rather than from whole kernels and soon his flakes proved a booming success. Later malt flavor, and then, against Doctor Kelloggs desires, he added sugar, producing a delicious breakfast food.

Perhaps the primary reason for William Keith's success was his brave plunge into advertising. The company soon became one of the nation's largest users of promotional media. It took a lot of advertising to convince Americans there was nothing strange about eating cereal cold, and housewives needed to be reassured they could serve nutritious good-tasting cereal without standing over a hot stove.

In about 1903 the phrase, "Not genuine without the signature of W.K. Kellogg" appeared on the cartons. It was probably necessary as a protection from the many imitators. But it was one of many problems that resulted in a court case between the brothers.

The most ambitious advertising scheme was the house-to-house sampling program. In several large cities newspapers ran ads announcing free Sanitos Toasted Corn Flakes. After the ads, delivery boys ran from door to door with the sample packages. With this and other advertising, the Kellogg's brothers business continued to grow.

During this period W.K. did the work in the food company while his brother practiced medicine, yet the doctor made it clear to the staff at the food company who was the employee and who was the employer. He required that he sign all checks and that three-fourths the profit go to himself and only one-fourth to his younger brother.

In February of 1906 the new Battle Creek Toasted Corn Flake Company was incorporated and later that year William finally, at the age of 46, squirmed from beneath the firm thumb of his elder brother. Financially he took a loss, but more important he gained his freedom.

With quiet confidence Will K. Kellogg (he officially changed his name) surveyed the future and began to move. Business became a game—fun, creative, and a chance to win.

It was about 1908 that the name of the corn product that made Will famous was changed from Sanitos Corn Flakes to Kellogg's Corn Flakes. Not until 1925 was the company named the Kellogg Company—the name it uses today.

Will K. Kellogg said he ran the company on intuition and it seemed infallible as one story illustrates. In 1927 three callers brought a new cold cereal for Will to taste. They poured it in a bowl, covered it with milk, then quietly watched as their boss ate the bowl of cereal. When he finished he tersely announced it "ate" well and would "go." That was all they needed to launch the new cereal—Rice Krispies. They totally trusted Mr. Kellogg's intuition and judgement; it had proved right time and again.

When Will became older, it was not enough that he founded the world's largest cereal company, he wanted to do something significant with the money earned from his company. The first third of his

life he had worked for his brother; the second third he worked for the company. The last third of his life was devoted to insuring that his philanthropic endeavors were useful to his fellowman, another job he did well. Will K. Kellogg died October 6, 1951 at the age of 91.

The Kellogg Company is of special interest to collectors of advertising dolls because it has consistently offered doll premiums, about 90, from the first four in Goldilocks series in 1925, to the Softina doll offered in 1978.

The following is a list of dolls offered by the Kellogg Company:

1925 **Goldilocks and Three Bears** (1st issue). Cloth; range in height from 15-inches down to 12-inches, printed on flat material in six lithographed colors; cost 10¢ plus one box top for one or 30¢ plus four box tops for the set of four.

A frightened *Goldilocks* doll, 14-inches tall, wears a lace trimmed dress and apron. Marks: "Kelloggs," on apron. $40.00.

Johnny Bear, 12-inches, looks startled. He wears polka-dot pants and holds a bowl marked "Kelloggs." $40.00.

The 1925 *Daddy Bear* is a big 15-inch fellow and is wearing green pants with blue window pane lines. His red jacket and the pants have yellow cuffs. Daddy holds a box of Kelloggs cereal in his paws. $40.00.

1926 **Goldilocks and Three Bears** (2nd issue). Cloth; all 13-inches tall, except

Mama Bear, 14-inches, is holding a bowl of cereal marked "Kellogg." She wears a red skirt, yellow blouse, and dust cap. $40.00.

This 1926 *Goldilocks* doll wears a different dress. It has a white skirt with red, green, and blue flowers. Marks: "Kelloggs," on front of waist: "Goldilocks," on back of collar. $40.00.

Johnny Bear, which is 10-inches; printed on flat material in six lithographed colors; cost 10¢ plus box top for one or 30¢ plus four box tops for the set of four. Very similar to the original issue, except for size and clothes.

Daddy Bear, 13-inches tall, wears a blue jacket with green trim, and yellow and red striped pants. Marks: "Daddy Bear," on back of collar. $40.00.

Johnny Bear, 10-inches, wears blue and white striped pants and a red shirt. Marks: "Kelloggs," on bowl; "Johnny Bear," on collar. $40.00.

1928 **Fairyland Series**. Cloth; 15-inches tall; printed on flat material in six lithographed

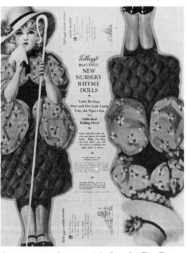

The 1926 *Mama Bear*, 13-inches, wears a dainty apron over her blue stripe dress. Marks: "Kelloggs," on bowl; "Mama Bear," on collar. $40.00.

An uncut sheet with *Little Bo Peep* includes verse printed on two pages of a cloth book that can be completed by purchasing the set of four dolls. *Bo Peep* is wearing a bright blue dress with yellow flowers, blue stockings, black shoes, and a straw hat. In one hand she carries a long staff, the other holds a hanky to wipe away the tears on her face. Marks: "Kellogg's," on back waist. P. Coghlan collection, Harry Sykora photographer. $45.00.

colors; cost 30¢ plus one box top from Kellogg's Corn Flakes; two pages for a cloth book were also printed on the background fabric; the pages had the corresponding nursery rhyme. **Little Bo Peep, Mary and Her Lamb, Red Riding Hood, and Tom the Piper's Son.**

The uncut sheet of *Mary and Her Little Lamb* is photographed with an old Kellogg's Corn Flakes package. The sheet includes two pages with the corresponding verse. *Mary* wears a short red pleated skirt, floral print blouse, green vest, and a white mop cap with a red bow. She is reading a book entitled <u>Kellogs Nursery Rhymes</u>. At her side is a white lamb. P. Coghlan collection, Harry Sykora photographer. $45.00.

1935 **Animal Series.** Cloth; about 12-inches tall; printed on flat oilcloth-like fabric; cost 10¢ each plus one Wheat Krispies box top or 25¢ plus four box tops for all four dolls. **Dinkey the Dog, Crinkle the Cat, Dandy the Duck, Freckles the Frog.**

1948 **Kellie Dog.** Cloth; 10-inches; required cutting and stuffing; cost 15¢ plus one Gro-Pup (dog food) box top.

Tom the Piper's Son, 15-inches tall, is lithographed in six beautiful colors, as are the other dolls in the Fairyland set. The background fabric has two pages for the cloth book with the verse. It also has the cover for the book entitled <u>Kellogg's Nursery Rhymes.</u> J. Varsalona collection. $45.00.

Red Riding Hood, approximately 15-inches tall, carries a basket containing boxes of "Kellogg's Pep" and "Kellogg's Corn Flakes." The printed sheet contains two pages for the book: "Kellogg's Nursery Rhymes." J. Varsalona collection. $45.00.

In 1935 Kellogg's offered four animals to advertise their Wheat Krispie cereal. *Dinkey the Dog* wears a blue coat and brown trousers. The ears and tail are cut and sewn on separately. Marks: "Kellogg's," on back of jacket. Playthings by the Yard, 1973. $30.00.

Dandy the Duck wears a derby hat marked "Kellogg's," brown trousers, a gray vest, and blue jacket. Playthings by the Yard, 1973. $30.00.

Crinkle the Cat is about 12-inches tall. It wears green pants, a brown plaid jacket, and red polka dot tie. Tail is cut separate. Marks: "Kellogg's," across back of jacket. Playthings by the Yard, 1973. $30.00.

Freckles the Frog holds his "hands" behind him. He wears brown pants, and a green coat. Playthings by the Yard, 1973. $30.00.

1948 **Snap, Crackle, Pop** ™.
Cloth; 12½-inches; require
cutting and stuffing cost 15¢
plus a box top from Rice
Krispies, the cereal they
represent.

In 1928 the first Rice Krispie
cereal was marketed by Kelloggs.
Capitalizing on the sound of Rice
Krispies in milk, they chose elves
named Snap, Crackle, and Pop for
the trademark. Twenty years later,
in 1948, they introduced the first
Rice Krispie dolls. Marks: "Snap!"
on chef hat. $15.00.

The Rice Krispie trio cost 15¢ each.
Marks: "Crackle!" on tall hat.
$15.00.

The dolls are printed in red, yellow,
blue, and green on white fabric that
had to be cut and sewn. Marks:
"Pop!" $15.00.

1949 **Chiquita Banana.** Cloth;
10-inches; requires cutting
and stuffing; cost 10¢ plus a
Corn Flakes box top.
(Rather poor quality doll
compared to other Kellogg
dolls.)

1952 **Howdy Doody.** Cloth; size
unknown; required cutting
and stuffing; cost unknown.

1953 **Sweetheart Doll.** Hard
vinyl; 16-inches; closed
mouth; open/shut eyes;
blonde rooted hair; cost
$1.00.

1953 **Howdy Doody.** Vinylite inflatable; 24-inches; $1.00
plus Rice Krispies box top.

1954 **Snap, Crackle, Pop** ™.
Cloth; 16-inches; required
stuffing and cutting; cost 15¢
plus a box top from Rice
Krispie cereal. These are the
same as the 1948 dolls, except larger.

In 1954 many requests were received for Kellogg's *Sweetheart* doll, the first vinyl premium doll offered by this company. She wears a red flannel skirt with suspenders and matching knit tights. The skirt is trimed with felt figures and narrow cord. The blouse and shoes are white. Marks: "ACE 393." E. Hess collection. $10.00.

The 1954 issue is 16½-inches tall, otherwise they are very similar to the 1948 dolls. Marks: "Crackle!" Playthings by the Yard, 1973. $10.00.

Rice Krispies' dolls were reissued in 1954. Marks: "Snap!" on hat. Playthings by the Yard, 1973. $10.00.

The dolls cost 15¢ each plus one Rice Krispies box top. Marks: "Pop!" Playthings by the Yard, 1973. $10.00.

1955 Majorette Doll. Soft latex (the type that disintegrates); 10-inches; closed mouth; dressed in white satin majorette outfit with leatherette boots and a tall hat with a feather plume; cost $1.00 plus one Raisin Bran box top.

1957 Walking Doll. Plastic; 8-inches tall; head moves as it walks; open/shut eyes; rooted blonde hair; cost $2.00. Dressed as a bride, four other outfits were available. (Doll similar to copies of the Ginny doll by Vogue.)

1958 Grown-up Doll. Vinyl; 10½-inches tall; closed mouth; open/shut eyes; rooted brown hair; dressed in long blue taffeta formal, three other outfits included: jersey sweater, skirt and beret, taffeta print dress, corduroy pants and blouse; cost $2.00 plus two box tops from Rice Krispies or Raisin Bran.

1959 Baby Ginger. Vinyl: 8-inches; nursing mouth; blonde or auburn/rooted hair; open/shut eyes; came with four outfits and a bath tub; cost $1.00 plus one box top from Rice Krispies or Raisin Bran.

1960 Little Miss Kay. Vinyl: 13-inches; closed mouth; open/shut eyes; rooted blonde hair; wears taffeta dress with matching bonnet and panties; several other outfits were included and others could be purchased with the doll; cost $2.00 plus two box tops from Sugar Frosted Flakes, Sugar Smacks, Sugar Pops, Cocoa Krispies, or Raisin Bran.

Kellogg's *Baby Ginger* is 8-inches tall with the nurse/wet feature, blue sleep eyes, and rooted hair that ranged in color from blonde to auburn. The offer included many extras as shown in the photo: bath tub, bottle, bunting, sponge, tray, back scrubber, and three outfits of clothing. The doll was manufactured by Cosmopolitan Doll & Toy Corp. A. Wolfe collection, David Nelson, James Giokas photographers $10.00.

Little Miss Kay was available in 1960 from several Kellogg's cereals. The 13-inch doll has soft vinyl "skin." The hair was advertised as hair that could be combed, curled, and washed. She came in several dresses, all fairly similar. The one in the photo is red plaid taffeta with a white nylon organdy pinafore. For $2.00 you could receive a skirt and blouse, pajamas, and a playsuit. Marks: "K4193." T. Baxter collection, David Nelson, James Giokas photographer. $6.00.

1961 **Baby Chris.** Vinyl; 13-inches, nursing mouth; open/shut eyes; rooted curly hair; came with nursing bottle and four different outfits, overalls and shirt, snow suit, sunsuit, and dress; cost $2.00 plus 2 box tops from Raisin Bran, Frosted Flakes, or Sugar Smacks.

1962 **Linda Lou.** Vinyl; 12-inches; closed mouth; freckles; open/shut eyes; dark straight hair with uneven bangs (called the pixie style at the time); three outfits included: coat, sleepers, dress with apron; four additional sets of

clothing were also available for $1.00; cost for doll and three outfits was $2.00.

Baby Chris came dressed in a blue nylon dress and bonnet trimmed with lace. Additional outfits were available in the $2.00 offer found on packages of Sugar Smacks cereal in 1961. The 13-inch doll is made of vinyl that is highly colored. B. McConnell collection, David Nelson, James Giokas photographers. $6.00.

1963 **Valerie.** Vinyl; 15-inches; closed mouth; turned-up nose; open/shut eyes; rooted platinum blond hair; pre-teen girl with small waist; three outfits included: dress, slack set, and nightgown; four additional outfits could be ordered for $1.00; cost of doll with three sets of clothes $2.00.

1964 **Magic Mary.** Two-dimensional paper doll with stand; outfit made of nylon, which adhered to the surface as if magnetic.

1964 **Calico Lassie.** Vinyl; 12-inches tall; teen doll similar to Tammy; closed mouth; painted side-glance eyes; rooted honey-blond hair with bangs and a double pony-tail; wears blue denim pants, striped blouse, and plastic sneakers; two other outfits were included with the price of the doll; three extra outfits could be ordered for an additional $1.00; cost of doll and three outfits was $2.00.

1964 **Toucan Sam** ^{TM}. Pre-stuffed cloth; 9-inches tall by 12-inches long; copied from the Froot Loop trademark character, a colorful toucan bird with a huge bill and feet; cost $1.00.

1964 **Hillbilly Goat.** Pre-stuffed cloth; 15-inches; trademark used by one of the Kellogg's cereals; wear lithographed pants held up with suspenders, a red shirt, black hat, and it has a slurping tongue; cost $1.00.

1966 **Woody Woodpecker.** Pre-stuffed cloth; 13-inches; brightly colored with blue suit, orange feet, red head, and orange beak; cost $1.00.

1969 **Mini People from Many Lands.** Wood; 3 to 4-inches tall; wear glued clothing made from cotton fabric, felt, and cardboard. Cost unknown. **Swiss Yodler, Spanish Pirate, Palace Guard, Venetian Gondolier, Wee Scotsman, English Policeman, Black Forest Man, and John Bull.**

1969 **Mary Kate.** Vinyl; 11-inches; nurser mouth; open/shut eyes; rooted hair; wears a pink dress with lace skirt, two other outfits included in the offer; cost $2.00.

Toucan Sam the trademark figure for Kellogg's Fruit Loop cereal, was Kellogg's first pre-stuffed cloth doll. It was introduced in 1964. "Sam" is 9-inches tall and measures 12-inches from the tip of his long bill to tail. Unmarked. S. Ricklefs collection. $6.00.

The *Hillbilly Goat* doll, 15-inches, was offered in 1964. We are not certain which cereal it represented. Unmarked. $6.00.

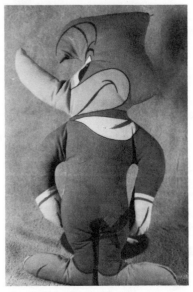

The 13-inch *Woody Woodpecker* doll was offered in 1966. The Walter Lantz cartoon has been a favorite for many years. "Woody" is red-headed with an orange beak and a blue body. Unmarked. $6.00.

In 1969 Kelloggs offered *Mini People from Many Lands*. These were small, 3 to 4½-inch wood dolls with painted faces. They were costumed in felt and cardboard. Eight dolls were available, including the *Venetian Gondolier* and the *English Policeman*. Unmarked. $2.00.

1969 **Banana Splits.** Pre-stuffed cloth; 9 to 11-inches tall; cost and the product they advertised are unknown, may have been Puffa Puffa Rice, a product no longer being sold. (Four cartoon characters.) elephant - **Snorky**; lion - **Drooper**; dog - **Fleegle**; bear -**Bingo**.

The Banana Splits, popular Saturday cartoon characters. *Snorky*, 9-inches tall, is gray with pink polka dot ears and green sunglasses. Unmarked. $4.00.

Kellogg's 12-inch *Drooper* is one of the "Banana Splits dolls offered in 1969. *Drooper* is dark gold with beige paws and mane. He has a red ball nose and also wears sunglasses. Unmarked. $4.00.

Fleegle, 10-inches, is another of the four Banana Splits characters. He is chartreuse green with a big red bow. Unmarked. $4.00.

The Banana Splits, *Bingo*, is approximately 10-inches tall. Unmarked. $4.00.

1970 **Little People.** Wood; 2-inches tall; clothes made of felt, cotton fabric, and cardboard; cost uncertain. **Pocahontas, Robin Hood, Oriental, Caballero, Friar Tuck, Red Riding Hood, Rip Van Winkle.**

In 1970 Kelloggs offered wooden *Little People* which were only 2-inches tall. They were made the same as the 1969 *Mini People from Many Lands* with painted features and glued on clothes. *Rip Van Winkle* has more detail than most of the dolls with his fur beard, wire glasses, and hat. Unmarked. $2.00.

Red Riding Hood and an unidentified companion were probably from this series. Unmarked. $2.00.

1970 **Tony the Tiger** ™.
Stamped cloth head with a plush body; 13-inches; wears a removable red neckerchief; cost $3.00 plus box top from Sugar Frosted Flakes, the cereal Tony represents.

A Kellogg's winner, *Tony the Tiger* was offered in 1970 for $3.00. The 13-inch doll has a cloth face with tiger markings and a slurping tongue stamped on the fabric; the body is a plush fabric. Beside the 1970 *Tony* is the 1972 *Tony* from the *Friendly Folk* series. The red neckerchief that is marked "Tony" is missing. $10.00.

1971 **Baby Michelle.** Vinyl; 9-inches tall; baby doll came in plastic carrier with bottle, blanket and wearing a flannel outfit; nursing mouth; drink/wet feature; rooted brunette hair; cost $1.00 for doll and accessories.

1972 **Friendly Folk.** Wood; 2½-inches; wear glued on clothing or painted; cost $2.00 plus two box tops for the set of five dolls. **Tony the Tiger, Og, Snap, Crackle, and Pop.**

Kellogg's *Friendly Folk* were offered in 1972 and were made from the same 2-inch wood base as previous small wood premium dolls. *Snap, Crackle,* and *Pop* were three of the five dolls in the set. $2.00.

The 2½-inch *Tony* was one of the *Friendly Folk* doll. $4.00.

The fifth *Friendly Folk* doll is named *Og*. $2.00.

1972 Miss America (Barbie doll). Vinyl; 11½-inch; closed mouth; painted eyes, long brunette wig and dark eyelashes; high-heeled feet; wears dress with gold lame bodice white skirt, "ermine" trimmed red cape, silvery crown and sceptor, carries red rose bouquet; cost $3.00. Offer didn't expire until January 31, 1975.

The 11½-inch vinyl *Miss America* doll is a Barbie doll manufactured by Mattel. The same doll sold for several dollars more at the retail level. Her gown has a gold lame bodice and a full white skirt. S. Ricklefs collection. $8.00.

1972 Uncle Sam Mini-man. Wood; 2-inches; felt costume, nylon fur beard; free with three Uncle Sam Stamps from packages of Frosted Mini Wheats.

A 2-inch *Uncle Sam Mini Man* doll was available free for collecting three Uncle Sam Stamps found on packages of Frosted Mini-Wheats. The doll has felt clothes and a white nylon beard. Unmarked. L. Maxfield collection. $2.00.

1973 Fun Fair Clowns (Three). Pre-stuffed cloth; 15-inches; each attired differently; cost unknown.

Three *Fun Fair Clown* dolls were offered in 1973 by Kelloggs cereal. The dolls are 15-inches tall and very colorful. Unmarked. $6.00.

Fun Fair Clown wearing a lithographed barrel. Unmarked. S. Ricklefs collection. $6.00.

Fun Fair Clowns, are unmarked. S. Ricklefs collection. $6.00.

1973 **Tony the Tiger** ™. Prestuffed cotton; 14-inches tall; lithographed red kerchief around the neck; ears not stuffed; slurping tongue to the side; Sold for $1.00.

1973 **Dig 'Em Frog** ™. Prestuffed cloth; 16-inches; trademark figure for Sugar Smacks cereal; green frog with yellow vest and large

side-turned white shoes; cost $1.00 plus two Sugar Smacks box tops.

Tony the Tiger, 14-inches tall, is made of pre-stuffed cotton fabric lithograped with tiger markings, facial features, and a red neckerchief. L. Zablotney collection, L. Zablotney photographer. $10.00.

Kellogg's 16-inch *Dig 'Em Frog* doll is constructed from a coarse fabric resembling canvas. It is lithographed in greens and yellow to resemble the trademark figure used by Sugar Smacks cereal. $6.00.

1974 **Tony the Tiger** ™. Molded vinyl; 8-inches; tongue to side of mouth in slurp fashion; molded kerchief with name imprinted; cost $1.50 plus two labels from Sugar Frosted Flakes, the cereal Tony represents.

The third *Tony the Tiger* doll offered as a premium for Kellogg's Frosted Flakes is molded/painted vinyl. The 8-inch *Tony* has the familiar slurping tongue and red neckerchief. It was available in 1974. Marks: "Tony," incised on neckerchief. $8.00.

1975 **Mini-People.** Wood; 2¼ to 4-inches; painted features with felt costume and nylon hair; free with three stamps from specially-marked packages of Pop-Tarts. **Robin Hood, Friar Tuck, Oriental, Red Riding Hood, Caballero, Rip Van Winkle, Pocahontas, and Uncle Sam.**

1975 **Toddler Twins.** Vinyl; 9-inches; rooted hair; painted eyes; wear matching red jumper for girl and overalls for boy; cost $3.50 for pair plus two Raisin Bran box tops.

The *Cute 'n Cuddley Kellogg Twins* were advertised on boxes of Raisin Bran in 1975. The 9-inch pair wear polka dot blouses and shirts, and red jumpers and rompers. The dolls also sold at the retail level. $8.00 pair.

1975 **Snap, Crackle, and Pop** ™. Vinyl; 8-inches tall; molded/painted features and clothing. Cost $1.00 each plus two box tops from Rice Krispies cereal.

Snap is an 8-inch squeeze toy from the set offered in 1975. $5.00.

199

Crackle. $5.00.

Pop. $5.00.

1978 Softina. Foam vinyl; 11-inches; nurse mouth; straight rooted hair; painted blue eyes; wears jumpsuit and carries a bottle; cost $3.00 plus two box tops from Raisin Bran.

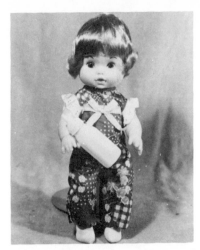

Softina **was offered on packages of Raisin Bran in 1978. She is made from a foam vinyl that is soft and cuddly. $4.00.**

Kelly Services, Inc. This agency, who supplies employees to companies needing temporary fill-in help offered a pre-stuffed cloth **Kelly Girl** doll in late 1971. The doll created a furor because feminists contended the message

In February, 1978 a cloth *Kelly Girl* doll was distributed by Kelly Services, an agency that supplies temporary help to employers. The small doll has removable green jumper and print blouse, yarn hair, and lithographed face with freckles. Marks: "Kelly Girl," on skirt. $8.00.

that accompanied the doll was filled with sexual overtones and double meanings.

The small freckle-faced doll had yarn hair, lithographed features and removable clothing consisting of a jumper and blouse. The skirt is marked **Kelly Girl**. In early 1978 35,000 dolls were distributed for this promotion effort. It was manufactured by Knickerbocker Toy Co.

C.D. Kenny Company.

The Kenny Company is another one that is no longer is business, therefore, information is scant. Several older people recall this company began by selling goods from wagons that were pulled about the country from one community to another. Later they had stores and were noted for selling tea and coffee.

Polk's Directory of 1891 states in 1870 Kenny had a dozen stores in the Baltimore area. This company continued until 1943 when it

A lovely old all-bisque doll advertising a company that once sold tea and coffee. The 4-inch doll is wire jointed at the shoulder. The doll has molded painted blonde hair with a blue bow to one side. The wrap dress or coat is white with pink labels and a soft green belt, all molded and delicately painted. Marks: "C.D. Kenny Co.," near bottom of coat back. R. Wernsdorfer collection. $45.00.

disbursed and was taken over by Consolidated Foods Corporation.

An advertising card found in a flea market read: C.D. Kenny Co./"Cheon"/The best tea in America/Sugar at cost/50 branch stores.

At one time they used a 4-inch all bisque doll as a premium. The company's name is stamped on the back.

Kentucky Fried Chicken.

Colonel Sanders, the man who received the recipe and method of cooking Kentucky Fried Chicken, is also the product's trademark. "My mug is my trademark." says Kentucky Colonel Harland Sanders. Smiling down from signs at thousands of take-out stores, the man in the spotless white suit with matching hair and goatee is synonymous with his "finger-lickin'" chicken.

In the 30's Sanders began fixing chicken in the back of a gas station. By 1953 his Sanders' Cafe had improved until it was worth $165,000. A comfortable retirement was in sight. Three years later because of a shift in a nearby junction, he was forced to sell-out at a third of the value. The future looked bleak until Sanders remembered selling his recipe and method of pressure-cooking chicken to a restaurant in Utah. The restaurant had done so well Sanders used them as a reference to persuade other restaurant owners to try his chicken and pay him four-cents for every chicken they sold using his recipe.

At the age of sixty-six, the Colonel launched a new career. He drove around the country cooking a sample of his chicken for restaurant owners. If they liked it, he made an informal agreement to receive the same amount he did from the first owners, four-cents per chicken. It took until the sixties before his new career became profitable. In fact by the mid-sixties it was such a job the Colonel remarked, "The popularity of Kentucky Fried Chicken was beginning to run right over me and mash me flat."

For that reason, Sanders sold Kentucky Fried Chicken, with the stipulation the new owners would protect his recipe and high quality. Until 1970 Sanders remained on the board of directors.

The new owners recognized the Sander's story was unique. Through wise publicity, the Southern Gentleman, became as famous as the chicken recipe he had created. Not one to spend his senior years in a rocking chair, Colonel Sanders traveled the country promoting Kentucky Fried Chicken.

As might be expected premiums were used that represented the Colonel. In the early 60's a 7-inch nodder doll was given to managers at a convention. The hard plastic doll holds a red bucket presumably filled with Sander's world famous chicken. The head is a good likeness of the Colonel.

In 1965 a 12½-inch plastic bank of the Colonel was sold at limited restaurants for $1.00. The bank represents a realistic Colonel dressed in a white suit and carrying a cane.

The *Colonel* doll is 7-inches high and holds a red bucket of chicken. As with most nodder dolls, the head is proportionally much larger than the body. The head is quite detailed with white goatee, mustache, eyebrows, and hair, and black horn-rimmed glasses. The "Colonel" wears his usual white doublebreasted suit. Marks: "Kentucky Fried Chicken," in raised letters on base.

A 12½-inch *Colonel Sanders* bank was sold at Kentucky Fried restaurants in 1965. The bank is a representation of Colonel Sanders wearing his white doublebreasted suit and carrying a can. Marks: "Ron Starling Plastics LTD/London, Canada 1965," on bottom; "Harland Sanders/Kentucky Fried Chicken," on front of base. $8.00.

The third premium found is also a likeness of the Colonel, 9¾-inches tall, but it is not as well done as the other two. It is all white, even the face and hands, except for some red on the tie and bucket.

Another *Colonel Sanders* figure is all white with a red tie, and stripes on the bucket. Marks: "COL. SANDERS," in raised letters on the base. $6.00.

Kentucky Tavern Whiskey.
This product has used a 13-inch paper mache snowman carrying a green broom with a red bow, apparently a Christmas promotion.

A *Kentucky Tavern Whiskey Snowman* made of paper mache is 13-inches tall. Marks: "Kentucky/ Tavern," in raised letters on front. K. Landsdowne collection. $1.00.

Kewpie Twins Shoes.
This company, which is no longer in business, used to advertise health shoes for children. The company's trademark figure was two Kewpies. The trademark was used for display dolls, but none of these were found. We did find two flat wood figures attached to a base. Whether these little 5-inch Kewpies were given with shoes or used for display is not known.

5-inch Kewpie figures were used to advertise children's shoes. Marks: "Kewpie Twin Shoes," inside the outline of a child's feet; "Health/ Shoes/for Children," stamped across stomach. M. Hiter collection. $12.00.

King's Food Host U.S.A.
This food chain sold a 2-inch vinyl boy doll with painted eyes, inserted hair, and felt crown.

A 2-inch vinyl doll with rooted hair and painted eyes was sold at the King's Food Host Restaurants. The doll wears felt clothing and a felt crown. Unmarked. $4.00.

King's Food Host Restaurants also gave free hand puppets to children in 1969. $1.00.

Kitty Pan Litter. This company offered a 7½-inch firm vinyl **Glamour Kitty** for $2.50.

Glamour Kitty a 7½-inch firm vinyl toy was available until early 1977. The cat was available in several colors. This one is black with green eyes, a red cloth cape and a gold crown. Kitty Pan Litter made the offer. $3.00.

Knorr Soup, a product of Best Foods. When introduced, this line of soup was advertised as Europe's best selling soups now made in America by Best Foods. To promote the European emphasis, dolls dressed in European costumes were offered. The dolls are similar to the fine souvenir dolls sold in Europe. They are not at all the usual International plastic doll offered today by many products.

The Knorr dolls are hard plastic, 7½-inches tall, open/closed eyes, European look faces with full lips, jointed and will stand alone. The dolls came in pairs, a boy and a girl. The costumes represent several countries. Each pair cost $1.50 and were available in 1963-64.

Kool Cigarettes. The penguin trademark for this menthol cigarette was found made of plaster of paris or a similar material. The penguin is 14-inches tall, has a hole in the mouth for a cigarette and was probably used for display.

Korn Krisp. A 26-inch cloth doll marked "My name is **Miss Korn Krisp**" was done with ribbon paints. It wears a chemise with ribbon draw string at the neck, striped stockings, and buckle shoes.

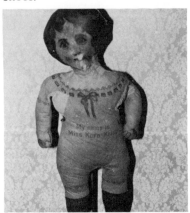

The 26-inch *Miss Korn Krisp* doll is beginning to show her age, which is probably about 70 years. She wears a gray chemise, red shoes, and black stockings. Marks: "My name is/Miss Korn Krisp," across front of waist. S. Ricklefs collection. $35.00.

L

H.D. Lee Company. Buddy Lee, the doll with a secret, who was the manufacturer? No one will tell. An even bigger mystery is WHY no one will tell. If the doll were poorly constructed it could be understood, but **Buddy Lee** is one of the better dolls. The Lee Company should be proud to name the firm who manufactured their doll and the firm should be proud to claim **Buddy Lee** as one of their products. In spite of two letters and several phone calls, the secret remains with the H.D. Lee Company in Shawnee Mission, Kansas.

The idea for **Buddy Lee** came from Mr. C.A. Reynolds in 1920. Retired Art Director for the company, Norm Tanner, said he does not know who actually sculpted the model for the doll, but remembers almost being fired for a comment he made. When he saw the first **Buddy Lee** he remarked it looked like a Kewpie. Mr. Reynolds was most adamant that Buddy Lee was no Kewpie lookalike.

The first **Buddy Lee** dolls are 12½-inches tall and made of breakable composition. The eyes are glancing to one side and the hair is molded/painted. A company in the east manufactured the composition **Buddy Lee**. We do know that much.

Buddy Lee was originally sold to dealers to use in display to promote Lee uniforms. The first price list to include the dolls was in 1922. It offered the Cowboy and the Engineer in two outfits, blue denim and striped denim. The dolls cost the dealers $13.50 per dozen.

The **Buddy Lee** dolls, dressed, in Lee clothing, were the first displayed in a window at the Dayton Company Department Store in Minneapolis, Minnesota. Later, stores throughout the country used the doll in their displays.

The company encouraged dealers to sell the dolls after they were through using them. The demand for the display dolls became so great, that soon dolls were provided to dealers to sell. The early dolls retailed for $2.50.

Of the 17 outfits manufactured by the H.D. Lee Company for their *Buddy Lee* doll, the Cowboy proved the most popular. It, and the Engineer outfit, are the first two outfits made. The first *Buddy Lee* dolls were composition, this one is hard plastic. All original except the scarf. Marks: "Buddy Lee," on back. $90.00.

According to company literature the original **Buddy Lee** dolls were the Cowboy (which was always the most popular doll), Engineer with blue denim, Engineer with stripe denim, plaid shirt and pants (sometimes referred to as the Farmer), and Unionall. The Union-all is a coverall originated by the H.D. Lee Company in 1913. The Lee people experimented by sewing an overall jacket and dungaree trouser together with buttons up the front. The name came from the old-fashioned one-piece union suit underwear. They were such a success it was the Army fatigue uniform for World War I doughboys.

The Engineer outfits came in either striped or plain denim. Along with the cowboy suit, they were the first outfits made by H.D. Lee Company to dress their *Buddy Lee* doll. All original, except the pipe. Marks: "Buddy Lee," on back; "LEE" on overall buttons and hat band. $100.00.

The dolls dressed in dungaree trousers and plaid shirts are sometimes called farmers. They may have come with a hat. The doll on the left is made of composition and is 12½-inches tall; the one on the right is plastic and 13-inches tall. The plastic doll replaced the composition one in 1949. H. Walas collection. $70.00 plastic, $80.00 compo.

Lee clothing has had several interesting firsts. They were the first to put a zipper fly on cowboy pants--that wasn't so long ago either--1926. They were the first to vat-dye jeans so the color was more stable. Remember how jeans always had to run through the very last batch of water because the water would turn blue, no matter how many times they had been washed.

Lee was first to have tailored sizes to insure good fit no matter what the width of waist or length of leg. That innovation was instigated in 1926 also. A decade or so later Lee came up with another improvement in fit. They asked several cowboys to make suggestions on how to improve the fit of the Lee pant. Included in the group of cowboys was Turk Greenough, champion cowboy, and husband of Sally Rand, the naughty fan dancer. Sally pinned a pair of jeans on Turk, thereby designing a tight fitting jean that was accepted as the best fitting cowboy pant on the market.

Lee provided uniforms for several large companies. Many of these uniforms were copied in diminutive size for the **Buddy Lee** doll. According to the company, seventeen outfits were made for the **Buddy Lee** doll. We can account for fourteen: 1. Coca-Cola, 1. Phillip 66, 3. Sinclair, 4. M M Man (which was a service station that advertised having Minute Men that could wash your windows, check your oil, and fill your gas tank in a minute--it may have been Shell Oil Company), 5. Standard Station, 6. John Deere, 7. TWA, 8. Cowboy, 9. Engineer in denim, 10. Engineer in stripe outfit, 11. Union-all, 12. and 13. two pant and shirt outfits.

Number 14. is questionable, Black Magic. I mentioned to Mr. Tanner that we had a photo of a black **Buddy Lee** in a uniform marked Black Magic and he said no black **Buddy Lee** dolls were ever manufactured. This leaves several possibilities: someone painted a doll black, the clothes are not Lee products, even though they have Lee buttons. The Black Magic Company (am unfamiliar with it) may have purchased dolls and painted them to fit the name of their company. If any reader knows of other uniforms please write and let us know.

A plastic *Buddy Lee* dressed in the Phillips 66 Uniform. This doll represented the Phillip's service station attendant when their colors were tan and orange. The round pin did not come on the doll, otherwise all original. Marks: "Buddy Lee," on back; "Phillips/66," emblem on hat and shirt. $90.00.

The **Buddy Lee** dolls were popular with dealers and children. In 1922 the H.D. Lee Company was told it was the second largest doll account in the country. Thousands of **Buddy Lee** dolls were being manufactured.

From an account in Novelty News, November 1924, we learn that **Buddy Lee** was also sold wearing a play suit. The article states, "The overall dress has been maintained but lately the Lee Company has sold thousands of the dolls dressed in play suits. This, as was the case with the overalls, has been used to feature the company's play suit line. The changes of the suit serves to keep the interest in **Buddy Lee** alive in the minds of youngsters everywhere."

The MM uniform was worn by a service station that prided itself on washing your windows, checking your oil, and filling the gas tank in a minute. Everyone I ask remembers they were called Minute Men, but no one can remember which company they represented. Original tan outfit. Marks: "Buddy Lee," across back; "MM," emblem on hat and shirt. $90.00.

Today's Lee employees are unfamiliar with what the play suit looked like and we were unable to locate one. A **Buddy Lee** doll with sculpted black slippers and colored anklet stockings was noticed at an auction. Perhaps this is the doll that wore the play suit because the usual **Buddy Lee** wears painted boots.

The composition **Buddy Lee** dolls were highly successful, but were easily damaged. Moisture or heat could crack the surface and make the paint peel or flake, and a hard knock or fall was sure to result in a break. The company

207

Buddy Lee **dressed as a cowboy, engineer, and the Coca-Cola man. This doll has not had the Coca-Cola emblems put on the hat and shirt** yet. **The uniform was white with green stripes. Courtesy H.D. Lee Company. Coca Cola doll $180.00.**

became tired of consumer complaints about the accident-prone composition **Buddy Lee**, and they were discontinued.

In 1949 a new **Buddy Lee** was introduced with slightly different proportions and made from a totally new material. Again, the firm who manufactured the doll is a mystery, but we do know they were located in Excelsior Springs, Missouri. The **Buddy Lee** is ½-inch larger, making it 13-inches high and is made from a hard plastic.

The proportions were changed to facilitate dressing. The legs are slimmer and slightly bowed and the hands are larger. The Lee Company made the first uniforms for the dolls, but the caps and accessories were always made by an outside firm. Originally a company in the east made them. Due to the

time and inconvenience involved in shipping the accessories from the east, this method of manufacturing accessories became unsatisfactory. The Kansas City Cap Company was selected to make the caps and in time they also made the doll uniforms because the Lee Company was too busy with orders for full-sized uniforms.

By 1962 the **Buddy Lee** doll had to be discontinued, for expenses had risen to the point that it was no longer profitable to sell the doll.

The H.D. Lee Company is well aware that the **Buddy Lee** doll has been a most valuable piece of advertising. From time to time they have considered issuing the **Buddy Lee** doll again, but the cost of labor to make the uniform alone would make it so expensive they feel it could not compete with other dolls on the retail market. At this time they do not plan to reissue **Buddy Lee**.

The one-piece unionall was created by the Lee Company by sewing an overall jacket and trousers together with buttons up the front. The suit is tan with red belt and collar. The hat is missing. E. Engleson collection. $70.00.

Note the slight differences in the composition and plastic *Buddy Lee* dolls. The 12½-inch composition doll is on the left; the 13-inch plastic doll is on the right.

Collectors are seeking out the **Buddy Lee** doll and are willing to pay from $100.00 to $150.00 for one dressed and in good condition. In less than perfect condition $75.00 is a price tag usually found. Surely a price like that would inspire the mystery manufacturer to step forward and claim **Buddy Lee** as his own.

Lee Rubber and Tire Corp. In 1929 this Pennsylvania company took out a patent for sponge dolls named, JolLeeJays and toy animals.

Leo Meats. In 1969 Leo's thin-sliced lunch meats offered a 2-foot tall inflatable lion. The toy cost $1.00 plus two labels.

Levi Strauss & Company. Denim, that wonderful fabric, "Columbus sailed it; Levi styled it; and the world wears it." In fact men have been wearing the same basic design that Levi Strauss invented over 100 years ago. Levi was a city dude who went west to seek his fortune in the California gold rush. He made his fortune alright, but from a pair of work pants he devised rather than from panning gold.

When young Strauss arrived in California he had hopes of selling tough canvas fabric for tents and covers on Conestoga wagons. When he told a miner what he had for sale the response was: "Should have brought pants." That started Levi to thinking. He took a few yards of his tough fabric and made them into a pair of work pants for the miner. And that is how the first pair of Levi's pants were created.

Levi's real popularity began in the 1960's when it seems everyone discovered the joys of wearing blue jeans. Baby diapers, cocktail dresses and men's suits were all fashioned from blue denim.

To capitalize on the blue jean mania Knickerbocker Toy Company manufactured a boy and girl designated the "Official Levis Denim Rag Doll." They sold at retail toy counters and from catalogs in 1974. Three sizes were available: 10-inch for about $2.00, 17-inch for about $5.00, and 25½-inch for about $11.00.

The dolls are made of blue denim, even the faces. Eyes, mouth, and freckles are painted; the nose is a rivet. The boy doll has orange yarn hair, the girl yellow yarn pigtails. Both wear removable blue denim jackets, the boy over a blue-striped shirt, the girl over a red-checkered shirt.

The boy and girl doll, 10-inch, authorized by Levi Strauss were sold in several sizes at the retail level. L. Zablotney. $5.00 each.

In 1974 Levi Strauss authorized the Knickerbocker Toy Company to manufacture the official Levi Denim Rag Doll. The doll was made entirely of pale blue denim. The only removable article of clothing is the jacket, which covers a red and white checked shirt. The hair is yellow yarn, eyes, mouth and freckles are painted, the nose is a rivet. The dolls came in three sizes: 10, 17, and 25-inch. This doll is the 17-inch. Marks: "Levi Strauss & Co./ by Knickerbocker Toy Co., Inc. 73/ Made in Taiwan," on label. $6.00.

Libby canned foods, products of Libby, McNeil & Libby. One of this canned food company's most successful promotions was **Libby** the talking doll. It was conceived by P.J. Peters, Marketing Services Director, and was produced by Mattel, Inc. It is interesting to note, the production and final delivery of the doll took approximately eight months. October, 1974 consumers heard of **Libby** on television commercials, Sunday comics, and on posters in stores that carried Libby brands.

The company was bombarded with requests for the $5.95 doll, far exceeding their expectations. Many people wrote, saying Libby was the name of their child and the **Libby** doll had special meaning for them.

The doll is 14-inches high, lithographed cloth, has yellow yarn hair, one tooth shows below her line-smile. Painted eyes glance upward, **Libby** wears a red blouse marked: Libby's Libby's Libby's.

By pulling a cord the doll says eleven different messages, including, "Will you tell me a story?" "Let's have a tea party for all our friends." And of course it says, "Libby's, Libby's, Libby's, on the label, label, label."

A *Doboy* doll was offered by a Texas company that produces Light Crust Flour. The 13-inch doll is lithographed with a gray Texas-sized hat, black cowboy boots, blue jacket and a string tie. The doll was probably issued in the early 70's. Marks: "DOBOY" on hat; "Light Crust Doughboys," on back. $6.00.

The 14-inch *Libby* doll was manufactured by Mattel for the company that sells Libby canned foods. The cloth doll has yellow yarn hair tied in two pony-tails, painted eyes, mouth showing one tooth, nose, and freckles. The red dress is also the body, it has a white ruffle around the bottom to match her white leather-like shoes. By pulling the cord the doll says eleven different sentences. Marks: "Libby's/Libby's/Libby's," on front of dress. $10.00.

Light Crust Flour. A prestuffed cloth **Doboy** doll was offered by a company producing this brand of flour. The doll was purchased in Austin, Texas, but no listing was found there for a Light Crust Flour Company. An old recipe booklet was found for Light Crust Flour that was issued by the Burrus Mill and Elevator Company at Fort Worth, Texas. This may be the company that produces the flour today.

The 13-inch doll is lithographed in Texas garb: cowboy hat, cowboy boots, blue jacket, and string tie. It is believed this doll was available throughout the southwest.

Lion Uniform Company. In 1947 the first **Lion Uniform** doll was introduced and it was used for approximately five years. The company conceived the idea, designed the doll, and manufactured the doll's uniforms, which are duplicates of their client's uniforms.

The concept of the dolls was to replace the usual calling card. Salesmen called on clients and gave them a doll dressed in that company's official uniform. Unlike a small card, the 13-inch doll was difficult to misplace. The dolls were also sold by mail and used as give-aways.

The doll resembles a young man and is made of hard plastic with molded/painted features and boots. An unusual feature of this doll is the open/closed mouth that shows a molded tongue.

The first **Lion Uniform** dolls were made from heavy plastic that was totally painted. The features were carefully painted and the labels on the uniforms were cloth rather than paper. On the bottom of one foot the older dolls are incised or have a sticker reading: "Old King Cole/Canton, Ohio," which may be the manufacturer. they were also marked LION, on the back.

The later dolls are made from the same mold, but from a lightweight plastic with faintly painted facial features. The later dolls wear uniforms with paper labels such as: Arco, Shell, Getty, and Citco.

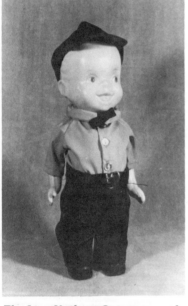

The Lion Uniform Company used a 13-inch doll as a calling card to obtain new accounts from 1947 to about 1952. Early dolls were made from heavy plastic and were totally painted. This model is a later copy and is lightweight plastic with faintly painted facial features and boots. The uniform consists of Navy blue pants and cap with a pale blue shirt and a black bow tie. Marks: "Made in H H," on soles of boots; "Made in Hong Kong," faintly stamped on back of neck; "LION," in center of back. $25.00.

The general office of the company in Dayton, Ohio have a display of **Lion Uniform** dolls showing the changes in trends, particularly in the style and construction of hats. The company generously mailed a doll for us to photograph for the book.

Listerine Antiseptic. This mouth wash had a list of premiums that could be obtained for certain amounts of points. The points were listed on the various sizes of mouth wash. In 1971 a **Raggedy Ann** doll was available for 100 points.

Panda Bears, Papa, Mamma, and **Baby,** were also available on this plan. The bears were black and white plush with a red bow around the neck. So many points were needed to obtain the premiums, it is doubtful many were redeemed. For example, it was necessary to purchase 15 medium-sized bottles of mouth wash to obtain the points needed for one Papa Bear.

Litter Green. In 1973 this brand of cat litter offered a cloth cat for $2.98. The cat measured 6-inches by 12-inches.

Little Crow Foods. This 75-year old Indiana company offered a **Gretchen** cloth doll on packages of their Coco Wheat cereal continuously from 1949 through 1966.

Gretchen first appeared in 1949 when the product she represents was ten-years old. The 13-inch doll was printed on a sheet of fabric to be cut, sewn, and filled for completion. The doll has yellow hair, a crooked smile, blue eyes, and arms and legs that are cut separate from the body.

The printed clothing consists of a red and white checked dress, white waist apron with ruffles over the shoulders, hair ribbon, and shoes with ankle straps. The doll is unmarked.

The 13-inch unmarked *Gretchen* doll was advertised on boxes of Coco Wheat cereal for 17 years, from 1949 to 1966. During that time the price only changed from 25¢ to 35¢. The cereal continues to be marketed by Little Crow Foods. The doll has yellow hair, a crooked smile, blue eyes, red and white checked dress, and a white apron. The doll was sold on a sheet of fabric to be completed by the owner. This seamstress chose to make the seam on the outside. Unmarked. Courtesy Ralph's Antique Dolls. $20.00.

Little Debbie Cakes. This brand of bakery goods offered a common 8-inch plastic doll with a stapled on taffeta dress and a straw hat. It is unmarked.

Lofties by Lawrence. This must be a line of fine quality women's clothing judging from the two outfits for this small display mannequin. The 24-inch figure fits on a pedestal and has molded painted features and shoes.

A 24-inch tall store mannequin wears an elegant two-piece boucle' suit. On the easel is a two-piece green wool suit trimmed in black. This mannequin must have been used to promote a top quality line of ladies' apparel. Marks: "Lofties/by Lawrence ® R." A. Wolfe collection, David Nelson, James Giokas photographers. $25.00.

Long John Silver's Seafood Shoppes. From 1972 through 1974 four cloth dolls were sold for $1.00 from their restaurants. The dolls were manufactured by Ike Sutton of Orange, New Jersey.

The first doll was a 17-inch **Long John Silver**, which is a copy of the character appearing on the company's logo. The lithographed doll has a peg-leg, a blue beard, and a patch over one eye. The clothing includes a pirate hat with skull and cross bones and a black jacket.

The second doll was a 13-inch **Parrot** wearing a pirate hat and a patch over one eye.

Next were a 13-inch **Boy** doll and a 12-inch **Girl** doll. Both wear a pirate hat and their arms and legs are cut free from the body.

The first doll offered, in 1972, by Long John Silver Seafood Shoppes was *Long John Silver* himself. It is 17-inches tall, has a peg-leg and patch over one eye. The doll is colorful with a black jacket, orange hair, and blue pants. Unmarked. $5.00.

The second doll offered by the Long John Silver Seafood Shoppes was a parrot. The *Parrot* doll is green with an orange beak. Unmarked. $3.00.

In 1974 a 13-inch boy and a 12-inch girl doll were offered by this franchise. Both wear a pirate hat and have arms and legs cut free from the body. The boy has yellow shirt, and blue pants to match the hat. Unmarked. $3.00.

The Long John Silver Seafood Shoppe girl doll wears a yellow dress, blue hat, has a watermelon mouth, circle eyes and a sprinkling of freckles. Unmarked. $3.00.

Lovable Bras. An 8-inch plush **Baby Bear** was used to promote a line of sheer bras by

Lovable called Baby Bares. The thumbsucking bear cost $2.00 plus 50¢ handling and the coupon included on the bra package.

The little bear has a vinyl mask face with an open mouth that fits his vinyl thumb. The painted eyes glance upward, painted knob nose, a few freckles dot the fat cheeks. This toy was available in the mid-1970's.

Baby Bear is plush with a vinyl mask face and hands. The distinguishing features of the bear is the open mouth that accomodates the thumb. Unmarked. $4.00.

Lucerne Ice Cream, a product of Safeway Stores. The common 7-inch plastic dolls were offered for $1.85 with each coupon and order blank in specially marked half-gallon cartons of Lucerene Ice Cream. Thirty dolls in native costumes were available in the early 1970's.

Lustre Creme. Two hard plastic dolls named **Starlet** and **Movie Star** were offered for $1.00 each by this shampoo, which is no longer being sold. The smaller doll, **Starlet** is 8-inches tall, has dark brown to blonde glued on wig, blue sleep eyes, and a closed mouth. The doll is jointed at the neck, shoulder, and hip and is a walker that moves its head from side-to-side when the legs move back and forth. **Scarlet** wears a pink dress, some are taffeta and some are cotton, both with blue trim. A booklet came with the doll that gave instructions for shampooing the doll's hair. Three Vogue patterns for doll clothing were also available.

The **Movie Star** doll is the same, except one-inch larger. It is dressed in the same style pink dress with blue trim. A 10-piece accessory set was also available with this doll.

In 1967 a pink long-fur fabric **Yorkie** dog was offered by this shampoo. The 11-inch dog is in a sitting position, has black button eyes, pom-pom nose, and red felt tongue. The dog cost $2.00 plus one Lustre Cream label.

Lustre Creme Shampoo offered the *Yorkie* dog in 1967. The dog is pink plush with long white hair. It has button eyes, black pom-pom nose, and a red felt tongue. Marks: "Yorkie Offer/See Other Side," under Yorkie's picture on front of paper tag around neck; "Yours For Only $2.00," on back of tag. A. Wolfe collection, James Giokas her. $6.00.

M

MD Bathroom Toilet Tissue, a product of Georgia-Pacific Corp. Several top quality cloth dolls have been offered by this product. In 1966 the MD twins **Maisy** and **Daisy** were introduced. The 17½-inch cloth dolls are dressed in a red jumper or a blue jumper. One doll is winking. Both have actual button eyes, yellow yarn hair tied with ribbons and removable jumpers and blouses. The body is pink cotton fabric with polka dot legs to match the blouses. The offer was extended to 1971. The dolls are unmarked, but can be identified from other issues of the twins by the eyes, hair, and mouth. The mouth on the doll with both eyes open is a red dot; the winking doll has a line smile.

The next edition (date unknown) of the twins is smaller, 16-inches, and varies slightly from the 1966 pair. This doll has yarn hair, button eyes, and a watermelon slice mouth. It wears either a pink outfit or an aqua one.

The MD Toilet Tissue twins changed a bit when reissued. They are 16-inches, wear pink and aqua, and the shape of the mouth is different. Unmarked. J. Ciolek collection, Visual Images photographer. $6.00.

In 1966 twin *Maisy* and *Daisy* cloth dolls were introduced by MD Toilet Tissue. The 18-inch dolls have yarn hair, button eyes, and removable jumper and blouse. The dolls were dressed in either red or blue. This doll is missing her clothing. The companion doll has a winking eye. Unmarked. $8.00.

MD Toilet Tissue's 1977 *Daisy* doll wears pink. Marks: "Daisy," on skirt. $3.00.

Older twin dolls had one twin winking, the 1977 pair both have open lithographed button eyes. Marks: "Maisy," on skirt. $3.00.

In 1977 the twins were offered again. They are 16-inches and wear aqua and pink, but have lithographed button eyes and lithographed hair tied with ribbons. The skirt of the removable jumper is marked **Maisy** or **Daisy**. The blouse is also the upper body.

Besides **Maisy** and **Daisy** dolls MD Toilet Tissue also offered two series of cloth dolls taken from famous children's stories. The first series, the *Wizard of Oz* characters, came out in 1971. The **Tin Woodman** and **Scarecrow** are 18-inches tall. The **Tin Woodman's** lithographed suit is gray with a bright red heart. The **Scarecrow** is a grouchy looking character. **Cowardly Lion** is 9-inches and **Dorothy** is 16-inches tall. She looks a bit like the MD twins. She has yellow lithographed hair, two dot eyes, dotted blouse, and a lithographed orange skirt. Each doll cost $1.00 plus a label. These dolls are unmarked.

In 1971 MD Toilet Tissue offered four "Wizard of OZ" dolls. *Dorothy*, 16-inches tall looks a bit like their *Maisy* and *Daisy* dolls. She has lithographed pony-tails, a triangle nose, circle eyes, and a line mouth. Her orange skirt and blouse are lithographed. Unmarked. $6.00.

MD Toilet Tissue's "Scarecow" doll is a frowning fellow, 18-inches tall. The Oz dolls cost $1.00 each plus labels. Unmarked. $6.00.

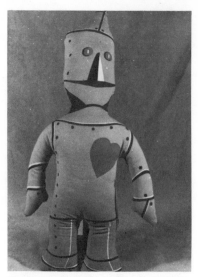

The gray *Tin Woodman* doll has a bright red heart and is 18-inches tall. Unmarked. $6.00.

The Oz series of dolls was so popular, in 1974 the company decided to offer another set of dolls, this time four characters from *Alice in Wonderland* for

$2.50 each. The 19-inch **Mad Hatter** has a removable felt jacket, **Cheshire Cat**, 11-inches, is a gorgeous three-dimensional creature in purple and orange

Mad Hatter is 19-inches tall with his high top hat. He wears a removable felt jacket and a big orange polka-dot bow tie. The numbers "10/6" are the only marks on the doll. The "Alice" series of cloth dolls cost $2.50 each. $6.00.

In 1974 MD Toilet Tissue offered four cloth "Alice in Wonderland" dolls. The *Alice* doll is the same as the 1977 twins, except the skirt is not marked *Maisy* or *Daisy*. *Alice* is 16-inches. Unmarked. $6.00.

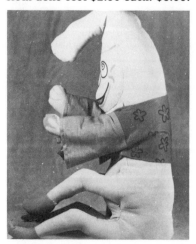

The six-legged *Caterpillar* doll is aqua with a removable red and blue vest. The "Alice" series is relatively intricate compared to most cloth advertising dolls. In the sitting position, the *Caterpillar* is 13½-inches tall. Unmarked. $8.00.

Cheshire Cat is a masterpiece three-dimensional doll. It is 11-inches long and made of purple fabric with markings like a striped cat. **Caterpillar** is 13½-inches with red and blue vest and six comically positioned legs. **Alice**, 16-inches, will look familiar; she is also the 1977 **Maisy** doll. Her hair is worn in pigtails with real blue satin ribbons, a blue removable pinafore or jumper with a lace border, worn over a blue and white polka dot body. Eyes are lithographed four-hole buttons. Dolls are unmarked.

Ma Brown Pickles. The **Ma Brown** doll is exceptionally well-designed and costumed. It is 15-inches high, all vinyl with grandmotherly features, platinum-gray rooted wig, and wearing glasses. She wears a long blue and white checked dress with a white dicky and a waist apron.

Ma Brown cost $2.95 plus two pickle jar labels.

and orange fabic lithographed to resemble a striped cat. Unmarked. $8.00.

Ma Brown of Ma Brown Pickles is a 15-inch vinyl grandmother-type doll. The gray hair is rooted, facial features are painted. She wears a blue and white checked dress with a long skirt that barely shows her white shoes. Over the dress is an organdy apron marked: ''Ma Brown,'' in script. $20.00.

Mack Truck Company. This company has used a bulldog trademark for many years. We found the trademark duplicated in a 10-inch red plush dog. The felt teeth gave it a ferocious look. Its white plastic collar is marked "Mack."

Magic Cow. This powdered drink mix offered a **Magic Cow** inflatable swim ring in 1978. The floating toy was a ring with a cow's head in front. It cost $1.50 and the offer expired in October of 1978.

Malted Cereal Co. Malt Breakfast Food, a cereal produced by this company, used a little Dutch girl trademark. To my knowledge the cereal has been unavailable for many years. A 1904 ad from The Designer announces a **Gretchen** doll to be given free to anyone sending the name and address of their favorite grocer.

A stipulation of the ad: "the doll is available only East of the Rocky Mountains," brings back memories of disappointments I experienced as a child living in Utah. It seemed either all magazine offers were unavailable or they cost more if you lived in that far-away land West of the Rocky Mountains.

The **Gretchen** doll provided to us by Mrs. Coghlan is different from the Dutch girl pictured on the ad and is also different from the girl on the label. The trademark pictured on the ad for the doll appears to be a toddler in a long dress. The 8-inch **Gretchen** doll is an older girl in a short skirt. It is printed full front and back with arms cut free from the body. The clothes consist of a blue jumper with a short, pumpkin-shaped skirt, wooden shoes, long stockings and a hat with a point at each ear and a third point in back that is made by sewing a dart.

The Malted Cereal Company also offered dolls printed by Art Fabric and games. The booklet describing the offer was printed in 1904.

In 1905 an 8-inch cloth *Gretchen* doll was offered free by sending the name of your grocer to The Malted Cereals Company. The doll wears a blue jumper with a short pumpkin-shaped skirt, wooden shoes, long wrinkled stockings, white hat, and white blouse. The face looks like a photographic process was used. The doll itself is unmarked, but since it is uncut, positive identification is possible from the background fabric. Marks: "GRETCHEN/The Malt/Breakfast Food/DOLL," plus the directions for completing the doll. P. Coghlan collection. $35.00.

Malto-Rice. See American Rice & Foods Manufacturing Co.

Manor House Frozen Pot Pies, a product of Safeway Stores. The common 8-inch plastic doll dressed in 30 different International costumes was available for $1.95.

Marquette Corp. See National Blue Ribbon Freezer Food Service.

Mary Merritt's Doll Museum. To advertise her doll

museum, it was natural for Marjorie Marritt Darrah to chose a doll. The 13-inch cloth doll is a fascimile of the museum's trademark doll--a dear bisque Jumeau. To me the cloth doll has an Amish look that is appropriate, because the museum is located in Pennsylvania, a state known for its Amish population.

The Mary Merritt Doll Museum in Pennsylvania has offered a cloth doll from 1974 to the present. The doll is a cloth rendition of the museum's trademark--a lovely bisque Jumeau. The 13-inch doll wears a red dress with a blue and white cape, black shoes, and a red hat that leaves no hair showing. Marks: "Mary Merritt Doll Museum," on the back. $2.00 still available.

The lithographed face is surrounded by a hat that leaves no hair showing. Printed attire matches her bisque counterpart: red dress with blue and white tiered cape, black shoes tied with a bow. The doll, in patriotic colors, fits in well with the nation's bicentennial celebration. It was manufactured in 1974 and was still available in 1980. The doll cost $1.95 and was ordered directly from the museum, rather than from the Chase Bag Company, who manufactured it and usually also handles the mailing.

Mason Mints, a product of Sweets Candy Company. **Peppermint Pattie** was one of four bean-bag type dolls named for candy products by the Hasbro Toy Company. The 10-inch doll wears a pink nylon tricot snow suit that is also the body of the doll. The body is filled with styrofoam pellets. A black and white scarf is wrapped around the neck and a stocking cap of the same material is sewn to the head. The face and hands are vinyl. The doll was sold at retail stores in 1973. Other dolls in the series were **Baby Ruth, Dots,** and Good and Plenty's **Choo Choo Charlie**.

One of four bean-bag dolls manufactured by Hasbro and named for candy products. The body and limbs are made from pink nylon tricot to resemble a snowsuit. The face and hands are vinyl. A black and white scarf is wrapped around the neck and head. *Peppermint Patty* was named for Mason Mints, a round mint candy bar, produced by the Sweets Candy Company. $8.00.

Maxwell House Coffee.

Three bears, sans Goldilocks, were offered in 1971 for $4.95. The price included all three brown plush bears in graduated sizes.

Another bear, a Koala, could also be purchased in 1971. The Koala cost $1.75 plus a proof-of-purchase.

The "Good to the last drop" coffee received its slogan from a president and its name from a hotel. Farm boy, Joel Cheek, when still in his twenties, was peddling a special blend of coffee he originated. Among his clients was the plush Maxwell House of Nashville, Tennessee. Cheek was assured success when the hotel's guests preferred his brew. He was quick to dub his blend Maxwell House Coffee.

The slogan came later when Theodore Roosevelt was a guest at the Hermitage, Andrew Jackson's old home. Asked if he wanted a second cup, Roosevelt exclaimed: "Will I have another? Delighted! It's good to the last drop."

One of three bears that were offered in 1971 by Maxwell House Coffee. The brown plush bear wears a striped shirt and night cap. L. Zablotney collection. $8.00.

Maypo Cereal.

This short-lived cereal offered a vinyl **Marky Maypo** figure that held a full-sized cereal bowl. **Marky Maypo** is dressed in cowboy attire, including a cowboy hat perched on protruding ears. The 10-inch molded/painted figure sits, his hands hold the bowl between his outstretched legs. The bowl was not included. Date unknown.

A clever *Marky Maypo* doll that would fit around a bowl of cereal was offered by Maypo Cereal. The 10-inch plastic figure is dressed in cowboy clothes including a red hat that sits on protruding ears; boots, gloves and scarf match the hat. Marks: "MARKY/MAYPO," on hat. A. Leonard collection. $10.00.

Mayrose Bacon,

a product of Swift & Company. In 1973 a **Marty Mayrose** doll of soft vinyl was offered for $1.25. The 7-inch molded/painted doll represents an old-fashioned butcher with a handle-bar mustache, straw hat, white bib apron (this one has a rose near one shoulder), black pants and a red shirt. The only moveable part is the head. Some literature has referred to this as a bank, but the one in my possession has no slot for money.

The 7-inch *Marty Mayrose* doll was manufactured in 1973 to advertise Swift & Company's Mayrose Bacon. *Marty* is an old fashioned butcher with a handle-bar mustache, straw hat, and a white bib apron with a rose at the shoulder. The molded/painted soft vinyl doll has a movable head. Marks: "Swift & Co./1973," incised on bottom of feet. $3.00.

McDonald Corporation.

This world-famous restaurant chain has offered several cloth premium dolls and they have also authorized toy manufacturers to produce McDonaldland characters for the retail market.

The clever trademark figures of this giant corporation are only a small part of McDonald's success story. The story began after World War II, when two New England brothers, named McDonald, started a hamburger stand in San Bernardino, California. Out of desperation trying to keep a full staff of help, they decided to eliminate the need for so many employees. Out went the long menu, the dishes, and the silverware. They offered only hamburgers, fries, and drinks. Everything was prepared in advance, was uniform, and was served on paper plates--the quick food restaurant was born. That was the first of many innovative ideas.

In 1954 the brothers were talked into selling franchises and in time a concept was devised for a franchise/tenant that provided additional dollars for the corporation. By now the restaurant's namesakes had turned the leadership over to others who had untiring ambition and total commitment. Departing from the usual preference for dependable fulltime help McDonald's chose a 90% part-time labor force of students and housewives, enabling them to staff heavily during rush hours. The public soon learned, if they were in a hurry, the place to go was McDonald's.

Dollars and imagination were invested in McDonald's advertising. At one point they were the second largest television advertiser. Billions of hamburgers have been sold since the first was served on a paper plate in San Bernardino. This corporation continues to amaze the business world with its records of success.

What part the trademark figures played in this success story is impossible to measure. The "real life" Ronald McDonald, "the McFriendliest fellow in town," to quote the song, made his public debut in 1966 in Washington, D.C., but it was five years later that the first **Ronald McDonald** doll was available. This 16-inch replica of the clown spokesman for McDonald's was offered to McDonald franchises for their exclusive use--as a premium to sell or to use as a giveaway. The first **Ronald** doll was available for three years, from 1971 to 1974. In many localities newspapers and radio advertised **Ronald** for $1.25 at McDonald Restaurants.

During that three-year period there were actually two dolls issued. They vary a bit--the first

223

has a pointed collar and a tab at the top of the zipper. The second has a rounded collar and no tab on the lithographed zipper.

Ronald McDonald introduced in 1971. He is copied from the "real life" clown spokesman for the giant chain of hamburger restaurants. Marks: a golden "M" on each of three pockets; "RONALD/ McDONALD ® " on the back. $5.00.

A reprinting of the "Ronald" doll resulted in a slightly different *Ronald.* Notice the points of the collar and the missing zipper tab. Marks: an "M" on each of three pockets. $5.00.

In 1972 the "real life" Ronald underwent some costume changes, but again it was five years before they were reflected in a doll. The third **Ronald McDonald** doll, which has the changes, was made available to franchises in February 1977.

The 1977 *Ronald McDonald* doll looks like a little brother to the other two. He is three inches shorter, 13-inches tall. The face is changed and the yellow zipper suit shows the red and white striped shirt at the neck. Marks: the Golden Arches on the pockets are black with "McDonald's" ® at the base; a large "M" ® on the back. $3.00.

The most noticable difference in the new doll is the size--it looks like a little brother, because it is three-inches shorter, 13-inches tall. The face and costume are different too. The face of the 1977 version looks like that of a real person painted to resemble a clown. The natural smile with teeth shows under the red-painted clown smile. The contour of the hair is different from the earlier dolls.

The major change in the costume concerns the placement and size of the pockets. Also the zippered suit shows the striped shirt at the neck of this doll.

Free hand puppet given in 1977. $1.00.

Correspondence mentioned only one cloth **Hamburglar** premium doll, but we found two. One is 17-inches tall and dressed in a

The 17-inch *Hamburglar* doll was sold at McDonald's Restaurants for only one year, 1972. The doll wears a jail-striped black and white suit, a long orange tie with yellow dots, eye mask, tricornered hat, yellow shoes, and a detachable cape. Marks: "McDonald's/Hamburglar." $7.00.

black and white jail suit with a detachable cape. The other **Hamburglar** is 15-inches tall and wears a purple outfit with a lithographed cape. The scale of body proportions and facial features differ, but both are unmistakably the same doll.

Another *Hamburglar* doll was found. This one is 15-inches tall and looks a bit different from the more widely known *Hamburglar* doll. It wears a purple hat and a purple lithographed cape. Marks: "M," on front of hat; "McDonald's/Hamburglar ® " on the back. K. Miller collection. $7.00.

A mystery is the 15-inch cloth **Big Mac** doll. The company mentioned no **Big Mac** premium doll, nor licensing one for retail sales. The owner recalls purchasing it at a McDonald's Restaurant so it is probably a premium that has been forgotten. The head of the doll is in the shape of the Big Mac hamburger with a tiny blue cap perched on top. It wears a blue suit with a star badge lithographed on the front.

The first McDonald character to be sold on the retail market was the **Big Mac** hand puppet that appeared in Montgomery Ward's Christmas catalog of 1974. The familiar vinyl hamburger-shaped head on a blue cloth policeman's jacket was offered, along with an entire McDonald Village.

This 15-inch *Big Mac* doll is a mystery. The company mentions no *Big Mac* premium doll nor giving authority for this *Big Mac* to be sold on the retail market. The doll wears a blue policeman's uniform with a star on the front and a lithographed whistle hanging from the belt. Marks: "M," on the small hat; "McDonald's/Big Mac $^®$" on the back. K. Miller collection. $7.00.

For the Christmas 1976 season Remco introduced seven McDonaldland characters from the McDonald television commercials. This was the first time McDonald licensed a toy company to produce the characters for consumer purchase outside the restaurants. The vinyl dolls range from 6 to 8-inches tall and are intricate in detailing and the design of clothing. The removable cloth costumes are careful copies of those seen on television and have tiny buttons, belts, and accessories. The characters are: **Ronald McDonald, Big Mac, Hamburglar, Grimace, Mayor McCheese, Captain Crook,** and the **Professor.**

Remco produced seven McDonaldland characters in 1976 for the retail market. *Ronald McDonald* is vinyl. The gloves, big shoes, and striped stockings are molded/painted. The suit is removable nylon knit. This *Ronald's* suit is missing the zipper up the front. Marks: a golden arch on the three front pockets, the lower one also has "McDonald's $^®$; REMCO 1976/ Pat. Pend/1976 McDonald's/ System, Inc./Made in/Hong Kong," on back of doll.

McDonald's *Hamburglar* wears a black cape and hat over a black and white striped suit. The tie is red with yellow dots to match the shoes. Similar to the other dolls in the series, the *Hamburglar* has a soft vinyl head with carefully molded/painted detail. Marks: "REMCO 1976/Pat. Pend./1976 McDonald's/System, Inc./Made in/Hong Kong." $5.00.

226

Big Mac's head looks like the bun, two hamburger patties and a slice of cheese. A molded vinyl hat looks very small on such a large head. *Big Mac* wears a blue policeman's uniform with a miniature plastic whistle attached to the collar by a cord. Marks: "REMCO 1976/Pat. Pend./1976 McDonald's/System, Inc./Made in/Hong Kong," on back of doll. $5.00.

Captain Crook is dressed like a pirate and carries a large sword. Marks: "REMCO 1976/Pat. Pend./ 1976 McDonald's/System, Inc./ Made in/Hong Kong," on back of doll. $5.00.

The mayor of McDonaldland is *Mayor McCheese*. The mayor wears a vest, jacket, and striped pants. In his hand are a pair of glasses on a string. The doll is constructed with a nob in the back that moves the head. Marks: "REMCO 1976/Pat. Pend./1976 McDonald's/System, Inc./Made in/Hong Kong," on back of doll. $5.00.

The *Professor* carries some unidentified gadgets in the pockets of his labratory coat. Marks: "REMCO 1976/ Pat. Pend./1976 McDonald's /System, Inc./Made in/Hong Kong," on back of doll. $5.00.

The McDonaldland dolls sold on the retail level for about $5.00 each, but were often available for less at discount stores. They were manufactured in Hong Kong and are marked.

Grimace is made of purple plush fabric with vinyl feet. $4.00.

Free hand puppets of *Mayor McCheese* were given at some McDonald restaurants. $1.00.

Saint Patrick's day was celebrated at McDonald's by giving free *Uncle O'Grimacey* hand puppets. $1.00.

McIntosh Country Apples. In 1969 two 16½-inch cloth dolls, **Betty** and **Billy** came from McIntosh Country, New York.

Billy is one of two 16½-inch cloth dolls used to advertise apples. *Billy* has red hair and wears a yellow shirt, and short pants. Marks: "Billy/From/McINTOSH/COUNTRY," printed in a red apple on the front of his shirt. A. Pfister collection. $6.00.

Betty the companion doll to *Billy*. Marks: "Betty/From/McINTOSH/-COUNTRY." A. Pfister collection.

Mennen Shaving Lotion. An exact replica of the Mennen Shaving Lotion bottle was produced in cloth. The 10-inch prestuffed replica is complete with lithographed label. Date and details are unknown.

This 10-inch cloth bottle is a copy of the Mennen Shaving Lotion bottle. How or when it was offered is not known. (For other Mennen dolls see Baby Magic dolls.) $3.00.

Michelin Tires.

A 25-inch, inflatable *Michelin Tire Man* used as displays in Michelin Tire dealerships. Doll is white with blue printing. $3.00.

Miller Beer. A gold-painted display figure was distributed to businesses selling Miller High Life Beer in the 1950's.

In 1950 Miller's High Life Beer distributed a 7½-inch display figure to dealers. The plastic figural is painted gold and depicts a young woman wearing a sombrero, a short full skirt, and boots. Marks: "Miller's/High Life Beer," on front of pedestal in red letters; "Form No. 70/Miller Brewing Company/Milwaukee, Wisc./Thomas A. Schutz Co./Chicago," on the back of base. K. Lansdowne collection. $18.00.

Minnesota Sales Co. As with so many old dolls, our information comes primarily from the doll itself. Mr. Ralph Griffith, in his fine doll museum, has a 21-inch cloth doll with a matching 6¼-inch doll. The original owner apparently saved some of the background fabric the doll was printed on and wrapped it around the doll to provide identification. The fabric reads:

MY DEAR DOLLY
(CLOTH DOLL)
c 1924
The Minnesota Sales Co.
Minneapolis, Minn.

The 21-inch *My Dear Dolly* and her 6¼-inch matching dolly were copyrighted in 1924. From a scrap of fabric wrapped around the doll we learn it was offered by the Minnesota Sales Company. The doll's dress is white with blue trim and yellow flowers. The black shoes are three-dimensional to allow the doll to stand. Marks: "MY DEAR DOLLY /(CLOTH DOLL)/ © 1924/The Minnesota Sales Co./Minneapolis Minn.," all printed on attached fabric. Courtesy Ralph's Antique Dolls. $35.00 to $50.00.

Further information on the **My Dear Dolly** was found in the August 1971 issue of Doll News. According to collectors several of these dolls have been produced in various sizes. The background fabric of some of these dolls state they were printed as early as 1918 by Saalfield Publishing Company and were designed by Frances Brundage. The doll offered by Minnesota Sales Company may have been printed by Saalfield, but was probably not designed by Brundage. It does not have the angelic face the other **My Dear Dolly** dolls have that are illustrated in Doll News.

Mission Macaroni Company. This Washington company offers many premiums including a cloth **J.P. Patches** doll for $2.50 plus two Mission Macaroni wrappers. The 14-inch doll represents a clown dressed in a patched suit.

J.P. Patches is one of several premiums offered by the Mission Macaroni Company. The 14-inch cloth doll is a clown dressed in a patched outfit. The high-top hat is marked. "J.P."J. Varsalona collection. $8.00.

Mobil Oil Company. A bendable foam rubber man representing a service station attendant holding a cardboard can of Mobil Oil in one hand and pointing with the other hand was found.

Dolls made from this material often begin to disintegrate after a few years.

The trademark figure used by Mobil Oil is not a service station attendant, it is Pegasus, the Flying Red Horse from Greek mythology. The trademark was originally used in 1911 by foreign subsidiaries. In 1933 it moved stateside and has been a dominant element in Mobil's advertising ever since.

The 5-inch *Mobil Oil* doll is made of foam latex and is beginning to disintegrate. The green suit is unpainted foam; face and hands are painted. The figure holds a miniature can of Mobil Oil. Marks: the flying red horse, Pegasus, which is the company's emblem is on the hat and shirt pocket. $4.00.

Mohawk Carpet Company. The trademark figure for this line of carpets is an Indian

Mohawk Tommy is the trademark for the Mohawk Carpet Company. Marks: "Mohawk/Tommy," on loin cloth; "Mohawk Carpet" on back. $6.00.

boy, **Mohawk Tommy**. A cloth doll copied from the figure was used sometime in the early 1970's. The 16-inch doll wears a single feather, a loin cloth, and carries a quiver filled with arrows, all printed on a heavy woven fabric.

Montgomery Ward. This company, largely noted for its catalog service, has sold at least two dolls that represent Montgomery Ward trademarks.

Carol Brent was available in doll form in the 1961 catalog. The doll, manufactured by Ideal, is 15-inches tall, jointed vinyl, has a closed mouth, painted side-glance eyes, and rooted upswept wig. Several costumes were also available.

The other trademark doll is **Wendy Ward** and it was available through the catalog in 1964. **Wendy** is 11-inches tall, jointed plastic and vinyl, closed mouth and open/shut eyes. The doll came with three wigs. Various outfits were also available.

Robert More Perfume Company. In 1925 an **Alice May** doll was given free by this Chicago perfume company in exchange for selling 20 bottles of perfume at 15¢ each. The doll is 1½-feet tall, with hair that is bobbed with bangs. It has a dotted Swiss Voile dress trimmed with lace and a cap to match. The doll has open/shut eyes and a cry box.

Morton Salt, a division of Morton-Norwich Products, Inc. Most everyone is familiar with the Morton salt trademark, a young girl carrying an umbrella and a can of Morton Salt with the slogan: "When it rains, it pours." The trademark is a natural for an advertising doll, but to our knowledge only two have been made, one a premium, the other for the retail market.

Morton Salt offered an 8-inch vinyl doll in the early 1970's. Unfortunately it does not resemble the much loved girl on their label. The doll has freckles, rooted wig, and side-glance eyes. She wears plastic boots, and a yellow or black raincoat with matching hat. Marks: "Hong Kong," on back of neck. $4.00.

Mattel's *Morton Salt Girl* is one of three Shoppin' Pal dolls manufactured for the retail market. The doll is cloth, 14-inches high, with yarn hair, painted facial features, and mitten-shaped hands. It wears a yellow dress and carries a miniature cardboard can of Morton Salt. $10.00.

The Morton Salt premium doll is 8-inches high, vinyl, with freckles across the nose, rooted wig, and eyes that glance to the side. The attire is the only clue that this is the **Morton Salt Girl**. It wears plastic boots, yellow or black raincoat, and hat. The doll could be ordered from the company in limited localitites in the early 1970's.

The other **Morton Salt Girl** doll was manufactured by Mattel for retail sales. It sold in 1974 for about $6.00 but the doll didn't reach some markets until 1977. It is 14-inches high, all cloth with yarn hair, painted facial features with side-glance eyes and mitten-shaped pink hands.

The bodice and sleeves of the yellow dress are the upper body and filled with polyester fiber; the skirt is cut to hang free from the body. The doll carries a tiny replica can of Morton Salt. The doll is one of three in Mattel's Shoppin' Pal series. The other two are the **Cracker Jack Sailor** and the **Chicken of the Sea Mermaid**.

Morton Salt has offered other premiums: salt and pepper shakers and a series of mugs printed with the different Morton Salt girls from a curly-haired blonde to a straight-haired brunette and then, finally to the current blonde with braids.

The **Morton Salt Girl** became a trademark in 1914 when the 50 year-old company was looking for a way to advertise their new free-flowing salt. An agency was hired and a dozen ads were presented to the company head, Sterling Morton, son of the founder. Nothing really caught his eye. One of the quick thinking ad men remembered in the nick of time three rough sketches that had been brought along as extras, so he pulled these out.

In Morton's own words: "I was immediately struck with one. It showed a little girl with an umbrella over her head, rain falling, a package of salt under her arm, tilted backward with the spout open and salt running out. Perhaps the fact that my daughter Suzette was occupying a lot of my time and attention at that period had something to do with my interest!

"But, anyhow, it struck me that here was the whole story in a picture--that the message that the salt would run in damp weather was made beautifully evident."

Mountain Dew. This carbonated beverage chose a delightful **Hillbilly** doll to capitalize on the name of their product. The 18-inch doll has a vinyl head with a small white beard, painted smile,

Mountain Dew's 18-inch *Hillbilly* doll is especially well designed and costumed. Marks: "Drink/Mountain Dew," on a large round cloth sticker on back. K. Miller collection. $20.00.

and upward glancing eyes. It is dressed in backwoods garb: floppy hat, patched denim trousers, ragged at the bottom with only one strap fastened diagonally to hold them up, and a long, long sleeved gingham shirt. The feet are bare, of course. The date and method of dispersal are unkown.

Mr. Bubble. This bubble bath soap was sold in a Mr. Bubble bank for a short time. The plastic container has molded/painted eyes, nose, and mouth.

Mr. Bubble is really a container for bubble bath. It is 10-inches tall and made of pink plastic. Marks: "Mr./Bubble/Bubble Bath/Bank/32 fl. oz. (1 qt.)" R. Keelen collection. $1.00.

Mr. Clean, a product of Procter and Gamble. This cleaning liquid offered a **Mr. Clean** doll in 1961. The small 8-inch doll, manufactured by Ideal Toy Corporation, wears white shirt, pants, and shoes. The head is bald, a green loop earring hangs from one ear. Muscular arms are folded across the chest.

In 1961 the Ideal Toy Corporation manufactured a *Mr. Clean* doll copied from the trademark figure widely seen on television commercials for the cleaning preparation of the same name. The 8-inch vinyl doll depicts a man with muscular arms folded across the chest, bald head, and a green earring in one ear. Marks: "P & G," on one foot. K. Lansdowne collection. $20.00.

Mr. Galeski Photo Center,

a local film company in Richmond, Virginia. In 1963 this company ordered 6,000 cloth dolls from the Chase Bag Company of North Carolina. The dolls were a self-liquidating promotion in their camera shops for about two years. Some were sold at cost and some were given away to good customers with small children.

The doll was a reproduction of the company logo: an elf-like fellow with a tam perched to one side of his head, pointed ears, and long pointed feet.

The centers were sold in 1973 and no dolls were saved so we were unable to obtain a photo of the **Mr. Galeski** doll.

Mr. Quick Burger Restaurant.

Mr. Quick hand puppets were given free at this reataurant.

Mr. Quick hand puppet was given free at Mr. Quick Restaurants. $1.00.

Mr. Turtle Candy, a product of De Met Company. A 20-inch inflatable **Mr. Turtle** toy was copied from the figure used on the candy label. The turtle is dressed in formal attire that includes tails and a top hat.

The inflatable *Mr. Turtle* toy was used to promote the De Met Company's Mr. Turtle candy. Marks: "Mr. Turle ® " on shoe. R. Keelen collection. $4.00.

Mrs. Butterworth's Syrup. In 1975 a **Raggedy Ann** doll was available for $3.95 plus two labels. The doll is not the usual cloth doll, but is made with a soft round vinyl head and a hard vinyl body. The unusual body construction includes joints at the hips, knees, ankles, waist, elbows, shoulders, and neck. The hinge joints are similar to those on the G.I. Joe dolls. The waist and neck rotate on a flange. The hair is rooted red yarn and the face is painted. The doll wears a removable dress, long striped pants, and vinyl shoes.

Some advertising doll collectors may want to include the figural Mrs. Butterworth's Syrup bottle in their collections. In 1978 the company offered a free exotic vaction to the person who could devise the most creative costume for the shapely syrup bottle.

Mrs. Filbert's Tak'em Tubs of Pudding. In 1972, this product offered Dolls of All Lands (Belgium, U.S., England, France, Greece, and a Bride doll) for $1.00 plus five product lids per doll.

Munsingwear. This manufacturer of underclothing used a 7-inch vinyl copy of their penguin trademark ca. 1970.

Mrs. Butterworth's Syrup offered an unusual *Raggedy Ann* doll in 1975. The doll has 14 joints including ankles, knees, waist, and elbows. The joints are similar to those on the G.I. Joe dolls. The body is a firm vinyl, the head is soft vinyl with painted features. The hair is rooted red yarn. The dress, long striped pants, and shoes are removable. Marks: "® 1975 The Bobbs-Merrill Co., Inc./Nasco Doll, Inc./Made in Hong Kong," on back of head; "U.K. Pat. N. 1372947/ U.S.A. Pat. Pending/Tong Ind. Co./Hong Kong," on lower back; "Raggedy Ann," stamped on apron; "Hong Kong" on soles of both shoes. $5.00.

The Munsingwear penguin trademark figure is 7-inches tall and made of hard vinyl. Marks: "Munsingwear," on back. S. Brunell collection. $5.00.

Myer Publishing Company. A cloth **Lerner Newsboy** doll was used by this company in 1970. The prestuffed doll is 13-inches tall, has a freckled face and is carrying a newspaper with headlines: Extra, Extra.

In 1972 **Lerner Newspup** doll was also offerd by this company. It is 12-inches high with a lithographed collar and tag. The dog is brown with a white muzzle and paws.

235

In 1970 Myers Publishing Company offered a 13-inch cloth doll. The *Lerner Newsboy* doll is a freckle faced boy carrying a newspaper with headlines that read: "Extra, Extra." Marks: "Lerner Newsboy," on brim of hat; "Myers Publishing Co. 1970," on back. $6.00.

A brown and white *Lerner Newpup* was offered by Myers Publishing Company in 1972. Marks: "Lerner/Newspup," on red collar tag; "© 1972 Myers Publishing Company," on back. A. Pfister collection. $6.00.

N

Nabisco. The Nabisco Company is a case in point of the "American Dream," where a good idea, hard work, and promotion can turn pennies into a fortune. That is the story of Nabisco. Back in the 1890's small bakeries all over the country were mixing and baking batches of crackers and cookies. These were deposited in large barrels, and delivered to stores by horse and wagon. If mice didn't nibble on the contents it was only because the cat slept in the barrel. Besides breaking into pieces, the cracker often picked up the taste of whatever it had been placed next to along the way-- kerosene, pickles, or soap.

A Chicago lawyer, Adolphus A. Green, was asked to represent some bakers who were concerned about modernizing their business. He saw a tremendous opportunity to revolutionize and improve the cracker bakeries in the area, and persuaded them to standardize a few of the really good crackers and cookies they made. The next hurdle was the big one--how to provide customers with a fresh tasting unbroken product. Green studied the problem, then abandoned his law practice, and began to concentrate full time on his newly merged industry, the American Biscuit and Manufacturing Company with offices in Chicago.

Meanwhile, another lawyer, William Henry Moore, saw the same opportunity in New York and merged many of those bakery firms under the name: New York Biscuit Company.

From the start, before either man had really had a chance to make any significant changes in the cracker industry, they became opponents. At first Moore tried to buy Green out, but Green preferred independence. War was on-- both cut prices trying to force the other out. At one point customers were even being paid to buy the products. It was only a matter of time until both would be financially ruined, when the depression of 1896 hit. Another company of Moore's, the meteorically successful Diamond Match Company, suddenly plummeted on the stock exchange. The company's collapse was so drastic that the stock market was forced to close for three months.

Green took advantage of his crippled foe and cut his prices again. Moore was forced to merge, and the official name of the company became the National Biscuit Company, with Green at the helm. The merger involved placing 114 bakery firms, each with their specializations, under one name and one boss. There were problems, but Green rallied to the challenge.

He realized the cracker barrel days were gone. He wanted to put on the market a superior cracker that would consistently have good taste, be uniform in size, and arrive fresh and unbroken. If the cracker could meet that standard, it would give the National Biscuit Company fame and fortune.

Green knew the universal best seller was a soda cracker, so he concentrated on perfecting a tasty soda cracker. After some recipe modification, he baked exactly what he wanted. Next it had to have a catchy name that everyone would remember and recognize immediately.

For days Green pondered over lists of names that could be used. Finally he settled on a list of ten to twenty names that he submitted to Henry N. McKinney, an advertising agent who had already established a reputation with such brand names as Karo, Keds, Necco, and Meadow Gold. Rejected from the list were such names as Pherenice, a Greek word that was pronounced in English "very nice;" Verenice, same pronunciation idea; Bekos; Trim; and Dandelo. McKinney did like one name on the list--Uneeda. It was patented in 1898, and became a household word in months.

After perfecting the recipe and selecting a name, Green devoted his attention to finding a way to keep his Uneeda Biscuit fresh, clean, and unbroken. Probably more important than the cracker itself was the ingenious moisture-proof package. It was made from a wax-impregnated paper that kept the crackers crisp and free from outside flavors. The container with its waxed inner seal was simple and obvious, yet very important to the success of the cracker. Green urged its creator Frank Peters to apply for a patent. When his associate returned from Washington, D.C. with the patent, Green knew his new company was assured success. The patent launched a revolution in food packaging in America. Soon other products moved out of bulk boxes and barrels and into clean individual packages--cheese, lard, flour, rice, pickles, coffee and tea.

Green wanted his new biscuit and company known to every potential customer in America. Many established companies used the catchy slogans that were household phrases: "It floats"- -Ivory Soap; "The Beer that made Milwaukee famous"--Schlitz; and "Absolutely pure"--Royal Baking Soda.

Not only were slogans popular, it was also the era of trademarks. There was the picture of a woman carrying a tray for Baker's Cocoa; the man dressed in Quaker garb for Quaker Oats, and two little black children for Gold Dust, the cleaning powder.

Always distrustful of another's ability, Green himself began the search for a company symbol. He found it in an antique book containing Medieval printer's symbols. The symbol that caught Green's fancy was a cross with two bars and an oval, representing the triumph of good and spiritual over evil and material. It is still used today on Nabisco products.

The next detail Green became involved with was choosing the package design. Here again he found what he wanted in one of his antique books. The border design on a hand-tooled binding was perfect as part of the package design.

The color Green chose for the box was purple with white lettering. Never able to delegate authority, Green sketched every detail of the package design himself.

Green's care paid off. Even though the Uneeda Biscuit cost a bit more than other crackers, customers believed it was worth it. They could depend on the quality and freshness of the Uneeda Biscuit.

The introduction of the Uneeda Biscuit to the public was as carefully orchestrated as a sonata. First potential customers were confounded by the word "Uneeda" appearing mysteriously on billboards and in street cars. No one knew what the word meant. In a few weeks the word was replaced with "Uneeda Biscuit." Next, "Do you know Uneeda Biscuit?" Then, Do YOU know Uneeda Biscuit?" Later came "Do you KNOW Uneeda Biscuit!!!" After that came, "Of course Uneeda Biscuit!!!" And last, "Uneeda Biscuit--certainly."

Only then did the National Biscuit Company provide stores with the wax-sealed purple box filled with quality controlled crackers, which had been masterminded from conception by Adolphus Green.

From the beginning the rewards of the advertising dollar were obvious to Green and he advertised aggressively. One effective advertisement followed another until the problem became supplying enough crackers to keep up with the demand.

In 1900 one of the assignments given to NBC's advertising agency was to find a trademark character to reflect, in an appealing way, their unique product and its advantage over other crackers. The copywriter given this assignment asked his nephew, chubby five-year-old Gorden Still, to pose for an advertising photographer. The child wore boots, yellow hat with matching slicker, and carried a box of Uneeda Biscuits under one arm. Perfect! The symbol had appeal and told the story. The Uneeda Biscuit Boy became one of the most widely used motifs in all advertising. It was reproduced on booklets, glasses, bookmarks, cards, and yes, as a doll.

The first **Uneeda Kid** doll was manufactured by Ideal in 1914 from a design by Morris Michtom of New York. The doll closely resembled the photograph of little Gorden Still. It was 15-inches tall, with composition head, black boots, and gauntlet arms and hands. The body was cloth. It had a painted closed mouth, yellow painted hair, and painted eyes. Yellow sateen was used to make the familiar raincoat and hat. Underneath the rain gear was a one-piece romper. One arm was bent to carry a miniature box of Uneeda Biscuits.

By 1916 the doll had been modified slightly to include jointed legs and open/close eyes.

That same year, 1916, the **Uneeda Kid, Jr.** doll was introduced. It is a bit different from the two earlier dolls. Most obvious, it is smaller, 11½-inches tall. The eyes are painted and the yellow sou'ester is molded/painted. The lower part of the body is composition painted black to resemble pants and rain boots. The **Kid** also has one arm bent to hold a small purple box of Uneeda Biscuits. The three Uneeda dolls cost $1.00 each.

The 16-inch *Uneeda Kid* was manufactured by Ideal in 1914 to advertise the National Biscuit Company's famous Uneeda Biscuit. The doll is photographed with other items using this popular symbol. The doll has composition head, gauntlet hands, and boots, with a cloth body. It is dressed in the famous yellow raingear made of sateen. Under the slicker is a pair of striped rompers. The eyes are painted on this doll, a later *Uneeda Kid* doll had open/close eyes. Marks: "Uneeda Kid/ Patented Dec. 8, 1914/Ideal Novelty & Toy Co.," on label sewn on sleeve of coat; "Ideal," in diamond on back; carries a miniature box of Uneeda Crackers. Margaret Strong Museum. $150.00.

After the phenomenal success of the Uneeda Biscuit, the National Biscuit Company developed other crackers and cookies, such as: Fig Newtons, Jinger Wafers, Nabiscos (sugar wafer), Animal Crackers, Social Tea Biscuits, Lorna Doones, Oreos, Ritz Crackers, and many more.

Another National Biscuit Company product that used a doll in its promotions was the ZuZu, a close cousin to the gingersnap cookie. Where Green found the name ZuZu, is uncertain. That it was a successful name is certain. Company records show many firms wrote for permission to use the catchy name, but all were turned down. The company used two promotions to popularize their ZuZu cookies. After choosing a clown as the trademark figure they manufactured clown suits, copied from the ZuZu Clown, and provided them free to children around the country to use for special occasions. Another promotion was the "Master ZuZu" doll.

Ideal manufactured the **Master ZuZu** doll in 1915 and it carefully resembles the ZuZu clown. The doll is 15-inches tall with a cloth body, and composition head, hands, lower legs and feet. The painted features include a coquettish smile and eyes that glance to one side. The clown costume is white fabric printed with stars. A tall pointed clown hat made from the same fabric partially covers the molded/painted hair. A miniature box of ZuZu gingersnaps with a string handle came with the doll. The ZuZu cookie is no longer being produced.

In 1917 Adolphus Green died. His company was no longer a one-boss establishment. It took many skilled administrators to manage the ever growing company. As the company grew the need to diversify became apparent.

Diversification began with a related product-the pretzel. Next came a cracker for man's best friend--Milk Bone. Ice Cream cones, Shredded Wheat Cereal, cake mixes, and presweetened cereals followed. A big stride was taken in 1961 when Nabisco purchased the Cream of Wheat Corporation. (See Cream of Wheat listing for cloth **Chef** dolls.)

In 1915 Ideal manufactured the *Master ZuZu* doll. The clown doll has composition head, hands, and lower legs, with a cloth body. It wears a yellow clown suit and pointed hat covered with red stars in two sizes. A miniature box of ZuZu ginger snaps is held in one hand. Photo courtesy Nabisco.

With the advent of radio, the famous N.B.C. initials were shared by two large corporations, a broadcasting company and a biscuit company. In the 1940's the name was changed to Nabisco, a name used for their first cookie, and interestingly one of the names being considered by Green for his famous Uneeda Biscuit.

Back in 1911 Green said if

N.B.C. were destroyed they'd be saved by a word--Uneeda. Mr. Green would be shocked today to know that many people have never heard the word Uneeda, nor tasted a Uneeda Biscuit. Somewhere along the line, probably late 1940's, Nabisco dropped the Uneeda Biscuit. With the name out of sight it is also out of mind for most people.

For many years no premium dolls were offered by this company. In the 1960's when presweetened cereal came on the market Nabisco introduced flavored cereals. To add to the appeal for the preteen consumer, Nabisco sold "Puppets" cereal in plastic containers shaped like Walt Disney characters. Carmel flavored Wheat Puffs came in a **Donald Duck** shape; Chocolate flavored Wheat Puffs came in a container shaped like **Mickey Mouse**.

In 1966 Nabisco's presweetened cereals came in 7 ounce plastic containers shaped like Walt Disney Characters. Two examples are Donald Duck and Mickey Mouse. $1.00.

To celebrate the Bicentennial, Nabisco Snack Crackers offered a plastic **Uncle Sam** bank. The mechanical-action bank is a copy of a bank made of cast iron in 1890. It is 9-inches tall and sold for $2.98.

We found two other Nabisco

premiums, but do not know the product that offered them, nor the exact date. The first, ca. 1972, was a **Raggedy Ann** which was manufactured by Knickerbocker, and also sold on the retail level. The second is a 17-inch plush kangaroo toy.

Gloria the official National Airlines doll, is similar to a Barbie doll. The stewardess doll is 11½-inches tall, vinyl with posable limbs and a twist 'n turn waist. Her stewardess outfit is a tan jacket with buttons down the front and a tan skirt. $4.00.

A 17-inch aqua blue plush kangaroo was offered by Nabisco. No details are known about the premium. $5.00.

Naptha Soap. This strong smelling soap that was deemed so necessary for a white laundry in the past offered a **Dolly Strong** in 1910. The doll had composition hands and head, that resembles the Kammer & Reinhardt #100. The body and limbs are stuffed plush fabric with joints at the shoulder and hip. Horsman was the manufacturer.

National Airlines. An **Official Stewardess Doll** was sold in 1973. The vinyl doll is the Barbie type, 11½-inches tall and jointed so she can be posed. The eyes are painted, with inset lashes and it has a long blonde wig. Clothing consists of a tan jacket and skirt. The box the doll comes in says: "Fly me, I'm Gloria."

National Blue Ribbon Freezer Food Service, a division of Marquette Corp. To

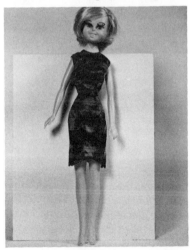

17-inch *Bonnie* doll has rooted blonde wig, open/closed mouth, painted eyes and long plastic eyelashes.Marks:"PerfeKta/Hong Kong." J. Ciolek collection, Visual Images, photographer. $20.00.

promote this food service the **Bonnie Blue Ribbon** doll was used in the 1950's. The doll is 17-inches tall and has rooted wig, open/closed mouth with teeth showing, painted eyes, and long eyelashes. The doll is jointed at hip and shoulder, has swivel waist, and hi-heeled feet. The doll wears a dress typical of the period, a tight-fitting straight dress called a sheath dress. The doll is occasionally mistakenly called the Blue Bonnet Margarine doll.

National Medicine Company.

This early mail order medicine company with offices in New York City and New Haven, Conneticut used to run small ads in magazines offering cloth dolls. Anyone willing to buy four boxes of their cold and headache tablet at 25¢ per box was eligible. Upon receipt of the $1.00, the doll would be sent free.

One such ad in the December, 1903 Delineator offers a demure doll with arms down to the side. The novelty of this doll is its size. The life-size 30-inch doll can wear real baby clothes. The ad explains it is an "exact reproduction of a hand-painted French Doll."

A 1901 premium list has the "Life Size" doll and a family of dolls dressed in Colonial costume. The dolls may represent George and Martha Washington, a boy, and a girl.

A "20th Century Premium List" includes five cloth animals: bear, elephant, lion, zebra, and camel. The 6 to 10-inch tall animals were copyrighted by Art Fabric Mills in 1900. The same list offered four pillow covers with various scenes lithographed on the top.

National Perfume Company.

In 1926 for selling 20 bottles of perfume this Chicago company would give a **Dolly Dot** doll free. The doll is probably cloth with a "Can't Break 'Em" head because it is guaranteed not to break.

Naugahyde, a product of Uniroyal, Inc. This vinyl material, that has been advertised as "The Great Imposter," is quite remarkable. It can resemble leather (only your taxidermist knows for sure), burlap, brocade, linen, wool, or most any other texture. In the mid-1960's the **Nauga** figure was introduced, whether it should be called a doll is questionable. It is shaped like a flat watermelon with cat ears, arms open wide, and it stands on short legs. The owlish face has a jack-o-lantern smile with jagged teeth, and the eyes, well, it has two.

Patterns were sold to make the **Nauga.** Many shops and stores made **Naugas** from their scraps of Naugahyde to sell or give to customers. Mothers made them for their children, and the com-

Nauga came in many sizes and many color combinations. Some were manufactured by Uniroyal from their leatherlike product Naugahyde. Others were made at home or by upholsters from scraps following a pattern that was available from the company. That helps explain the wide variation in the character. The dozen we found ranged in size from 10 to 15-inches high. Marks: "Naugahyde Vinyl Fabric/Uniroyal, Inc. 1967." $4.00 to $8.00.

pany also manufactured them. We found about a dozen, each a different size, from 10 to 15-inches tall, and each a bit different color combination. A few were stamped with the company name and 1967, so they were probably factory made **Naugas**.

Neo-Mull-Soy Formula,

a product of Syntex Labratories. In 1974 to promote their soy bean formula for babies who are allergic to milk Syntex offered a **Davee Duck** cloth toy. The yellow duck is 12-inches tall with orange lithographed beak and features. It wears a checked suit with a script D on the front. The toy cost $1.50 and was available until June 30, 1975.

To promote their soy bean baby formula, Syntex Laboratories offered the 12-inch cloth *Davee Duck*. The yellow duck has an orange beak and features. He wears a red checked suit marked with a "D" on front. Marks: "Neo-Mull-Soy ® Formula/© 1974 Syntex Laboratories, Inc.," on one foot.

Nesling's Crib Blanket.

To advertise the quality and design of an unusual blanket this product offered a diminutive blanket and a small bisque doll. The crib blanket was fashioned with a zipper opening in the center and a hole for the

baby's head to stick out. The blanket is well marked.

Nestle Company. This company is one of the oldest still in business. At the turn of the century it was selling baby food. A 1904 magazine ad said: "Nestle's Food points to three generations of happy, sturdy Nestle's Babies as its best recommendation to the young mothers of today." If the company had fed three generations of babies by 1904, it must have begun business in the mid-1800's. Judging from magazine ads the company of Henri Nestle sold only baby food at this time. The slogan was: "When the stork has brought the baby, Nestle's Food will keep the baby." That was way back when storks made home deliveries.

An early 7-inch cloth doll stamped "Nestle's Baby Food" in fading purple ink was located. Mrs. Elizabeth Fisher, the owner, believes the doll is 1916 vintage. It was purchased in a flat sheet to be cut, sewn, and stuffed by the purchaser. The small doll has printed underwear, shoes, stockings, and a red ribbon in her blonde curly hair.

We found no other Nestle dolls until 1969 when the **Little Hans** doll was used as a promotion. By this time the company no longer sold baby food but sold many other food products including a powdered chocolate drink. A figure used in television commercials for this beverage was "Little Hans, the Chocolate Maker." A 12½-inch vinyl doll was manufactured to represent this figure. The doll has a round bulbous nose, painted wire frame glasses, and a rooted red mustache that fans out from the nose to the bottom of the face. The doll is well dressed in a yellow molded hat, black boots, fake leather lederhosen trousers, yellow suede shirt, and red knit stockings. Only 2,000 of these top quality dolls were produced.

A year later a prestuffed cloth **Little Hans** doll was offered. It is also 12½-inches high, with a lithographed costume including black trousers, yellow shirt and hat. The doll was available for product labels in 1970.

To promote the speed of making Nestle's Quik, chocolate drink, a rabbit trademark was used. The **Nestle Quik Rabbit**, as seen on television commercials, was offered in 1976-77 for $4.95 plus proof-of-purchase. The 2-foot high rabbit is brown and tan plush with a large "Q" stamped in blue on its chest.

Nestle's also offered free plastic hand puppets with **Little Hans** printed on one side.

In the 60's Nestle used Little Hans, the Chocolate Maker in television commercials, to promote their powdered chocolate drink. In 1969 Nestle ordered 2,000 *Little Hans* dolls. The 12½-inch vinyl doll has a round bulbous nose, painted wire frame glasses, and a rooted red mustache. The yellow hat and black boots are molded/painted. Marks: "1969 The Nestle Co.," on back of neck; "AE", low on back. $20.00.

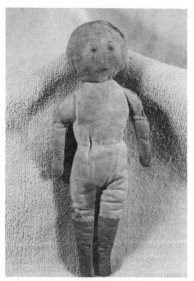

A small 7-inch muslin doll was offered about 1916 by Nestle's Baby Food. The much loved doll has printed lace-trimmed underwear, black boots with laces, red stockings, and a red ribbon in her yellow curly hair. These details hardly show in the photograph. Marks: "Nestle Baby Food/The/Unsweetened Food/for Babies," stamped in fading purple ink on the back. E. Fisher collection. $25.00.

In 1970 a second *Little Hans* doll was offered by Nestle. Marks: "TM Nestle Company, Inc." $8.00.

A *Little Hans* hand puppet was given free. Esser collection, Bruce Esser photographer. $1.00.

By 1976 *Nestle Quik Rabbit* dominated Nestle commercials. The idea was to emphasize the speed of making the chocolate drink. A premium rabbit was offered in 1976 and 1977. The *Nestle Quik Rabbit*, 2-feet tall, is brown and tan plush with a bright pink nose. The eyes and two front teeth are vinyl fabric. Marks: "Q," stenciled in blue on chest; a cloth label states the toy was manufactured by Animal Fair and gives other figures and information. $5.00.

New York and New England Apple Institute. In 1976 the New York and New England Apple Institute offered a 30-inch inflatable **Johnny Appleseed**. The doll has large bare feet and can stand alone. **Johnny** wears ragged pants, a shirt, and an unbuttoned vest. A package of apple seeds was included in the offer.

Johnny Appleseed was offered by the New York and New England Apple Institute. The 30-inch inflatable doll wears ragged pants, a vest, and cap. Notice the large bare feet that enable the doll to stand alone. A bag worn over one shoulder was for seeds. $3.00.

Nickerson Farms Restaurants. This roadside restaurant, gift shop, and service station complex is known for the delicious honey it sells and serves. Some of the buildings have a bee hive for customers to observe through glass. To emphasize this feature Nickerson Farms sold a 13-inch cloth **Queen Bee** in early 1970. The lithographed detail includes a crown and wings that are placed like ears. The bee doll is well marked.

In the early 1970's a 13-inch cloth *Queen Bee* was sold at Nickerson Farm Restaurants. The bee is yellow with black markings and a bit of red. Marks: "N/F/"BEE"/MY/HONEY," on the front. $3.00.

North America Moving Company.
An 11-inch vinyl doll, much like a Barbie, was given by this company.

Notaseme Hosiery Company.
In March, 1921, this Philadelphia company patented a **Binkie** doll. The following year a patent was registered for a **Kim** doll.

The Nugget Casino.
This Sparks, Nevado casino has used **Nugget Sam**, a beguiling old prospector, as their trademark since they opened in 1951. **Nugget Sam** has a white beard, a smile with one lone tooth showing, and wears western garb. The dolls representing this figure were sold to customers of the casino.

The first doll was a 5½-inch nodder made of paper mache with a wood base and was sold in 1953. His beard and a tuft of hair are fake fur.

The second doll, 12-inches, was made of rubber with molded/-painted features and clothing.

Nugget Sam is the trademark for the Nugget Casino in Sparks, Nevada. Clothing and features are molded/painted. Marks: "Dick Graves/NUGGET/Sparks, Nevada." K. Lansdowne collection. $12.00.

In the late 1950's a 12½-inch rubber *Nugget Sam* doll was sold at the Nugget Casino. Marks: "The NUGGET Sparks, Nev.," across brim of hat; "Rempel, Mfg. N.C./Akron, II, Ohio USA/© Roscoe Reading," on back of hat. K. Lansdowne collection. $8.00.

Nutrena Mills, Inc.
This old Kansas Milling Company sold sacks printed with a **Trena** doll. The doll, circa 1915, is rather crude, simple, and printed in two colors, red and navy blue. **Trena** is 14-inches high, with an open-mouth and wide eyes.

O

Old Crow Whiskey. This product has used three figures representing their trademark, a formally attired crow. The earliest figure, 1950, was a 4½-inch hard plastic bird dressed in a molded high-top hat, shoes with spats, and a red cummerbund. A gold-handled walking stick is tucked under one wing and plastic white glasses fit over the beak.

The 1956 *Old Crow*. Marks: "OLD CROW," incised on front of base; "Kentucky Straight Bourbon Whiskey/Distilled and bottled by the famous Old Crow Distillery Co./Frankfort, Ky.," in small letters on back of base. K. Lansdowne collection. $20.00.

In 1950 Old Crow Whiskey used a 4½-inch hard plastic *Old Crow* figure. The crow wears a top hat, shoes with spats, a red cummerbund, and a gold handled walking stick is tucked under one wing. Until 1956 all Old Crow symbols wore glasses as this figure does. Unmarked. K. Lansdowne collection. $8.00.

The second crow is a 14-inch vinyl figure with no glasses, therefore it was issued after 1956. From that date forward glasses were discontinued on the Old Crow trademark. The crow wears a high top hat, spats, and a vest rather than a cummerbund.

The most recent Old Crow display item, 1970, is a 28-inch black felt bird with a red vest.

The 28-inch felt *Old Crow* doll is in formal attire: high top hat, detachable bow tie, tails (wings of felt with white lining), spats, and a red vest, rather than the usual red cummerbund. The bird is in profile, only one side has detail; the other side is solid black felt. Ca. 1970. Unmarked. K. Lansdowne collection. $15.00.

247

Orange Crush. A tiny, 3½-inch, **Orange Crush Man** was used by this bottled soda pop.

A 3½-inch bisque doll was used to advertise Orange Crush soda pop. The *Orange Crush Man* has an orange shaped and colored head, black top hat and shoes, and a green suit. No date or marks. A. Wolfe collection, David Nelson, James Giokas photographers. $15.00.

Orange Plus. In the 1970's a round plush **Orange Plus** toy was sold to advertise the soda drink. The toy represents an

Orange Plus, an orange plush toy was a promotion of the drink by the same name. The figure is round with arms, legs, pom-pom nose, felt smile, and big plastic eyes. The plastic hat has a " + " on the front. $4.00.

animated orange because it is made of orange plush fabric in the shape of an orange with protruding arms and legs. It has large plastic eyes, pom pom nose, and a felt smile. The black derby hat has a green plus mark.

Orkin Exterminating Company. The largest pest control company in the world uses an **Otto the Orkin Man** trademark, which is a character made from a chemical tank. It looks like the rounded end of a bomb with arms, legs and facial features.

A 7½-inch paper mache **Otto** bank has been offered, possibly given free to children of potential customers.

Otto, the Orkin Man is a paper mache bank copied from the exterminating company's logo. The tank is white with black features and it stands on a green base. Marks: "Pennies/A Day/Keep Pests Away!," on back; "Orkin/® " in diamond-shaped seal on base. $5.00.

Oscar Mayer Company. This company has used two inflatable display items that were later offered as premiums to customers for a limited time, a **Little Oscar** and a **Hot Diggity Dog**. We also found an interesting Oscar Mayer pull-toy.

In 1972 the *Little Oscar* inflatable was distributed to stores selling Oscar Mayer meat products. Shortly afterwards, it became a mail-in premium. *Oscar* is 29-inches tall including his chef hat. He wears a white outfit. Marks: "LITTLE/OSCAR," on hat; Oscar/Mayer," on front of suit. K. Miller collection. $3.00.

Hand puppets such as "Mr. Green Jeans" were free from Oscar Mayer in 1966. $1.00.

The inflatable **Hot Diggity Dog** became available via coupons at point-of-sale in 1978. The weiner is about three-feet long and is marked with a yellow band just like the edible kind. Each weiner cost $1.50 plus two labels from any one-pound package of Oscar Mayer Wieners or Franks. The expiration date is January 31, 1979. Meat markets often had this inflatable weiner hanging from the ceiling. Perhaps it was requests for the display that prompted the premium.

In 1972 a **Little Oscar** inflatable doll was distributed to stores and quick-food stands selling Oscar Mayer products and later it became a mail-in premium. The 29-inch chef cost $1.00 plus proof-of-purchase.

Oster Corporation (sub. of Sunbeam Corp.) In 1972 Oster was known for its electric blender, the Osterizer. To introduce a new appliance, the Super Pan, the company offered a

In 1972 the 19-inch *Super Pan* doll was used by the Oster Corporation to introduce their new electric cooker, the Super Pan. The doll wears an aqua suit with orange letters and a red detachable cape. Marks: "Oster/SuPer/Pan," on front of the suit. J. Varsalona collection. $8.00.

249

cloth **Super Pan** doll. The appliance consisted of a pan that fit on a heating unit and could be used for fondue, casseroles, tempura and a chafing dish.

The 19-inch doll is a Superman character with a removable cape. The arms and legs are cut free from the body, and the feet turn to the side. The comic face gives the effect of a ¾ profile.

The **Super Pan** doll was one of several items available for joining the Super Pan Super Fan Club. Other items included a watch, book, bag, and bib. The doll cost $2.69.

Oxol, a product of J.L. Prescott Co. "To make your wash white and free from stains add Oxol to the soap and water in tub or machine." Oxol is one of many products almost forgotten because it is no longer found on grocery shelves. It will be remembered by those lucky enough to own the **Oxol** doll. It is printed on a sheet of fabric, to be completed by the owner. The 17-inch doll is dressed in clothing resembling the Oxol bottle: with a diamond-checked jacket of red, white and blue and the word "Oxol" in block letters across the front and back. The black hair is cut in the "windblown" style of the depression years. It has rosy circles on the cheeks, a rosebud mouth, and eyes with prominent lashes. The **Oxol** doll was a premium in 1931.

In 1931 a cloth *Oxol* doll was offered by this laundry product. The doll wears a red, white, and blue checked jacket that resembled the label on the Oxol bottle. Marks: "Oxol," in large letters across the front and back of the jacket. Playthings by the Yard, 1973. $35.00.

P

Pacific Power & Light Company. In 1973 this company offered a cloth **Col. Watt** doll to urge customers to economize on energy. The 15-inch doll reminds me of Teddy Roosevelt. He has a mustache, little round glasses, and wears a western style hat. The doll was printed on muslin to be assembled by the owner. How the dolls were dispensed is not known.

Col. Watt, 15-inches, was offered by the Pacific Power and Light Company to urge customers to economize on energy. The doll is lithographed on muslin in orange and black. Being a good guy, he wears a white hat. Marks: "Col. Watt says: Use what you need. . . but save all you can," written across the back; "© PP&L 1973," on back of pants. $4.00.

Pals Vitamins, a product of Miles Laboratory. To encourage children to take vitamins, this company produced colored swallowable vitamin tablets in the shape of a pink fish, orange owl, purple turtle, green cat, and brown squirrel. In 1974 to further promote Pals Vitamins, 1½-inch vinyl toys were made in the same colors and shapes as the vitamin pills.

Pan Am Airlines. A ball and a cylinder of wood with four small dowels represents a simple 3½-inch doll. It has no detail, only a Pan Am sticker on the cylinder.

Pan Am Airlines used a simple 3½-inch doll-like toy perhaps as a gift to children. The wood cylinder has a Pan Am logo. A. Pfister collection. $2.00.

Pappy Parker's Chicken House. A 6½-inch molded/-painted vinyl doll was purchased in

The *Pappy Parker* doll is photographed with the take-out box used by this quick food restaurant. The vinyl doll is 6½-inches tall, and represents a hillbilly with a tall hat. J. Ciolek collection, Visual Images photographer. $4.00.

the Washington, D.C. area from this restaurant about 1973. The doll represents a **Hillbilly** with a tall hat that covers the eyes. The mouth is open/closed showing two teeth and bordered on three sides by a mustache. The arms are molded to the body.

Peabody Overalls, a Canadian company. A cloth doll that appears to be very old is marked "Peabody's Guaranteed Overalls." The doll is 17-inches tall and is dressed as a railroad engineer in striped overalls with matching shirt and cap. The face is the old photographic type, with a full mustache. Arms and legs are cut free from the body. No further information is known.

The 17-inch cloth *Peabody Overall* doll is an interesting example of an early advertising doll. No information was found on either the doll or the company it represents. It appears to be a railroad engineer with matching cap, shirt, and overalls. Marks: "PEABODY'S/Guaranteed/ OVERALLS." P. Coghlan collection, Harry Sykora photographer.

Pepperidge Farm. To promote Gingerman Cookies a **Gingerman** doll was offered for

$1.00. The brown cloth doll is shaped like a gingerbread boy cookie with just slight curves to represent legs. Eyes, nose, and buttons are lithographed candies of red and white. A line mouth and two circles complete the facial features. The foam-filled doll was sold from Chase Bag Company in North Carolina.

A 16-inch long gold cloth **Goldfish** was offered to promote Peppridge tiny goldfish-shaped crackers.

The *Gingerman* cloth doll was offered by Pepperidge Farms to introduce their Gingerman cookies. Marks: "PEPPERIDGE FARM ® " on bottom of one leg; "GINGERMAN COOKIES," on other leg. L. Zablotney collection. $4.00.

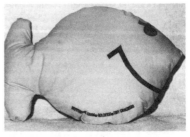

Pepperidge Farm's *Goldfish* was a promotion for their tiny goldfish-shaped crackers. The 16-inch long fish is made from gold cotton cloth. Marks: "Pepperidge Farm ® , Goldfish ® , Tiny Crackers." L. Zablotney collection. $4.00.

Penman Company. This Canadian knit underwear factory sold a 7-inch cloth doll about 1910. The little girl was ready for a cold Canadian winter in her long-legged suit of underwear with a back drop. The doll is marked with the Penman trademark, a triangle with a bottle of ink and a feather pin.

Pepsodent, a product of Lever Bros. Two vinyl dolls are known as **Miss Pepsodent**, one is 15-inches and the other 23-inches tall. Both have an unusual feature: two rows of teeth on a ball that rotates from white teeth when upright to yellow teeth depending on the position. The dolls have open/shut eyes, open-mouth, and a dynel wig.

The 15-inch doll was licensed by Lever Bros. in 1953. It is marked "A-E" on the back of the head.

The 23-inch doll was manufactured by Imperial Crown, date unknown, wears a ribbon marked "Miss Pepsodent."

Pepto Bismol. This pink remedy for diarrhea and vomiting

The *24-Hour Bug* doll was a clever premium of Pepto-Bismol, the medicine advertised to coat and soothe the stomach. J. Ciolek collection, Visual Images photographer. $12.00.

offered a soft vinyl bank called the **24-Hour Bug**. This sickly green creature is 7-inches high, has black spots, pink eyes, and a wavy smile. The arms are crossed in front. It was manufactured by Niagra Plastics in Pennsylvania.

Peter Pan Ice Cream. A cloth **Peter Pan** doll was manufactured for this ice cream store chain by Chase Bag Company in 1972. The 18-inch doll is a very thin representation of the famous character, obviously he needs to eat more ice cream. **Peter Pan** was sold at the ice cream stores for $1.00.

Peter Pan doll. The doll wears an orange and blue tunic top over long red stockings. The doll is unmarked. A paper sticker on the back identifies the manufacturer as the Chase Bag Company of Reidsville, N.C. S. Ricklefs collection. $6.00.

Peter Paul Candy. The ordinary 8-inch plastic **Dolls of the World** were offered for $1.00 plus a wrapper from a Peter Paul Candy bar.

Peters Weatherbird Shoes. An interesting 1920 type doll with composition head and arms was found that has a label identifying it as a promotion from this brand of shoes. The doll is approximately 22-inches tall and has a mohair wig. It is not known how the doll was offered or if it was used for display.

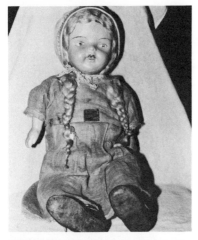

This 22-inch doll has a label on the front of the dress from Peters Weatherbird Shoes. The head and arms are composition with a cloth body. Courtesy Rummerfield Antiques.

This all bisque doll is only 2½-inches tall. Her carelessly painted dress is brown, beads and headband are silver. Marks: "Weather Bird/Shoes," incised on back. B. Glass collection. $18.00.

A tiny, 2½-inch, bisque doll was found marked: "Weather Bird Shoes." It is the frozen type commonly manufactured in Japan.

These dolls were often free to children when they purchased a new pair of shoes.

Pfeiffer Brewing Company, Detroit, Michigan. This brand of beer used the trademark figure of a boy playing a fife. It has been made in plaster 5½-inches tall to use for display at bars.

Philip Morris, Inc. At least three dolls have been manufactured to represent Johnny, the diminutive bellhop who advertised Philip Morris cigarettes. The company has no knowledge of the dolls, but were generous with information on their legendary trademark Johnny.

To anyone who has heard Johnny's call on the radio, no reminder is necessary as to who Johnny is or what his call was, for who could forget that jaunty little bellhop with his precise enunciation and melodic tone as the call rang out, "Call for Phil-leep Morrees."

To someone who has never heard the Philip Morris call it is difficult to adequately describe. Philip Morris' officials recognized Johnny as some one special and his call unique the first time they saw and heard him.

In April, 1933 at the Hotel New Yorker two company officers stood mesmerized by a 48-inch bellhop strutting across the lobby paging hotel guests. The company's trademark, a snappy bellboy, had been established about 10 years earlier. Now, right before their eyes was the personification of their trademark. After listening to him page several more guests they decided to conduct a most unusual radio audition.

They handed Johnny a dollar bill and asked him to locate Mr. Philip Morris. As Johnny later told the story. "I had no idea that Philip

Morris was a cigarette. I just went around the lobby yelling my head off, but Philip Morris didn't answer my call."

To officials, Johnny wasn't yelling, "That call was beautiful. It came across in a perfect B-flat that had an unforgettable ring. He cupped his hands to his mouth and with great enthusiasm gave a resounding 'Call for Phil-lip Mor-rees."

15-inch *Johnny* doll sold at retail stores. The composition head has a wide open/closed mouth and bulgy eyes. The body is cloth with felt hands. Johnny wears his bellhop uniform and a removable pillbox hat. Unmarked. L. Shearer photographer and collector. $75.00.

Twenty-year old Johnny Roventini was reluctant to quit his successful hotel job and said he'd have to ask his mother whether to take a radio job with the Philip Morris Company. He couldn't imagine being paid such a wonderful salary for doing so little. Later that year Johnny signed a lifetime contract with Philip Morris, one of the few lifetime contracts in advertising history.

Johnny became as familiar to Americans as any prominent figure in the country. His radio debut was April 17, 1933 on the Ferde Grofe Show, a program bill-ed as the "finest orchestra that ever struck Broadway."

That evening Johnny, who had never been in a radio studio, stepped to the microphone, his call for Philip Morris blending with the final tone of the composition from "Grand Canyon Suite." A unique sound had entered the folklore of American advertising.

Stardom for Johnny came over night and sales for Philip Morris brand cigarettes skyrocketed to fourth in the nation.

By 1940 the war was on and Johnny tried to enlist in the Coast Guard Auxillary, but his diminutive size made it impossible. He was honored for his genuine effort and given an "A" draft classification, the only person in the United States to receive such an honor.

After the war the great radio shows gave way to television. For a time Johnny introduced early Philip Morris video shows. Then he became a roving ambassador for the company, always with that familiar smile, that outstretched hand and that sincere warmth that have been his personal trademark. Because of his unusual career Johnny met many talented entertainment stars, famous political figures, and sports heros. At 68 years of age Johnny continues to be the pride of the Philip Morris Company.

Any fan of Johnny, and there are many, would be pleased to own a **Johnny** doll. Of the three we know about two have composition heads, cloth bodies, and cloth limbs. One is 15-inches tall with a wide open/closed mouth, thin body with removable jacket, pants, and hat. The other one is 11-inches tall with a closed mouth, the body is also the bellhop uniform and is well padded.

The third doll is a 5-inch bisque figure of **Johnny** carrying an open drum to hold cigarettes. The dolls all wear a small red pillbox hat and a bellhop suit with buttons. No dates or manufacturers are known.

An 11-inch *Johnny* doll has a closed mouth and is probably dated 1940's. The head is composition with a molded/painted pillbox hat. The body is cloth and is made to resemble a red bellhop uniform. The doll is unmarked, but had a paper tag on the suit that has become undecipherable. $65.00.

Phillips Petroleum Company.

Stations selling Phillips 66 gasoline offered the **Buddy Lee** doll in 1947. The doll was actually created to advertise H.D. Lee uniforms, but was purchased in large quantities by Phillips Petroleum Company to advertise their service stations. The uniform was tan and orange, the company colors at that time.

In later years, individual dealers were allowed to use promotion dolls, which they would order and disperse. The head office has no record of these dolls. We located two Phillips 66 dolls, there are undoubtedly others.

One is a 7-inch molded/painted composition nodder with the head on a spring. The **Phillips 66 Man** doll is winking, has a white

mustache, and gas nozzles in both hands. The Texas-sized hat, and kerchief around the neck gives a clue that this doll may have been commissioned by a Texas dealer. The doll was made in Japan.

The other doll is a more recent doll made of hard plastic. The doll is 15-inches tall and almost that wide. Facial features are molded, but not painted. The tan and orange uniform is marked on the pocket and the hat is marked with a Phillips 66 emblem.

Many false stories are told about why Phillips Petroleum Company named their gasoline 66. Some stories say it referred to the octane, that there are 66 books in the Bible, or because Frank Phillips the organizer was 66 years old. None of these are true.

In 1927, when the new company was ready to market their gasoline, they needed a name. It had been suggested that 66 would be apt. The fuel gravity was close to 66 and the refinery was near highway 66, but these suggstions were ignored.

On the eve of the big meeting where a final name for the gasoline would be selected an official was road-testing the new fuel. He proudly reported, "This car goes like sixty."

"Sixty, nothing," responded the driver. "We're doing sixty-six!"

At the meeting the next morning the conversation was retold. The officials decided the third omen made it destined that their gasoline should be known as Phillips 66.

Pillsbury Company.

Information on the advertising dolls of this company comes from the dolls themselves and what ads could be found. The Pillsbury Doughboy dolls were especially confusing to sort out. It is possible there are corrections and additions.

In 1965 cloth **Flip** (girl) and **Flap** (boy) dolls were offered for 75¢ plus a Pillsbury Pancake Flour boxtop. The cloth dolls were round like a pancake and measured 14-inches in diameter. We did not find these dolls.

Sometime in the 1960's Pillsbury introduced the **Pillsbury Doughboy** symbol. It is a little all-white fellow with a big smile and a chef hat that especially appealed to children. My research shows he began appearing in Pillsbury television commercials and print ads in the late 1960's.

Apparently the first **Pillsbury Doughboy** doll was offered in 1968 and was an all vinyl doll that would "feel like a roll of biscuit dough." We found this doll in two sizes, 5½-inches and 7-inches. I believe the 5½-inch doll was offered first. Then the 7-inch doll was offered for $1.50. The 7-inch doll was sold at retail stores in the

In 1971 the first cloth *Pillsbury Doughboy* doll was offered. It is 16-inches tall from the tip of the hat to the toe. It is white with blue facial features. The cap and neckerchief are detachable. Marks: "Pillsbury," in logo on chef hat. $6.00.

early 1970's. The one I purchased is marked "1971."

Two cloth **Pillsbury Doughboy** premium dolls were found. One is 16-inches tall measuring from the tip of the 2-inch hat to the toe. The hat and neckerchief are removable. The doll cost $3.00 plus proof-of-purchase from two Pillsbury frosting or cake mixes. The offer expired December 31, 1971.

The other cloth doll is 15½-inches tall from the tip of the hat to the toe, but the hat on this doll is an extension of the doll and is stuffed. The doll is made from white fabric with blue details. It cost $2.00 plus labels. We found several of these dolls and all were alike except for size. Some were wide and some were narrow, perhaps because of variation in the seam allowance.

In about 1972 the ads quit calling the mascot the Pillsbury Doughboy and began using the name **Poppin' Fresh**. Soon a mate was added named **Poppie Fresh**. Both were offered as dolls by the company in 1972 for $2.95 plus two labels from Refrigerated Dough Products. The dolls were made of knit velour and were advertised as being, " . . . soft, cuddly dolls, machine washable." The fabric was placed over a molded foam core with indented mouth and protruding nose. Eyes were plastic. Each wears an attached hat, the girl wears a removable blouse and the boy a removable scarf. These were also available in Sears catalog in 1973 for $3.47.

Pillsbury widely advertised the popular symbol. Salt and pepper shakers were offered in both ceramic and plastic. The ceramic pair was a retail item; the 3½-inch plastic shakers were a Pillsbury premium. They were free for 50 labels from refrigerator biscuits or $2.00 with four labels.

By 1972, the name had been changed to *Poppin' Fresh*. The doll is knit velour over a foam core. The nose and mouth are molded and the eyes are plastic. The eyes and disk at the front of the hat are blue. $6.00.

In 1972, the popular *Poppin' Fresh* doll was given a companion, *Popie Fresh*. The dolls cost $2.95 each and were available with labels from any Pillsbury Refrigerated Dough Product. $5.00.

In 1974 an 11-inch ceramic cookie jar was available for $5.95 plus refrigerator cookie labels.

In 1972 Pillsbury included free plastic **Poppin' Fresh** hand puppets in some products.

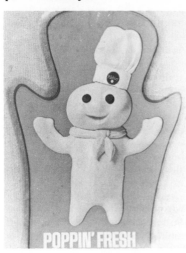

In 1972 some Pillsbury products included a free hand puppet. $1.00.

In 1974 the Pillsbury Doughboy Family was enlarged. **Granmommer** and **Granpopper** dolls, 5-inches, were introduced. They were made of the same soft white vinyl with movable heads and arms. Both wore molded square-rimmed glasses and had touches of blue.

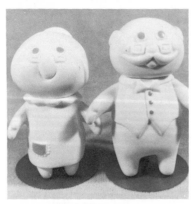

In 1974 the family was enlarged to include *Granmommer* and *Granpopper*. The dolls are 4 7/8-inches and 5¼-inches tall respectively. They sold in Penney's catalog for $2.97 each. $5.00.

Finger puppets of the Pillsbury family include from the left to right: *Bun-Bun*, the little girl of *Poppie* *Fresh* who is in the middle, and their pet *Cupcake*. $2.00 each.

Poppin Fresh stands between his son *Popper* on the left and the pet dog on the right. These are all vinyl finger puppets. $2.00.

The children of **Poppin' Fresh** and **Poppie** were **Popper** and **Bun-Bun**. They were 4-inches tall and made in the same manner as the other members of the Pillsbury Doughboy Family.

The children had a pet cat named **Cupcake** and a **Doughbear**. They were about 2½-inches tall.

The children and the pets were made to fit over a child's finger for a puppet.

The last member of the family is **Uncle Rollie** complete with a car that has a rumble seat that opens and closes. The headlights on the car are eyes that open and close also.

259

Uncle Rollie came in a car with an open/close rumble seat and headlights that work like open/close eyes. The doll is 3-inches tall and wears a molded yellow hat with an orange brim and a molded green scarf. $6.00.

In Penney's 1975 toy catalog the entire Pillsbury family and a 17-inch three-story playhouse that doubled as a carrying case was featured.

Poppin' Fresh and *Poppie Fresh* were available in Penney's 1975 catalog for $2.97 each. The *Poppin' Fresh* is 7-inches tall and may be the same one offered by the company as an earlier premium. *Poppie Fresh* is 5½-inches tall. All clothing and features are molded with a bit of blue paint for eyes and logo. Marks: "Pillsbury," on boy's hat and girl's dress. $5.00.

Poppin' Fresh and **Poppie** hand puppets came in a replica of the Pillsbury refrigerator biscuit cans. The heads were white molded vinyl and the bodies were cloth. They sold for $3.88 in the 1974 Montgomery Ward catalog and were also available at other retail stores.

Poppin' Fresh pops out of a can much like the can used for Pillsbury refrigerated biscuits. His companion "Poppie Fresh" was also available in a can. The dolls have a vinyl head and half body. The lower body is cloth, made to fit over a child's hand. The hand puppets sold for about $4.00 each, in 1974. $7.00.

Lazy Lion was offered in 1977 to promote Pillsbury Bundt Cake mixes. The 23-inch long lion is orange plush with a gold mane and a white nose. L. Zablotney collection. $6.00.

The latest Doughboy offer appeared in December 1978 magazines. **Poppin' Fresh** and **Poppie Fresh** were available for $2.00 plus one label from their Slice 'n Bake Cookies for one doll. The second doll was free for an additional four labels from the cookies.

To promote Pillsbury Bundt Cake mixes in 1977 a 23-inch **Lazy Lion** was offered for $5.99. It was orange with a gold mane and a white nose.

Pine Sol. This liquid household cleaner offered the **Pine Sol Bears** for $9.99 in 1978. The bear is made of a fur fabric with extra long "fur." It is in a sitting position and measures 15-inches by 15-inches.

Selmore and *Semore* is a reversible cloth doll offered by the Pioneer Seed Company. The 14-inch doll represents two feed store salesmen. They wear lithograped clothing including blue slacks, red jacket, and yellow cap. Marks: "Selmore," near label of jacket; "Pioneer," near bottom of jacket. A. Wolfe collection, David Nelson and James Giokas photographers. $8.00.

The *Pine Sol Bear* measures 15 x 15-inches and is in a sitting position. It was available in 1978. $15.00.

Pioneer Seed Company.
An interesting reversible cloth doll was used by this Coon Rapids, Iowa, company. The 14-inch doll represents a salesman, rather than a farmer it seems, named **Selmore** on one side and **Semore** on the other. Each has a distinct expression.

The other side of the Pioneer Seed Company's doll. Marks: "Semore." A. Wolfe collection, David Nelson, James Giokas photographers.

Pizza Hut. In 1969 a hardplastic "Pizza Pete" bank was provided to Pizza Hut franchises. The

7½-inch bank was a facsimile of the company logo: a fellow with a large nose, a handle-bar mustache, and his arms folded contentedly across his stomach. **Pizza Pete** wears a small black hat, neckerchief, and oversize shoes.

For one year, 1969, a 7½-inch plastic *Pizza Pete* bank was offered from Pizza Hut Restaurants. Marks: "Pizza Hut," on stomach. $5.00.

A *Pizza Pete* hand puppet given at Pizza Hut restaurants. $1.00.

Each restaurant could disperse the banks however they chose. Usually they were given away with the purchase of two large pizzas. The figure was designed by Ed Pointer, a Witchita, Kansas artist. Pizza Hut's headquarters are also in that city.

A paper mache version of **Pizza Pete** was used for the illustrations in the company's 1972 annual report. It was not offered for sale or display.

Pizza King. The **Pizza King** doll is 15-inches tall, white fabric, and shaped like an overweight bowling pin with arms and feet. A detachable ruffle is tied around the lower bulge for an apron. A small white chef hat and blue and red kerchief are detachable. The ears, mouth, nose, and mustache are made of felt. Date unknown.

A rather humorous looking doll was used to advertise the Pizza King Restaurants. It has the body of a fat bowling ball, arms, feet, and little round ears. The white cloth doll wears a small white chef hat, an apron, and a blue and white neckerchief. Marks: "PIZZA KING," on black ribbon label sewn on front of doll. $6.00.

Plaid Stamp Company, a division of E.F. McDonald Stamp Company. In 1968 a

20-inch plastic **Bonnie the Plaid Lassie** was offered through the Plaid Stamp catalog for 2 books. The doll, manufactured by Skippy Doll Corporation, wears Scottish clothes and has red rooted hair.

Bonnie the Plaid Lassie was both a retail item and an advertising item for the Plaid Stamp Company. The 20-inch plastic doll wears a red and black plaid shawl and skirt, blue jacket and hat, and a white blouse. Marks: "This doll Bonnie; the Plaid Lassie" is made exclusively for E.J. MacDonald Stamp Company, Dayton, Ohio." L. Yagatich collection, Donald G. Vilsack photographer. $15.00.

Planter's Peanuts, a product of Standard Brands, Inc. Several **Mr. Peanut** dolls, facsimiles of the trademark, were located. The company official I spoke with on the phone was surprised to learn of the dolls, he was only aware of two, the fairly recent cloth dolls.

Perhaps the oldest is a 4-inch bisque **Mr. Peanut** connected to a flat dish. The figure is marked: made in Japan.

Another old **Mr. Peanut** doll is made of wood beads strung together with elastic. This type of doll was commonly available in the late 1930's. The 8½-inch wood **Mr. Peanut** has a yellow peanut-shaped body, black arms and legs, white hands, and a blue top hat. The doll's features are painted and include the famous monocle.

The earliest *Mr. Peanut* doll we found was made of wood beads and strung with elastic. This type doll was very popular in the 30's. The 8½-inch doll has a yellow peanut-shaped body, black arms and legs, white hands, and a blue top hat. The face has not changed at all through the years. Marks: "Mr. Peanut," across hat. J. Keelen collection. $35.00-50.00.

The third **Mr. Peanut** doll is made from paper mache and is a 6½-inch nodder. The doll is well made with detailed painting. It also copies the trademark. The long-legged peanut doll stands on a base.

The fourth doll is really an 8½-inch bank made of hard plastic. It was made between 1960 and 1970. Today flea markets abound with this form of the trademark. It is molded in one color, usually peanut tan, but some were blue, green, or dark red. It is interesting to note the wide range of prices found on this particular item. In the past year I have bought several for 25¢ and have also seen several marked at $20.00 and $25.00. The value is in the eye of the seller in this case.

Mr. Peanut was also made as a nodder doll. The 6½-inch doll is made of paper mache and is well done. Notice the broken mache at the bottom of the peanut body. That was our only casualty in mailing dolls back and forth for the book. The body is peanut tan; hat, arms, legs, and base are black. Marks: "Mr. Peanut," across hat; "©Lego," on base. Ken Lansdowne collection. $20.00.

Two cloth **Mr. Peanut** dolls have been issued. The original one is 21-inches in length and was available in 1967. The doll was shortened to 18-inches a few years back. According to the company the cloth dolls have been offered as a premium on the cellophane packages of Planter's Peanuts continuously since that date. In the first decade of the offer, 450,000 had been redeemed. The dolls cost $1.00 plus two bags or wrappers from any Planter's product. The cloth dolls have the face printed on both sides. They are constructed of yellow cotton fabric with black printed detail.

Between 1960 and 1970 an 8½-inch hard plastic *Mr. Peanut* bank was offered on Planter's Peanut products. The entire bank is made in one color, usually tan, but sometimes blue, green, or dark red. Marks: "Mr. Peanut," across band of hat; "BANK," on front of pedestal; "made in U.S.A.," on back of pedestal. $5.00.

The original cloth *Mr. Peanut* doll is 21-inches tall and was offered in 1967. The doll is taller and slimmer than the later issue. Both sides of the doll are identical. Marks: "Mr. Peanut," across hat band. $5.00.

In the 1970's the *Mr. Peanut* doll was shortened to 18-inches. This edition is a bit plumper than the original. Both are yellow and black. Marks: "Mr. Peanut," across hat band in front. $2.00.

While doing research for the book, we noticed many **Mr. Peanut** items such as various sizes and colors of salt and pepper shakers, cricket toys, metal bowls, glass containers, and a toy peanut-butter maker in the form of **Mr. Peanut** himself. Recently efforts have been made through the Antique Trader to start a Planter's Peanut collecting organization. There seems to be plenty of items to collect from Planters and the company and the trademark have an interesting history.

An Italian-born fruit stand operator, Amedeo Obici, was the force that elevated the peanut from its status of "monkey food" to respectability. He and a partner pioneered packaging peanuts in glassine and cellophane packages and vacuum-packed candy. From a humble start Obici convinced the American people that the 5¢ snack food was both good and good for them.

The master stroke came in 1916 when the company sponsored a contest for a trademark. A schoolboy--now forgotten--won with the sketch of a peanut in the shell with a smiling face and spindly arms and legs. A commercial artist added the cane, hat, and monocle, giving "Mr. Peanut" that debonair flair that developed into such priceless property for the peanut company.

The word Planters has no siginificance at all. Obici picked it because it sounded "important and dignified." The name Planter's and the Mr. Peanut trademark were kept as part of the tradition when they became the property of Standard Brands, Inc. in 1960.

Mr. Peanut has marched in parades, been introduced in all sorts of toys, been lighted up in a mammouth sign, and served in every way imaginable. After over 60 years Mr. Peanut shows no sign of slowing down.

Play Doh, a product of Rainbow Crafts. Packages of this clay-like substance advertised the **Play Doh Boy** doll in 1969 for $1.00.

The *Play Doh* doll wears a red outfit with hat and white side-turned shoes. Marks: "Play Doh Boy," on back of one foot; "Rainbow Craft Inc. 1969," on other foot. $8.00.

265

The cloth doll was 15-inches tall and represented a smiling boy with arms raised up to show fists full of Play Doh. The doll wears lithographed clothes consisting of a red suit and hat, and white shoes turned to the side with laces.

Plymouth Chrysler Corporation. A 7½-inch inflatable **Roadrunner** was used to advertise for this make of automobile. The toy hangs on a string attached to a suction cup.

The 7½-inch inflatable *Roadrunner*, used by Plymouth Automobiles, is hung from a string that is attached to a suction cup. The toy is pink and gray. Marks: "Roadrunner," written on cloth strip attached to string. K. Miller collection. $2.00.

Poll Parrot Shoes. We found three dolls known to have been given by this company. Two of the dolls are made in Japan, all bisque with legs, body, and head in one piece, arms attached with elastic.

One is incised Poll Parrot and has gold painted hair. The other has pale yellow hair and is stamped on the front Poll Parrot.

The third doll, approximately 20-inches tall, has composition head and arms and cloth body with a woven label on the front of the dress.

From the 20's through the early 40's Japan produced thousands of these bisque dolls. Poll-Parrot Shoes gave them to children who purchased their shoes. The hair is pale yellow and the waist band is green. Marks: "POLL-PARROT/SHOES." $20.00.

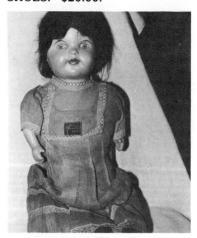

An interesting old composition and cloth *Poll Parrot Doll* wears original dress with label on front. The arms are rather short for the 20-inch doll. It has painted eyes, painted closed mouth, and mohair wig. Marks: "Poll/Parrot/Shoes," on label front of dress. Courtesy Rummerfield Antiques.

Pom Pom Candy, a product of Nabisco. In 1977 a cloth **Fonz** doll was offered on boxes of this candy. See Junior Mints for full description and illustration.

Pond's Cosmetics. In 1956 Citro Manufacturing Company was licensed to make the **Polly Ponds Beauty Doll.** The 25-inch vinyl doll has poseable legs, rooted hair in an upsweep style, open/shut eyes, and high heel feet. **Polly** is marked "1325-1/Made in USA."

Popeye Puffed Wheat, Popeye Puffed Rice, Popeye Popcorn, products of Purity Mills, a division of Stokely-Van Camp, Inc. October 1, 1974 a cloth **Popeye** doll was advertised on the poly bags these products are packaged in. The 15-inch doll was manufactured by the Chase Bag Comapny and is a facsimile of the famous Popeye cartoon character. In order to receive the doll, the consumer would send in

$1.50 (the price rose to $1.75 in 1976) and a coupon from the back panel of the package.

After dispersing several thousand in the three years they were available, the company decided to change the back panel to a different premium. The present offer is a Popeye coin bank that is actually a 20 oz. popcorn can with a slotted lid. The offer has been on the bags since October, 1977 and is presently on all three products. The price of the bank is $1.00. Included with the delivered bank are four 25¢ coupons good on the next four purchases of Popeye popcorn.

Post Cereals, a division of General Foods. Because of General Food's policy of not providing information on their premiums, the information on

A 15-inch cloth *Popeye* doll was used to advertise Popeye Puffed Wheat from 1974 to 1976. Unmarked. J. Ciolek collection, Visual Images photographer. $4.00.

Post Cereal's *Sugar Bear* was introduced in 1972 and offered intermittently to 1976. The bear is 12½-inches tall and made of rust colored plush with a felt face and an aqua shirt, which is the upper body. The doll is copied from the character used to advertise Super Sugar Crisp and Super Orange Crip Cereals. Marks: "Sugar/Bear," stencilled on front of shirt. $5.00.

premium dolls offered by Post Cereals may be incomplete. To our knowledge, except for the Sugar Bear all Post dolls have no product tie-in and are also sold at the retail level.

The one exception, Post's Sugar Bear, is a likeness of the "coolest bear in the forest." This bear figure was used to advertise Super Sugar Crisp and Super Orange Crisp cereals. (The latter is no longer found on grocery shelves in my area.) Intermittently from about 1972 to 1976 a fur-cloth bear has been offered that is 12½-inches tall, and cost $2.00 plus two boxtops.

In 1978 the bear was changed, the new Sugar Bear is 16-inches tall and cost $4.75 plus two labels. It is made of Acrylic plush fabric and is washable. The offer expired July, 1979.

In 1978 a Sugar Bear watch was also offered, for $7.95.

Other known dolls offered by Post Cereals include:

1969 4-inch **Storykin Cinderella** and coach, vinyl manufactured by Hasbro.

In 1969 Post Cereals offered a series of 4-inch vinyl dolls, which were manufactured by Hasbro. *Storykin Cinderella* is photographed beside her pumpkin coach. S. Esser collection, Bruce Esser photographer. $3.00.

1969 4-inch **Storykin Goldilocks** and table, vinyl manufactured by Hasbro.

Storykin Goldilocks came with a table, three bowls, three chairs, and a bear. S. Esser collection, Bruce Esser photographer. $3.00.

1969 4-inch **Storykin Sleeping Beauty** and bed, vinyl made by Hasbro.

Storykin Sleeping Beauty was another doll offered by Post Cereal. S. Esser collection, Bruce Esser photographer. $3.00.

1970 5-inch finger puppets, vinyl, manufactured by Remco in 1969. Puppets have vinyl torso, head, and arms, use fingers for the legs of the dolls. Boots were included.

1971 4½-inch **Monkee Finger-Ding Doll**, vinyl head, cloth body.

1972 3-inch **Dolly Darling**, vinyl, 60¢ plus two Post

Alpha-bits symbols, or free with five Post Alpha-Bits symbols.

1973 11½-inch **Malibu Barbie** complete with sun-bathing accessories cost $2.00 plus boxtop from Frosted Rice Krinkles, (another cereal no longer being produced, to my knowledge) Alpha-Bits, Cripsty Critters, or Honey-Combs.

1974 **Action Jackson**, vinyl.

Date? 10-inches, **Linus the Lion**, plush fabric, offered by Crispy Critters.

Linus the Lion was offered by Post's Crispy Critters cereal. It is gold plush and approximately 10-inches tall. Marked on a sewn on label: "Linus the Lion from Crispy Critters." $4.00.

Prairie Farms Butter offered a 40" x 25" inflatable yellow cow (date unknown).

Prince Macaroni. In 1965 a 6-inch Italian doll, direct from Italy was offered for $1.00 plus a coupon from Prince Macaroni Products. The ad says 20 cities are represented. Handmade with handtinted face, native hairstyle, and costume.

Princessa Shoes. A free doll was given with the purchase of a pair of Princessa Shoes in 1965. Eight different dolls were available. No further information is known.

Princeton Partners, Inc. In 1972 a clever cloth doll made from what looks like a thumbprint was manufactured for this company. The doll, 13-inches high, is oval with two tiny legs protruding from the bottom, and one arm lithographed on the front that holds a red heart printed: THUM-BODY/LOVES YOU. Black line eyes and mouth are the only facial features.

Procter & Gamble. In this book dolls are usually listed by the product they represent, except cereals, rather than the large company that manufactures the product. An exception is Procter &

Mary Makeup was manufactured by American Character and is 11½-inches tall. She has light blonde hair and no facial coloring. The owner was to provide color from a makeup kit and a hair coloring kit, which came with the doll. D. Matney collection. $8.00.

Gamble because this company has offered several dolls, which involve many of its products.

For a limited time in 1965 an 11½-inch **Mary Makeup Doll** was free for sending in seven labels from certain Procter & Gamble products. Customers were warned all the listed labels were required for one doll. This same doll was also sold at retail stores. Some of the products required were: Oxydol, Joy, Mr. Clean, Camay, and Downy.

That same year, a 3-inch "Wanda the Witch" troll doll was also offered free. This doll required a mail-in coupon found on many Procter & Gamble products. The doll had 7-inch long hair made of sheep fleece, green jewel eyes, and wore a witch costume.

In 1975 six Pogo cartoon dolls were sold with boxes of various Procter & Gamble products depending on the locality. The figures were: Howland Owl, Pogo, Uncle Albert Alligator, Beauregard Montmingle Bugleboy III (dog), Churchy La Femme (Turtle), and Porky (Porcupine). They range in size from 4 to 6-inches and are made of molded vinyl.

The year these were offered by Procter & Gamble was the year Walt Kelly, the creator of the Pogo comic strip, died. Many families kept mighty clean in 1975, in order to obtain all 6 of the Pogo dolls found in such products as Biz, Spic & Span, Oxydol, Tide, and Cascade.

Procter & Gamble is a mammoth enterprise, said to be the nation's biggest advertiser. Their corporate symbol, a circle with 13 stars and the profile of a Neptunish man-in-the-moon, is found on most of their products. Look closely and you may find it on such products as: Tide, Oxydol, Joy, Dreft, Dash, Crisco, Fluffo, Folger, Duncan Hines, Crest, Gleem, Head and Shoulders, Secret, Big Top and Jif.

The year Walt Kelly died, 1975, Procter & Gamble products were sold with small vinyl figures representing Kelly's beloved Pogo characters. The figures were from 4 to 6-inches tall and were quite detailed. From left to right: Churchy La Femme (turtle), Pogo (possum), Uncle Albert Alligator, Beauregard Montmingle Bugleboy III (dog). J. Ciolek collection, Visual Images photographer. $4.00.

Vinyl finger puppets were sold with various Procter & Gamble pro- ducts. These three are characters from the "Wizard of Oz." $1.00.

The trademark goes back to when a Mr. Procter, who made candles, and a Mr. Gamble, who made soap, teamed up to start a company back in 1837. One of their earliest major products was candles, which they loaded by the case on freight boats traveling the Ohio and Mississippi rivers from their river port city of Cinncinnati.

For identification, illiterate longshoremen would scrawl a star on each case of these candles. Later the star was enclosed in a circle, then more stars were added. Procter decided that because the first American flag had thirteen stars his company's symbol should have that same number, so the number of stars was fixed at thirteen. No one seems to remember why the man with the beard was added, but he is still there.

In time the candle line was dropped, and the company decided the trademark was rather meaningless, and it should be dropped too. Customers quickly changed their minds by insisting the trademark be retained and today if you look closely you can find this symbol that originated in 1837 on boxes of Procter & Gamble candles.

Puritan Flour. Making the most of the company name, Puritan Flour offered a cloth doll representing a Puritan gentleman. The 15½-inch doll is old, probably pre-1920. The printing on the fabric is done by a photographic process that produces an especially nice face. The costume is typical of what school children draw on pictures of the first Thanksgiving.

Puritan Flour offered an excellent quality *Puritan* cloth doll. The 15½-inch doll was probably used before 1920. It wears black pants, jacket, and hat, the collar is the large square kind. The belt, hat and shoes have large buckles. Marks: "PURITAN FLOUR," on the front collar; "PURITAN," each letter on one of the seven buttons down the front of the jacket. L. Edmundson collection. $30.00.

Q

Quaker Oats Company.

This company has grown along with America, claiming several firsts including: first to market a breakfast cereal nationally and first to register a cereal trademark. Many of its promotion ideas were also first in the advertising field.

The company started in the 1850's selling Quaker Oats, a hot cereal still on the market today, symbolized by the frugal trustworthy man in Quaker garb. By 1966 Quaker Oats was the largest seller of breakfast food in the world. Today the Quaker label is found on over 200 products: corn meal, grits, dog and cat food, livestock and poultry feeds, chemical, and baked goods.

Henry D. Seymour chose the name Quaker while searching through an encyclopedia because "the purity of the lives of the people, their sterling honesty, their strength and manliness" impressed him. His partner William Heston probably is responsible for the trademark figure. His version is, one day while walking he noticed a picture of William Penn and was struck by Penn's clothing and character as connoting just the qualities he was looking for.

The Quaker Oats man used a hundred years ago is much different from the one on today's packages. Originally he was a frail man dressd in dark drab garments. Today, the Quaker Oats diet must have paid off, he has emerged a genial, ruddy cheeked fellow.

After selecting a name and a trademark, Quaker went on to improve their sales by merchandising through premiums either in the package, or offered for labels, coupons, or boxtops. Who can forget carefully wriggling fingers down through a big box of oatmeal to discover which piece of china was enclosed. In addition to china Quaker has offered a fortune teller calendar, spoons, crystal radio, comic books, rings, a snap cannon, cartoon cookie cutters, one-inch square of Yukon Territory, coffee maker, scales, electric train, banks, and of course dolls, although to our knowledge no Quaker doll was ever offered.

The premiums were self-liquidating, meaning none of the advertising dollar went to the premium itself, all went to the consumer product. The premium had to be a bargain or a novelty to inspire people to send for it. Quaker acknowledges receiving 2,500,000 boxtops in a single year.

One of the most successful premiums was the Aunt Jemima doll. It was a novelty that was unavailable in stores and it was a bargain. Quaker Oats Company purchased Aunt Jemima Pancake Flour in 1926. Since that time it has offered two sets of dolls: a cloth doll in 1929 for 25¢ and a set of plastic dolls in 1948 for $5.00. (See Aunt Jemima Pancake Flour.)

Two other older cloth Quaker dolls are eagerly sought after by collectors. **Puffy** the 16-inch cloth soldier boy was a premium for Puffed Wheat and Puffed Rice, the cereals advertised as "Shot from Guns." The attributes of the puffed cereals were carried via radio from Babe Ruth and prominent male and female movie stars including Shirley Temple and Bing Crosby.

Puffy was introduced in 1930 during a lag in interest, after the excitement of the St. Louis World's Fair and before the advertising centered on the baseball hero Babe Ruth. The little soldier is standing at attention, with his gun at his side and his hat brim almost covering his eyes.

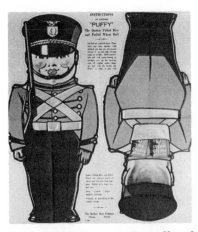

Quaker Oats Company has offered many premiums since they began selling cereal in 1850. One of interest to doll collectors is *Puffy*, the little cloth soldier used to advertise Quaker Puffed Rice and Quaker Puffed Wheat. The 16-inch doll wears a military uniform with blue pants, red jacket, and blue hat. The doll was printed in 1930. Marks: a box of Quaker's Puffed Wheat and Quaker's Puffed Rice in a knapsack hung on his back. Playthings by the Yard, 1973. $35.00.

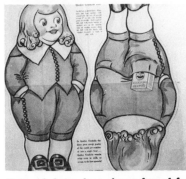

Several dates have been found for Quaker's *Crackels Boy* doll. The earliest is 1924, the latest 1930. Perhaps it was offered through that span of six years. *Crackels* is 16½-inches tall wears a lavender suit with soft green vest. The buttons are gold and the shoes brown. A box of Quaker Crackels, the short-lived cereal, is sticking out of his hind pocket. Playthings by the Yard, 1973. $35.00.

Quaker is well-known for its long term products, but occasionally products fizzled out and are now forgotten. One of the casualties was Crackels, which was introduced as a ready-to-eat cereal in 1924. The advertising was done by heavy-weight boxer Max Baer. Most of the cereal's premiums appealed primarily to boys--such as a hand-grip excercisor.

Sometime shortly after the cereal was introduced a chubby **Crackels Boy** doll was offered. The cloth doll had long yellow curls, and carried a box of Crackels in his hind pocket. The **Crackels Boy** doll had an even shorter life span than the cereal he represented.

To our knowledge it was over forty years before Quaker offered another doll. In the early 1960's competitors were pushing pre-sweetened ready-to-eat cereals for the young children's market. The Quaker Oats Company had no presweetened product, so began to consider marketing one. A bumbling sea captain named **Cap'n Crunch** was chosen for the name and the trademark. A product was needed to live up to the name preceeding it. What evolved was toasted pillow-shaped cereal coated with sugar.

During the next few years, eighty percent of Quaker's advertising budget was used for the new Cap'n Crunch cereal. In the early days, national prominence could be achieved for a promotional cost of $100,000. The introductory cost of Cap'n Crunch in the 1960's was five million for a single year. The advertising paid off, in two years it was one of the most popular presweetened cereals offered to the pre-teen market.

In 1975 a hard plastic bank of the old sea captain was offered for $1.50 plus two boxtops. The 7½-inch bank is well marked.

A 7½-inch hard plastic bank of *Cap 'n Crunch* was offered by the Quaker Oats Company in 1975. The old sea captain wears a molded blue jacket and hat with yellow trim. Marks: "Cap'n Crunch," indented in ½-inch letters on back; "C", on front of hat. K. Lansdowne collection. $4.00.

A 7½-inch plastic bank of *Jean LaFoote* was also offered by Quaker Oats Company in 1975. He wears a green pirate suit and hat and is barefoot. Marks: "Jean La Foote," in small print on back. K. Lansdowne collection. $4.00.

Cap'n Crunch's enemy, Jean La

Foote, was also offered in bank form in 1975. The **Jean La Foote** bank represents a pirate and is the same size and cost as the "Cap'n Crunch" bank.

In 1978 an all fabric **Cap'n Crunch** doll was offered in a packet offering free coupons, magazines, and other items. The doll cost $5.95 plus two labels from Cap'n Crunch cereal. Animal Fair, Inc. manufactured the doll exclusively for the Quaker Oats Company. It is a 15½-inch three-dimensional doll made from a wool-like fabric, that is synthetic. Epaulets, eyes, mustache, and other trim are made from felt.

In 1978 an all-cloth *Cap'n Crunch* doll was offered by Quaker Oats Company. The 15½-inch doll is made from a wool-like synthetic fabric. The jacket and hat are blue, face and hands are flesh, pants are white, and the boots are black. Trim and facial features are felt. Marks: "C", on front of hat; "Exclusively made for/The Quaker Oats/Company," on one side of cloth label sewn in boot; "Animal Fair, Inc./Copyright 1978," plus some other information on other side of label. $6.00.

After the success of Cap'n Crunch cereal, Quaker tried several other presweetened cereals for young children. Quake, "for earthquake power," was sold for a few years. Its trademark figure was a strong man in profile and a doll was manufactured to represent the figure. The 11-inch cloth **Quake** doll is unmarked, except for a "Q" on the chest.

An 11-inch cloth doll of a man flexing his biceps was offered in the late 60's by Quaker's Quake Cereal, a product that only sold for a few years. The doll's head is in profile, but the body is full-front. The only mark is a "Q" on the chest. $8.00.

Possibly because of consumer concern that many sugared cereals on the market were not providing adequate nutrition to young children, Quaker introduced "vitamin powered sugary cereal Quisp for Quazy energy."

The trademark figure chosen for this cereal is an outerspace fellow with a propeller atop his head and carrying a gun. A cloth **Quisp** doll was manufactured to resemble the trademark. The 15-inch doll has a pink head with crossed eyes, propeller, and green suit with a "Q" on the buckle.

A 7-inch **Quisp** was also offered. It is made of paper mache with high-gloss paint. The propeller on the bank could be mistaken for a hair ribbon. It cost $1.00 plus proof-of-purchase seal.

Quisp Cereal's outerspace creature *Quisp* was offered in fabric with lithographed features and clothing. His green suit has a belt with a "Q" buckle. The head and propeller are pink. $7.00.

A 7-inch *Quisp* bank of paper mache was offered by Quisp cereal. The bank looks ceramic because of its high-gloss paint. *Quisp* wears a green suit with a black belt and a large "Q" buckle. The round head is pink with a propeller that resembles a hair bow. Marks: "Taiwan," on bottom of base. $7.00.

R

RCA. Before RCA purchased the Victor Talking Machine Company, a 15½-inch **Sellin' Fool** doll was used to advertise their radios. The dolls were manufactured for display. The limbs were wood beads strung on elastic, the bead for the hands was slotted to hold display cards that could be changed.

The *Sellin Fool* doll was used for display in 1926 by dealers selling RCA products. The 15½-inch doll has a composition head and upper body. The limbs and lower body are wooden beads; slits in the bead hands could hold display cards. The major colors of this doll are red and yellow. Marks: "RCA/Radiotron," on tube hat; "RCA Radiotrons," on ribbon worn diagonally from one shoulder;" Art quality Mfg./Cameo Doll Co., N.Y.," on one foot. Margaret Woodbury Strong Museum, Barbara Jendrick photographer. $150.00-200.00.

Joseph L. Kallus, the well-known doll artist, created the doll from a figure conceived by Maxfield Parrish. The doll had a com-

position head with molded/painted hair showing under a tall radio tube hat. The thin-lipped mouth is smiling, eyes are painted. The composition upper body fits onto a wood ball that completes the lower body. A molded/painted collar at the neck is the only indication of clothing other than boots. The doll is well-marked.

In 1960 RCA promoted their television repair tubes with a rotund **Service Man** bank, dressed in a molded/painted gray uniform. The hard plastic bank is 5-inches tall. Facial features are molded, but not painted.

In 1960 the *RCA Service Man* bank was used to promote television repair tubes. The 5-inch bank is hard plastic with molded facial features that are unpainted. The suit and hat are molded/painted gray with black belt, visor, and shoes. Marks: "RCA/We use RCA tubes," on the hat and shirt front; "Made in USA," on back. $4.00.

Ralston Purina Company. This St. Louis company has used the red and white checkerboard as a trademark since the late 1800's, when founder, William H. Danforth, first noticed the eye appeal of the checks. It seems a thrifty family who patronized his small feed store all wore clothing made from a bolt of red and white checked fabric. The visual impact was unforgettable.

When Danforth launched his Purina Chows product line, he remembered those checks and adopted them for his trademark. Today the checks are still an important part of Ralston Purina packaging. The checkerboard trademark is registered in 79 counties and is carried on about 550 products in this country alone.

According to a company spokesman, the name Ralston Purina is divided by products. Ralston is used when referring to foods produced for human consumption, such as Ralston Chex Cereals. Purina is used when referring to food produced for animal consumption, such as Purina Puppy Chow.

Years ago Purina feed of various kinds sponsored Tom Mix, the old cowboy idol of the movies. Many small Tom Mix premiums were offered by the company.

More recently Ralston Purina Company has produced several products that have offered doll or animal premiums. In 1965 the Chex line of cereals offered the Purina **Squarecrow from Checkerboard Square**, as seen on television commercials. It is a 23-inch doll with a cloth body, and a vinyl head and hat. The nicely molded and painted face depicts a smiling open/closed mouth scarecrow with a red triangle nose. The body has lithographed clothes including patched pants and a patched jacket with a rope belt. The "Squarecrow" was available for $1.50 plus a proof-of-purchase from any of the Chex cereals.

In 1973 to promote Raisin Bran Chex cereal, an ugly raisin-looking cloth doll was offered. The 15-inch doll is egg-shaped, the lithographed arms crossed in front, tiny legs

and feet attached to the bottom, and a red petal hat is sewn to the top of the doll. Purple, brown, and black lines are used to represent the wrinkles of the raisin, one eye is winking.

In 1965 the *Squarecrow from Checkerboard Square* was offered by Ralston Purina's Chex line of cereals. Marks: "R.P. Co." $12.00.

In 1973 the Ralston Purina Company offered a cloth raisin doll to advertise their Raisin Bran Chex cereal. Unmarked. $8.00.

Raisin Bran Chex was a short-lived cereal that was probably marketed before its time, before it became fashionable to include fiber in the diet. The doll was a limited offer, therefore this doll is difficult to find, even though it is fairly recent. The doll cost $1.00 plus proof-of-purchase.

In the mid-70's one of seven different plastic characters were enclosed in boxes of Ralston's Freakies Cereal, a line of cereal aimed at young children. The idea was to buy lots of cereal in order to obtain all seven characters: 1½-inch purple **Gargle**, 1¼-inch green **Boss Moss**, ¾-inch orange **Grumble**, 1-inch blue **Snorkledorf**, 1¼-inch olive **Cowmumble**, **Hamhose**, **Goody-Goody**. The last two we do not have, so do not know the size nor color.

Ralston Purina Company offers a variety of animal feeds that are listed under the company name rather than the product name.

In 1976 Purina's Meow Mix offered a 4½-inch yellow cat free on packages of dry cat food with proof-of-purchase requirements. The toy is yellow vinyl with black markings and was intended as a toy for pet cats.

In 1978 this same product offered five cat toys: a ball, mouse, butterfly, fish, and pull-toy. They were free with required proof-of-purchase seals.

Purina Cat Chow annually offers a cat calendar that results in thousands of requests.

Purina Dog Chow offered a **Doctor Dolittle** marionette in 1968 to coincide with the **Doctor Dolittle** movie. The marionette was part of an adventure set that included eight small rubber animal erasers. The 10½-inch marionette resembles Rex Harrison who played the lead role in the movie.

In 1977 Purina Dog Chow offered a 21-inch white plush dog named the **Shaggy DA** after a dog and a movie of the same name. The dog wears a man's red tie. It was available for one weight circle and $6.75.

The 4½-inch vinyl *Meow Mix* cat was a free offer on packages of Meow Mix dry cat food. Marks: "© 1976/Ralston Purina Company," on back; "MEOW/MIX," across chest. $2.00.

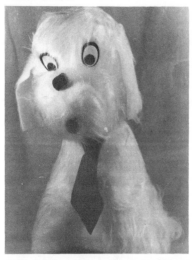

Ralston Purina Company's Purina Dog Chow offered the *Shaggy D.A.* in 1977. The 21-inch white plush dog has felt eyes, nose and tongue. It wears a man's red tie. V. Jones Collection. $7.00.

In 1975 a one-piece vinyl *Chuck Wagon* and team copied from the set used in TV commercials to advertise Purina's Chuck Wagon Dog Food was made available. The toy is 8-inches long and 3¼-inches tall. The horses and wood on the wagon are shades of brown. The wagon top is painted with Ralston Purina's famous red and white check. Marks: "Ralston Purina Company © 1975," on bottom. $2.00.

A sleeping bag made to look like a bag of Purina Dog Chow was available first through the Ralston Purina Company, and later through Sears stores.

Although not dolls or animals it might be noted that Purina Chuck Wagon Dog Food has offered several premiums modeled after the team of horses and wagon that race through their television commercials. One was a kit to make a wooden covered wagon, another was the familiar wagon made to house a transistor radio.

In 1975 the Doyle H. Spencer Company manufactured a one-piece vinyl **Chuck Wagon** toy. The toy is 8-inches long and 3¼-inches tall. (See Chicken of the Sea, another Ralston Purina Company product.)

Razzles Dubble Bubble Gum, a product of Fleer. Television commercials for this gum used a character called Razzle. In the early 1970's a 13-inch cloth doll was made to represent this trademark figure.

The doll was available for $2.00 plus 10 Dubble Bubble Gum wrappers.

In the early 1970's *Razzle* advertised Razzles Double Bubble Gum. The 13½-inch white cloth doll has blue shoes and purplish-red trim on the shirt. The brown hair has a cowlick in back. Marks: "R," on front of shirt; "Razzle" on back. K. Lyons collection. $6.00.

Red Barn Restaurant.

For a limited time, some restaurants of this quick-food franchise offered three plush characters. The toys were manufactured by R & R Toy Mfg. Co., Inc. and were introduced in March 1970.

Hamburger Hungry is plush fabric with a felt hat, eyes, and mouth. The body and arms are felt, and it wears a scarf. Marks: "Hamburger/Hungry"; plus the company logo, on the front. A. Wolfe collection, David Nelson, James Giokas photographers. $10.00.

Big Fish Hungry, 22-inches, is in the shape of a fish, with arms and facial features. The body is royal blue plush; the head is gray felt with felt eyes and mouth and a pom pom nose. Marks: "Big Fish/Hungry," plus the company logo. A. Wolfe collection, David Nelson, James Giokas photographers. $10.00.

Chicken Hungry is shaped like a 22-inch drum stick, with arms. The plush premium is the color of golden brown fried chicken. The hands, mouth, and eyes are felt. It was photographed beside a cardboard Red Barn take-out box. Marks: "Chicken/Hungry." A. Wolfe collection, David Nelson, James Giokas photographers. $10.00.

Red Rose Tea Company.

In 1950 a puppet monkey was offered by this tea company that sells primarily in Canada and some northern states. The monkey has a vinyl head with protruding ears, dark sun glasses, and a molded hat. The clothing consists of a jacket over a shirt and a string tie, made to accomodate the hand of the puppeteer. The hat is marked: "Red Rose."

In the early 1970's various 1 to 2-inch ceramic animals such as a turtle, rabbit, and cat were enclosed in boxes of Red Rose Tea.

Reddi-Wip.

Since 1965 this whip cream-like topping has offered the common 8-inch plastic dolls that so many other products also offer. In 1965 the dolls cost $1.50 plus the pull tab from a can of Reddi-Wip.

The November, 1972 issue of Family Circle carried an ad for the dolls that said they were dressed in 30 different costumes including Pocahontas, Cinderella, Betsy Ross, and Annie Oakley.

In 1976 the same dolls came with a cardboard tag that said: Bicentennial Dolls. Sometime between 1972 and 1976 the cost inflated to $2.00 per doll.

Revlon, Inc. In 1950 Revlon, "The people who help make the world a little more beautiful!" allowed Ideal Toy Company to manufacture vinyl dolls named after their cosmetics. Several sizes of Revlon dolls were produced until 1958, when they were all discontinued.

In 1950 Ideal Toy Company manufactured a 10½-inch vinyl *Little Miss Revlon* doll. The doll was well made and proved a favorite with little girls. The doll wore nylons, shoes, garters, and a bra. It was usually sold in a cotton print dress with a gathered skirt, but many other outfits were available including a bride outfit. The doll has rooted hair, nail polish, high-heel feet, swivel waist, pierced ears, small bust, open/close eyes. Marks: "Ideal Doll/VT 10½." M. Beahon collection. $20.00.

The earliest **Little Miss Revlon** doll, is 10½-inches high, has high-heel feet, pierced ears, and a swivel waist. The rooted Saran wig came in many shades ranging from light blonde to dark brown. The doll is made of top quality vinyl with excellent detail. Each finger is separate and has polished nails. The blue eyes open/shut; mouth is closed. Several outfits were sold to fit the **Little Miss Revlon** doll including a bride dress and veil.

The 10½-inch doll was sold until 1956 when a larger **Miss Revlon** doll was manufactured. The new 18-inch **Miss Revlon** body resembles the smaller one and it has all the same features: swivel waist, high-heel feet, separate fingers, closed mouth, and pierced ears. This doll came with a comb, hair curlers, and Revlon Satin Set hair spray. Several outfits were available.

In 1956 an 18-inch *Miss Revlon* doll replaced the smaller doll. It resembles the earlier "Little Miss Revlon" and has the same features. The doll came with a comb, curlers, and hair spray. Marks: "Ideal," on back; "Miss Revlon Doll Ideal," on ribbon label at waist. K. Lyons collection. $22.00.

In 1958 a new model **Miss Revlon** and her mother **Mrs. Revlon** were manufactured by Ideal. The mother and daughter are the same 19-inch doll, except the mother's wig is gray and it has a touch of purple eye shadow around the eyes. These two dolls have a different face than the two previous **Miss Revlon** dolls: the chin is smaller, and the lower part of the face is narrower. They do have the same mechanical features: jointed waist, high-heel feet, pierced ears, and closed mouth. On these dolls both the finger nails and the toe nails are polished. The 19-inch **Miss Revlon** was available in several short cotton dresses with full gathered skirts.

Ideal's 1958 *Mrs. Revlon* doll is 19-inches and is the same doll as the *Miss Revlon* doll made by Ideal that year except for two differences. *Mrs. Revlon* has gray streaked hair and wears heavy eye shadow. She wears the original dress, but is missing her shoes. The doll body, arms, and legs are in one piece, with no joints. Marks: "14R," on back of neck; "VH-19 2," incised on one foot; "A," on lower back. $22.00.

Rexall Drug Co. Patent records show a patent was obtained in 1914 for a Rexall doll and toy. No further information is known.

A vinyl baby doll of fairly recent vintage was found that is marked with the company name. How or when it was used is unknown. The 7½-inch doll is a one-piece squeak toy with very short arms, hands curled in a fist with thumbs extended upward, curved legs, and a bald head except for a few molded/painted lines on the forehead. It wears a molded diaper and miniscule bib. The facial features are simple, but emit a personality. Eyes are closed, mouth U-shaped and it has two pink circles on the cheeks.

Little is known about Rexall Drug Company's 7½-inch vinyl doll. It wears a molded diaper and tiny bib with a scalloped edge. The facial features include painted eyes that are closed, pink circles at the cheeks, and a few lines on the forehead for hair. The legs are bowed and the tiny arms are outstretched. K. Brunell collection. $3.00.

Right Guard. In 1972 the **Love Doll** by Hasbro was offered for $2.75 plus a cap label from this deodorant. The doll represented the young people who were protesting the Viet Nam War. One of their slogans was: "Make Love not War." The 9-inch **Love Doll** is vinyl with posable legs, jointed at the neck, shoulders, waist, and hips. The eyes and mouth are painted, inset lashes, rooted synthetic wig.

Ring Clear Hosiery. An 8-inch plastic doll, the common type, was free with three pair of this brand of nylons. The dolls were dressed in a long gown with ribbon bodice, felt hat with a feather. No date.

Rodkey's Flour, a product of the Eagle Milling Company. This Edmond, Oklahoma company printed a cloth doll on their sacks of flour. **Rag Darling** really is darling, her face is sweet, and she wears a dress with a bow at the waist.

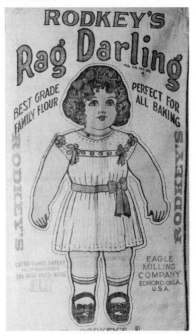

Printed on bags of Rodkey's flour was their *Rag Darling*. The flour was a product of the Eagle Milling Company of Edmond, Oklahoma. M. Rice collection. $30.00.

Rose Marie Reid Swimsuits. A rather unusual doll was either used for display or as a premium by this line of women's swimwear. The 7-inch hard vinyl doll is all green with molded hair and facial features. It wears a modest one-piece swimsuit decorated with a rhinestone brooch. No date.

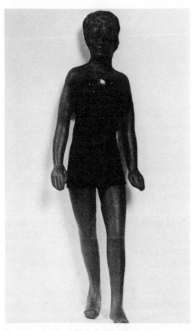

Rose Marie Reid Swimsuits used this 7-inch hard vinyl doll. Whether it was a premium or a display doll is unknown. It wears a modest one-piece swimsuit in black with a rhinestone brooch. J. Ciolek collection, Visual Images photographer. $10.00.

Royal Blue Food Stores. The Susie Q figure used on ads from this store became available in doll form for Christmas of 1948. The 15-inch jointed plastic doll wears a royal blue dress with white cuffs and collar, and a checked waist apron. The black wig is worn in braids, eyes open and close. The doll was sold at the stores and cost $3.79.

Royal Crown Cola. An inflatable **Zippy** doll with a crown was used by this carbonated beverage.

Zippy is an inflatable doll used by Royal Crown Cola. $4.00.

Royal Gelatin. A 9½-inch vinyl bank called **King Royal** was offered by this brand of gelatin. The figure is dressed in robes and a crown.

A comical looking bank named *King Royal* was used to promote Royal Gelatin. The 9½-inch bank is made of vinyl and is shaped like a king with a huge nose. No further information is known. Marks: "King Royal." $6.00.

S

Salerno Butter Cookies. In 1956 a **Cookie Bear** was offered by this brand of cookie. The bear was 14-inches tall and cost $5.50 plus a coupon from a package of cookies. No further information is known.

Sambo's Restaurant. In 1957 the name Sambo's was chosen for a new restaurant franchise, because the name Sambo combined the first syllables of the two men who started the restaurant. They chose a trademark that represented characters in the book: Little Black Sambo, Sambo and a tiger.

According to one of the vice-presidents, the **Sambo** dolls and **tigers** were introduced for their restaurants in 1966. Since that time **Sambo** dolls and **tiger** figures have been made in many sizes and from several materials.

In our search for advertising dolls we found several **Sambo** dolls and several **tigers**, there are probably others. Individual restaurant managers had the option of ordering dolls. The **Sambo** dolls found range from 7 to 18-inches high and are made from vinyl or nylon. The tigers range from 4½-inches for the little cub to a 48-inch plush stuffed tiger that cost $50.00. The tigers are made from plastic, rubber, velvet, and cotton fabric.

The **Sambo** doll most often found is sitting, has a nylon face with painted features. It comes in three sizes 7, 10, and 12-inches. The doll has a closed umbrella that resembles a tree in one hand. The other hand holds a plate of pancakes. On the head is a turban with a red paper jewel and feather. A tag on the jacket identifies the doll.

In 1978 many Sambo's restaurants stocked plush tigers manufactured for the franchise by R. Dakin & Company. These were sold with other advertising items near the cash register. One tiger was the bean-bag type that was filled with styrofoam pellets.

Sambo's Restaurants sold several *Sambo* dolls, this seems to be the most common. The doll, 10-inches tall, is fabric, with a nylon face and felt limbs. One hand holds a closed umbrella. The other hand holds a plate of felt pancakes. In keeping with the famous children's story *Sambo* wears crimson shoes, and a little red jacket. Being a child from India *Sambo* wears a turban with a fake jewel in front. Marks: "Dream Doll/R. Dakin & Co./Prod. of Japan," on cloth label; same information on a paper tag. $6.00.

Sambo Restaurants sold several sizes of this tiger. It is made of knit velvet stretched over a firm base. The facial features are made with felt. Marks: "Dream Pets/R. Dakin & Co.," on cloth label plus other information; "Dream Pets," on paper tag. $3.00.

A rubber *Sambo* doll, 5-inches tall, sold at Sambo Restaurants. Marks: "© 1972/Kings Import/Spain." $3.00.

A 7-inch *Sambo's Tiger* sits on his back legs. The tiger wears a little chef hat marked "Sambo's," has a fuzzy beard and has felt facial features. Marks: "Created Exclusively for Sambo's/R. Dakin & Co." $6.00.

A 7-inch sitting stuffed tiger from Sambos Restaurant. It is felt and came in other sizes. $3.00.

One of the older rubber tigers, 4¼" sold at Sambo Restaurants. Marks: "© 1972/Kings/Import/Spain." $3.00.

Hand puppets were given free at restaurants where the manager ordered the promotional items. J. Varsolona collection. $1.00.

The *Mother* hand puppet from Sambos. J. Varsolona collection. $1.00.

Sandies Restaurant. A nodder football doll was a promotion for this hamburger restaurant. (In our area the name was changed in 1977 to Bucky's.) The 7-inch molded/painted doll is composition with a spring neck that allows the head to nod. **Sandies** is painted on the base.

Sanitary Cloth Toys by Art Fabric Mills. An ad in The Youth's Companion, October 5, 1905, offered a small free cloth doll to anyone writing in for one.

Schiaparelli. An 8-inch doll with jointed knees was offered by this company, whether it is a line of clothing or hosiery is not certain. The box the doll came in says, "This doll is created especially for you by Mme. Elsa Schiaparelli, world famous designer."

The doll is hard vinyl except the head which is soft vinyl. The eyes open/shut, mouth closed, and the wig is rooted. It wears a blue felt jacket over a dress. Plastic boots with roller skates attached, complete the doll costume.

Scott Paper Company. An "Election Selection" promotion with two stuffed animals was

In 1972 an 11-inch donkey or a 9-inch elephant could be ordered from the Scott Paper Company free with seals from their paper towels or tissue. The animals are made of royal blue plush fabric with a cotton fabric trim that is white with stars. There is no identification relating the animals to Scott paper products, only a paper tag explaining the materials used, care, and the manufacturer, which is "A & L Novelty Co." L. Yagatich collection, Donald G. Vilsack photographer. $2.00.

advertised at point-of-sale for a limited time in 1972. In addition to choosing either McGovern or Nixon for president of the United States, Scott offered either a **donkey** or an **elephant** free for 10 decals from Scot Towels or 5 seals from Scotties Facial Tissue. The blue plush animals were manufactured by the A & L Novelty Company. The **donkey** is 11-inches high, the **elephant** 9-inches.

In 1976 **Scottie Dog** was offered free for 15 seals from boxes of Scotties Facial Tissue. The dog, 7-inches, came in either black or white plush fabric, with a plaid bow around the neck.

Scottie was free for 15 seals from boxes of Scottie Facial Tissue in 1976. $2.00.

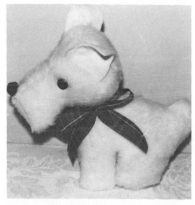

Scottie in white plush. J. Varsolona collection. $2.00.

Sea Island Sugar, a product of Western Sugar Refinery Company. During the 1930's this San Francisco refinery sold sugar in cloth sacks with dolls printed on them. The dolls were usually stamped in two or three colors and these would rapidly fade with each washing. Most of the dolls represented children from other lands and they were usually printed on the 10-pound sack.

There were many Sea Island Sugar dolls. A few were: **Jong-yi**, the Korean girl; **Chung**, the Chinese boy; **Gobo**, the African boy; **Gretchen**, the Dutch girl; **Dusty**, the Cowboy; **Fifi**, the French girl, and **Abdul**, the Arabian boy. The dolls on this size sack were 8-inches tall. The dolls were unmarked. Luckily some people saved the entire sack. From this we found the dolls were

Gobo, the South African boy. Many of the Sea Island Sugar dolls were printed with only two colors, this doll uses brown for the skin, dabs of red and blue for the skirt and other details, and black for the hair. The sack is 10 x 16-inches; the doll is 8-inches. Marks: "Gobo/South African Boy," on back. P. Coghlan collection, Harry Sykora photographer. $6.00-10.00.

copyrighted in 1935. Other names of dolls mentioned on the sacks were: **Haru, Fatima, Pat, Hulda, Jock, Carmen, Chief, Little Bear, Tanya, Hula, Minka, Scotty** and **Uluk.**

In 1935 the company also took out a copyright for a large **Uncle Sam** that was printed on a larger sack, probably the 25-pound size. We were unable to locate one of these dolls.

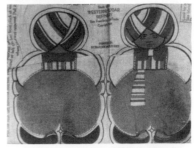

Sea Island Sugar's *Abdul, the Arabian Boy,* doll is printed in red, blue, and brown. $6.00-10.00.

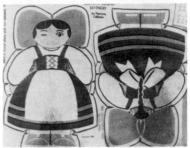

Fifi, the French Girl looks like she might be Dutch on first glance. Notice her wink. $6.00-10.00.

Franz, the Tyrolean Boy is another Sea Island Sugar doll. $6.00-10.00.

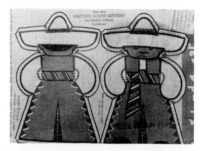

Pedro, the Mexican Boy wears a huge sombrero. $6.00-10.00.

Sea Island Sugar's *Tanya, the Russian Girl* doll. $6.00-10.00.

A departure from Sea Island Sugar's usual international dolls, this is *Dusty, the Cowboy*. $6.00-10.00.

Chief Little Bear from Sea Island Sugar. $6.00-10.00

Seabrook Farms Prepared Foods. The common 8-inch International Dolls were offered by this brand in 1974.

Sears. For about 15 years Sears Stores and Catalog has used Winnie the Pooh as a trademark for a top quality line of children's wear. The Milne creation lives in a huge paper mache tree in the center of the children's department at many large Sears Stores. He is found on labels, and displayed in various ways throughout the store and catalog.

The little bear and his friends play a big part in Sears advertising on this line. They are offered for sale in every imaginable size and from many materials. At one time Sears gave free a 5½-inch seated **Pooh Bear** doll. The soft vinyl bear is eating from his famous honey pot.

Seiko Watches. A robot figure is used as a trademark for

The 21-inch inflatable *Seiko Robot* was intended for store displays. Because many were requested by customers they were made available to jewelry managers for $2.00. The robot symbolizes the mechanized assembly plant in Japan that makes the Seiko watch. $5.00.

289

this large Japanese watch company.

In 1977 the robot was made in a 21-inch inflatable size to celebrate the company's tenth anniversary. Many stores ordered extras to sell to the public for $2.00, others used them only for display.

Sergeant's Sentry IV Flea Collar. In 1976 to promote their novel pet collar, Sergeants, the "Pet Care People," offered three stuffed animals for $5.00 each.

The three toys were manufactured by the Fable Toy Company of New York and were patterned after characters used in Sergeant television commercials.

Dirty Dog, 20-inches, is gray plush fabric with plastic half-ball eyes, plastic nose, and felt tongue. It wears a vest marked DIRTY DOG.

Sergeant Dog, 20-inches, is made of gold plush with the same type features as "Dirty Dog."

Glamour Puss, 20-inches, is a pink plush cat with the same type features as the other two animals.

Sergeant Dog was offered in 1976 by Sergeants, "The Pet Care People." The gold plush dog is 20-inches tall. Marks: "1976 Mill/Morton Co. a subsidiary of A.H. Robins Co./Richmond, Va 23230," on a cloth label. $6.00.

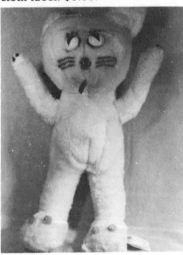

A companion to *Dirty Dog* and *Sergeant Dog* is *Glamour Puss*, a 20-inch pink plush cat. The three animals cost $5.00 each. $6.00.

20-inch *Dirty Dog* is made from a long gray plush fabric, the eyes and nose are plastic, and the tongue is felt. It wears a vest marked: "Dirty/Dog." $6.00.

Seven-Eleven. In 1979 two inflatable characters advertising Seven-Eleven's frozen soft drink were offered. In June **Koala Kola Bear**, a 3-foot gray bear with black features was given to the child, under 12-years of age, winning a coloring contest.

In July the offering was **Renegade Lemonade**, approximately 4½-feet tall. The inflatable Indian wears an orange hat, green vest and loin cloth with red trim, and yellow pants. Both characters are marked with their name and the store's logo in the circle.

Seven Up. Before the company used the very clever promotion selling this carbonated beverage as the UNcola, they used Fresh-Up Freddie and the Zorro television show to sell 7-UP.

Freddie is a rooster cartoon character, created by Walt Disney Studios. In 1957 company representatives met at the studio to select an advertising figure from a collection of cartoon characters that had been featured in Disney productions.

The character that caught their eye was Panquito, a rooster who appeared with the parrot, Jose Carioca, as one of the "Three Cabelleros." In that movie Panquito was "fresh, light, and sort of bubbling with enthusiasm," perfect for a drink with the same qualities.

The little rooster had to be modified for 7-Up's use. He was too scrawny, his comb needed clipping, and his bill needed to be adapted for dialogue. A company publication says, "Where Panchito was a trifle goofy and brainless, Freddie had to have a mind of his own, a hefty IQ and yet still be a wryly humorous fellow."

In time he was ready to make his debut with the voice of Paul Frees, who also recorded most of the voices of the characters in the cartoons. In June of 1958 Fresh-Up Freddie was introduced to the public via television commercials on the Zorro show and on posters used to advertise 7-Up.

In the fall of that first year, the **Fresh-Up Freddie** doll, a 24-inch cloth figure with a rubber head, was given as an attendance prize at a 7-Up convention. About 700 of these dolls were distributed to local dealers to use for display.

Seven Up's first *Fresh up' Freddie* doll was a 24-inch cloth doll with a molded/painted rubber head. The doll was given as an attendance prize at a Seven Up convention in 1958. Marks: "7up," in logo; "Fresh up"/Freddie,"on front of shirt. Photograph provided by Seven Up Company. $25.00.

The next year the company sponsored a contest--managers were to find, "The most imaginative way to use the **Fresh-Up Freddie** doll in promoting Zorro and 7-Up." (Freddie and Zorro would make quite a match for the Lone Ranger and Tonto.) First prize was $500.00 worth of credit with Diners Club. This inspired managers to bring the doll out of the back room and into an imaginative display.

Eventually **Freddie** could be purchased for $6.00, which was quite expensive at that time. The cloth and rubber **Freddie** was developed by Earle Pullan Company of Canada.

A second **Freddie** doll was manufactured in 1959. It was a

9-inch squeeze toy made of molded/painted vinyl or rubber. It is not certain how or where these sold. Company literature mentions a St. Louis bottler that sold over 6,000.

In 1959 a second *Freddie* doll was manufactured and sold primarily at retail stores. It was a 9-inch squeeze toy made of molded/-painted vinyl or rubber. The Walt Disney inspired character holds a bottle of 7up in one hand, the other hand on his hip. "Freddie" wears green short pants and a white shirt. Marks: "1959," on one foot; "The/ Seven/Up/Co.," on the other foot; "7up," in logo on front of shirt. Photograph provided by Seven Up Company. $10.00.

In the 70's Seven-up offered the *Undeer* hand puppet. It is 10-inches tall and made of rust colored plush with plastic red horns. R. Keelen collection. $3.00.

Years later, after the big "UN" campaign was underway a 10-inch "UNdeer" puppet was sold as a holiday promotion. The puppet is made of plush fabric with plastic horns, and sold in the early 70's.

The information used here was sent by the company in a cardboard envelope sealed with a large sticker saying: UNdoit.

Shakey's Pizza Restaurant. Two **Shakey Chef** dolls, representing the Shakey logo, have been used to promote this pizza restaurant. One doll is 18-inches high, all-white cloth, with some sparce lithographed detail. The hands are in front, hat is stuffed as an extension of the doll, facial features include a mustache. This doll has also been found printed on yellow fabric.

The other **Shakey Chef** doll is 10½-inches high on a pedestal, and manufactured by Ashland Rubber Product Company. The doll is molded white plastic with a few red and black details.

The 18-inch *Shakey Chef* doll is printed on white fabric with lines outlining the apron, hands, and facial features. The top of the chef hat is sewn on separately. Marks: "S," on front of hat. $6.00.

Shakey's Pizza Parlors were given a 10½-inch plastic figural of the *Shakey Chef*. Marks: "Shakey's Pizza Parlor/Ye Public R," on the front of the pedestal; "Ashland Rubber/ Product Co./Ashland, Ohio," on bottom. K. Lansdowne collection. $3.00.

Shaklee Products. A 6½-inch **Small Wonder** bunny was used by this company. The toy is made of soft vinyl.

Small Wonder is pink and white with blue writing, bow, eyes, and nose. Marks: "Shaklee Products/ Hayward, California/94544," on back. J. Ciolek collection, Visual Images photographer. $3.00.

Shamrock Oil Company. A 15-inch lithographed cloth **Leprechaun** doll was offered by Shamrock Service Stations.

The Shamrock Oil Company used a 15-inch cloth *Leprechaun* doll in the 1970's. It is a red-headed fellow in a green suit and hat; a stick is carried over one shoulder. Unmarked. $5.00.

Shoprite Stores. In the 1970's this chain of stores sold a

Scrunchy Bear advertises Shoprite stores. The bear is brown plush with a yellow shirt. It measures 16-inches sitting down. Marks: "Shoprite," in circle logo. B. Welch collection. $7.00.

293

Scrunchy Bear. It measures 16-inches sitting down. The brown plush bear's upper body is constructed of a yellow knit fabric to resemble a shirt.

Simplicity. In 1943 a 12½-inch **Simplicity Mannequin** doll was manufactured by Latexture Products for the retail market. The mannequin is made of a substance similar to composition, but more durable. Features are molded/painted, with brown hair and blue eyes. To aid in fitting the miniature Simplicity patterns the arms are moveable. Molded high heel shoes fit into a pedestal. A Simplicity sewing book also came with the doll and patterns.

A *Simplicity* doll shown in the original box with the original contents. The 12½-inch doll had molded high heel shoes and removable arms to facilitate fitting clothing made from Simplicity patterns. The hair is molded/painted brown. According to the box, it is a Latexture product. M. Rice collection. $25.00.

Sinclair Refining Company. In the early 1930's this company began to use a green dinosaur in its advertising. At the Chicago Exposition in 1933 and at the Dallas World's Fair in 1935, Sinclair's life-size dinosaur model was a hit. To further Sinclair's association with dinosaurs, they sponsored dinosaur bone expedi-

tions into the Rockies and Texas.

One of their first premiums, a Dinosaur Stamp Album, capitalized on their symbol. In 1930 four million albums and ninety-six million stamps were printed for this promotion.

For some unexplained reason it wasn't until about 1960 that the decision was made to adopt the dinosaur, brontosauras (order Sauropoda), as the official Sinclair trademark.

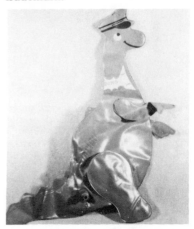

A 14-inch inflatable green dinosaur offered at Sinclair Stations in 1978. Marks: "Dino," on neck; "Sinclair," on back. Still available.

Another wise move was the adoption of the name Dino for Sinclair's regular gasoline and for their trademark figure. Through the years Dino has been offered to customers in many sizes and from several materials. We were only able to find the premiums being sold in 1977 and still available at some stations.

With the purchase of gasoline the customer could purchase either a green inflatable **Dino** that looks like the brontosauras used for the trademark, (except it's wearing a cap) or a **Dino** of the upright Tyrannosauras, wearing a cap. The two dinosaurs come in two sizes, the larger size, 48-

inches from head to tail cost $2.98, the smaller size, 14-inches cost 98¢.

Six Flags over Texas.

This resort area gave free hand puppets away to advertise their attractions. The puppet is the plastic mitten type with a cowboy on the front and a description of the resort on the back.

A shootem' up Texas cowboy puppet advertises the popular Six Flags over Texas recreation spot. $1.00.

Skookum Packers Association of Wenatchee, Washington. The **Skookum** doll used by this company looks nothing like the more common **Skookum** Indian dolls with stern mouths, tiny side-glance eyes, and blankets. The apple packer's **Skookum** resembles their trademark: a mischievous looking Indian with a hole for a feather. The 16-inch doll has composition head and hands and wears felt jacket and pants. In 1916 an exclusive license was granted to Louis Amberg & Son to manufacture **Skookum, The Bully Kiddo** for the Northeast Fruit Exchange.

The word Skookum was registered by Mary McAboy in

1917 and 1919 with a note that the word had been used since 1913. On her dolls was a sticker that explained the word Skookum meant "Bully Good" in Siwash.

The *Skookum* doll used to advertise the Skookum Packer's Association of Wenatchee, Washington in no way resembles the stern looking *Skookum* dolls patented by Mary McAboy in 1917. The apple packers' doll has a smiling mouth and wrinkled eyes. Its head and hands are composition and the body is cloth. It wears original clothing consisting of a red felt jacket, blue pants with orange felt fringe, black and white shirt, and leather shoes. Date unkown. Marks: "Skookum/Apple Indian/ Reg. U.S. Patent office by/ Skookum Packers Association/ Wenatchee, Washington." $75.00.

Smaks Restaurant. A seal puppet named **Smaky Jr.** is patterned after their trademark. The 11-inch seal was manufactured by Animal Fair, Inc. and made of plush brown fabric, with tan plush nose, a pom-pom on the tip. The eyes are black plastic on a felt background.

This *Smaky Jr.* hand puppet is copied from Smaks Restaurant trademark. The 11-inch seal is brown plush fabric with a yellow knit shirt. $3.00.

Snoboy Apples. A **Snoboy** doll, copied from the trademark figure was available to customers buying a bag of Snoboy apples. The 12-inch white plush doll, manufactured by Princess

A delightful copy of Snoboy Apple's trademark is the 12-inch *Snuggly Snoboy* doll. Except for red earmuffs the doll is made of snow-soft plush fabric with a felt snowman face. Marks: "SNOBOY" plus other information on a cloth label. $10.00.

Toy Company of Minneapolis, represents a snowman wearing red earmuffs. The doll cost $1.95 plus the coupon inside the bag of apples.

Snow Crop Orange Juice, a division of Coca-Cola Co. Four **Teddy Snow Crop** offers have been used to promote this brand of orange juice. In the 1950's an 8½-inch plush hand puppet with a gray vinyl face was offered.

This well-worn *Teddy* has been around since the 1950's. The 10-inch toy is white plush fabric with a gray vinyl mask face. A. Leonard collection. $6.00.

That same decade a 10-inch **Teddy** made of plush with a gray vinyl face resembling the one used for the hand puppet was offered.

In 1972 a 14½-inch all terry cloth **Teddy** with felt features was offered. The toy has a blue ribbon that reads, "Hi, I'm Teddy Snow Crop."

A 17-inch plush stuffable pajama bag represented **Teddy** was also a premium mail-in offer. It cost $2.25 plus a plastic opening strip from a can of orange juice.

A 14½-inch terry cloth *Teddy Snow Crop* toy was offered by Snow Crop Orange Juice in 1972. The bear is white, with felt features. Marks: "Hi, I'm Teddy Snow Crop ® " stamped on a blue ribbon worn around the neck; "Stuart Inc./St. Paul, Minn.," on another cloth label. K. Miller collection. $5.00.

White plush *Teddy Snow Crop* was a mail-in premium for Snow Crop orange juice in the mid-1970's. Marks: "Hi, I'm Teddy Snow Crop," on ribbon around neck. K. Miller collection. $5.00.

So-Lo. In 1972 this low-fat milk offered a plastic **Pudgie** hand puppet.

This hand puppet is a *Pudgie* from So-lo low-fat milk. $1.00.

Sony Corporation. This Japanese manufacturing company used a molded plastic **Sony Boy** doll for a promotion during the 1960's. The doll figure came in four sizes: 4, 8, 12-inch, and a large one of unknown size used as

During the 1960's Sony Corporation used vinyl *Sony Boy* dolls to advertise their products. The dolls were available in three sizes; 4, 8, and 12-inches, plus a large display figure. These 4 and 8-inch dolls have brown shoes, green pants, yellow shirts, and brown hair. The neck is jointed. Marks: "SONY," in orange letters across shirt. P. Coghlan collection, Harry Sykora photographer.

a display figure. The dolls, all identical, wear brown shoes, green pants, a yellow shirt with orange letters, and they hold their hands behind their back. The trademark figure was probably intended for the United States market because there is no hint of an Oriental look.

SpagettiOs, a product of Franco-American O's Products, a division of Campbell Soup Company. The **Wizard of O's** doll, 8-inches tall with his tall pointed hat, is made of soft vinyl with moveable head. It is dressed in molded/painted hat, long coat, and bow tie. The bow tie and hat are decorated with what looks like pasta O's from a can of SpaghettiO's. The doll was available for $1.00 plus two labels from any variety of SpaghettiO's or Raviolios.

The two-piece vinyl 8-inch *Wizard of O's* doll was offered in 1978 and 1979. The long coat and hat are SpagettiO's sauce, red with white O's on the hat. Marks: "WIZARD OF O'S" T.M. CAMPBELL SOUP CO.," on bottom. $2.00.

Spic and Span, a product of Procter and Gamble. In 1912 a pair of dolls dressed in Dutch costumes were known as the **Spic and Span** dolls, named for the cleaning product of the same name. The dolls had composition heads and hands with cloth body and limbs. The hair, eyes, and mouths were molded/painted. The man is dressed in a double-breasted jacket, wide trousers, and a hat. The woman wears a jumper, blouse, and the typical white Dutch hat. Both have wooden clogs. Marked: "Spic and Span/Amberg Doll" on base.

Star-Kist Tuna. In 1959 Star-Kist Tuna began using a new label, a fisherman wearing an earring and a yellow sou'wester hat and slicker. To impress consumers with this change a 16-inch vinyl doll was offered that was dressed in a yellow sou'wester, slicker, and boots similar to the fisherman on the new label. Under the rain outfit the doll wore a red checked dress and matching panties. The doll had sleep eyes, closed mouth and rooted "poodle-cut hair." Remember that style? It cost $2.50 plus two Star-Kist Tuna labels.

By the 1970's, the emphasis was off the fisherman with the earring, and on **Charlie** a caricature of a blue tuna with a smart-aleck lip. Anyone who watches daytime television is sure to hear a comical commercial showing how genteel Tuna are turned down when they ask to be a Star-Kist Tuna because **Star-Kist Tuna** must be more than a Tuna with good taste; it must be a Tuna that tastes good. The fisherman remains on the can label today, but the advertising concentrates on **Charlie**.

During 1969 and 1970 almost every month a new ad appeared in magazines offering a premium from Star-Kist Tuna. Each premium featured **Charlie**.

One of the first offers was for a huge 3-foot pillow made in the shape of a fish.

A *Charlie the Tuna* pillow was the first premium using this trademark. The 3-foot fish is blue with an orange hat. Marks: "Charlie," across front of cap. $7.00.

In 1970 a talking **Charlie** pillow was introduced, "A genuine Talkin' Patter Pillow by Mattel" the ads read. **Charlie** is cotton fabric, 15-inches tall, with a blue body, lithographed mouth, glasses, and orange cap. It resembles many of the cloth adver-

A 15-inch *Charlie* pillow that could talk was offered by Starkist Tuna in 1970. It is blue with an orange hat. Marks: "Charlie," on hat. $7.00.

tising dolls, except this one has a pull string to activate "nine different under-water cracks," such as "Hi! Did you ever hear a talking fish before?" The fish cost $4.00 plus three Star Kist Tuna labels.

Other items offered during this 1969 to 1970 period were: A rug for $3.00, a lamp with **Charlie** as the base for $4.50, bath towels two for $4.50, jewelery $1.25 each, and more recently a wrist watch for $9.95.

In 1973 Product People of Minnesota manufactured a 7-inch vinyl **Charlie the Tuna** complete with molded/painted glasses and a removable hat. This doll was apparently sold only at retail stores.

One of several dolls manufactured by **Product People**, this 7-inch vinyl *Charlie* was intended for the retail market. The hat is removable. Marks: "CHARLIE," in raised letters on hat. $5.00.

Gebruder Stollwerck.

This German confectionery firm offered as a premium a 3-inch long tin buggy with a frozen charlotte doll inside. Date unknown.

This adorable yellow and brown tin buggy and 1¼-inch frozen Charlotte doll were a premium of a confectionery firm in Germany. Marks: "Gebruder Stollwerck, Koln./ Chocoladen & Zuckerwaaren," on side of buggy. $50.00.

Stoney's Beer. A display figural for this beer was given to managers of bars and also to customers in some localities. The molded plastic bartender **Stoney** is 8-inches high including the base. It was manufactured by Sculptural Promotions Inc.

A Stoney's Beer figural is 8-inches high, including the base. Marks: "Stoney's Beer," on front of base. L. Yagatich collection, Donald G. Vilsack photographer. $20.00.

Sue Flakes Beef Suet. A 12-inch cloth doll, **Miss Sue** was printed by Dean's. The English cloth doll manufacturer, for this suet company, which is also based in England. **Miss Sue** is marked on the band of her chef hat. She also wears an apron over a dress that has the letter "s" printed in circles. A spoon is held in one hand. Date unknown.

Sunbeam Bread. This product with bakeries in Minnesota and other states has offered at least two advertising dolls. In 1959 a 17-inch doll copied from the face used on their bread wrappers was used for a promotion. **Miss Sunbeam** has a vinyl head and arms, plastic body and legs, yellow rooted wig, blue sleep eyes, dimples and an open/closed mouth showing a line of straight teeth. The doll is dressed in a cotton print dress with a waist apron

Miss Sunbeam was manufactured by Eegee for Sunbeam Bread, in 1959. The 17-inch doll's face was copied from the face found on their bread wrappers. The open/closed mouth shows a line of teeth, synthetic wig is rooted, and the eyes open and close. Doll wears original clothes including a white organdy apron marked "Miss Sunbeam." Marks: "Eegee," on head; "A," on body. N. Ricklefs collection. $25.00.

stamped Miss Sunbeam. The doll was manufactured by Eegee.

This doll has been mistakenly identified as representing Sunbeam Appliances.

The second doll, **Little Miss Sunbeam** is a 17-inch prestuffed cloth doll with lithographed blonde hair and lashed blue eyes. It wears a short blue dress and blue Mary Jane shoes; arms stand out from the body. The apron is marked. No date.

Cloth doll offered by Sunbeam Bread is copied from the girl used on their bread wrapper. The 17-inch doll has yellow hair, blue eyes with long lashes and wears a short blue dress with matching mary-jane shoes. Arms and legs are cut free from the body. Marks: "Little/Miss Sunbeam," on front of lithographed apron. $10.00.

Sun-Maid Raisins. A 14-inch vinyl doll dressed in fabric printed with boxes of Sun-Maid Raisins sold at better department stores for $14.00 during the 1973 Christmas season. The doll has a rooted wig with long ringlets, closed mouth, and open/shut eyes. It wears a poke bonnet and jumper made from the raisin print fabric over a yellow blouse. The doll was

sold along with a line of children's clothing using the same printed fabric. The small girl's clothing was styled the same as the clothing on the doll. Fun Frill, Inc. of New York City produced the dolls.

Some companies, like Sun-Maid, are fortunate to establish a successful trademark early that they can keep and use for generations. In 1911 the Sun-Maid symbol, which tells a story, was created. It depicts a lovely young girl carrying a tray dripping with lucious grapes to be dried into raisins by the sun in the background.

The name metamorphosed from "sundried" to "sun-made" into the final name "Sun-Maid." The trademark was so successful that the California Associated Raisin Company changed its name to match their product, it became the Sun-Maid Raisin Growers of California.

Sunoco Service Stations. A 25-inch **Little Brute**

The 6½-foot inflatable *Brute* football player is used for advertising by Sunoco Service Stations. The 25-inch "Little Brute" was sold at their stations for $2.00. These inflatables are used by other establishments for display and advertising. L. Yagatich collection, Donald G. Vilsack photographer. Still available.

inflatable doll was offered at these gasoline stations. The doll is a football player manufactured by Gem Giftwares in Taiwan. It cost $2.00.

A large six and a half-foot **Brute** inflatable was distributed to Sunoco dealers for display use. These were not for sale.

Sunshine Animal Crackers.

Two rather old looking cloth elephants were located that advertised this brand of children's cookie. One elephant is 6½-inches long and is printed the same on both sides. Between the legs is an outdoor scene with grass, trees, and sky. A lithographed banner worn over its back reads: "Today! Sunshine Animal Crackers at your Grocer."

Another Sunshine Elephant, somewhat larger, three-dimensional with four legs, attached ears, and tail. Mebane collection. $40.00.

Swanson International Dinners.

To introduce their International line of TV dinners. Swanson offered the ordinary 8-inch plastic dolls wearing international costumes. The dolls came in a plastic bell-shaped container.

A cloth elephant 5½-inches tall and 6½-inches long was used to advertise Sunshine Animal Crackers. Date unknown. The elephant wears a red blanket with yellow trim. Marks: "Today!/Sunshine/Animal Crackers/at your/Grocer," on blanket. P. Coghlan collection, Harry Sykora photographer.

The other elephant is somewhat larger, the shape of the banner is different, and it is three-dimensional with four legs, attached ears, and tail. The trunk is longer and straight.

For a limited time Swanson International TV dinners offered 8-inch plastic dolls in international costumes. $3.00.

Sweet 'N Low.

In 1979 this sugar substitute offered two plush

animals, **Sweetie** dog and **Sweetie's Friend** another dog. **Sweetie**, 12-inches tall, holds a free package of Sweet 'N Low. The cost is $4.50 plus $1.25 for postage and handling.

Sweetie's Friend, size unknown, wears an apron hand-printed with the name of your choice. Cost is $6.75 plus $1.25 for postage and handling.

Swiss Miss. This powdered chocolate drink mix has used a girl in blonde pigtails as the Swiss Miss character in various forms since 1960. In 1972 the figure took the form of a puppet and has been used extensively in advertising. Doll collectors have long wondered why the product didn't

The 17-inch *Swiss Miss* doll was offered in 1978 by the chocolate drink mix of the same name. The doll has yellow yarn hair with two felt flowers in front and ribbons on the bottoms. The face has tinted cheeks and darts at the cheeks to give it a contour. The body is made of flesh fabric to the waist; white fabric is used for the legs and lower body. The blue jumper, white apron and blouse are removable. Unmarked. Still available.

offer the figure as a doll premium. Finally in 1978 a cloth **Swiss Miss** doll, designed to resemble the puppet, was offered.

Sylvania Soft White Light Bulbs. In 1974 Sylvania offered a 12-inch talking **Bugs Bunny** doll manufactured in 1971 by Mattel. The cartoon character has a gray plush body with a molded/painted vinyl head. By pulling the string eight flippant phrases are activated including the famous, "What's up Doc?"

In 1974 Sylvania light bulbs offered a 12-inch *Bugs Bunny* doll that was manufactured by Mattel. The doll also sold on the retail market. By pulling the string, the smart-lipped rabbit would speak eight phrases. The head is vinyl; body is gray gabardine with a white fuzzy tummy; yellow hands hold a felt carrot; the ears are pink plastic; and the bow tie is green. Marks: "Mattel 1971," on label. $3.00.

Bugs was a bargain, costing only $2.25 plus the bottom panel from a two-pack of bulbs. Sylvania was overwhelmed with requests and had to turn many down. The toy also sold at retail stores, but the cost was considerably higher.

T

Tame Creme Rinse. See Gillette Company.

Tastee-Freez International. In 1955 a "Miss Tastee-Freez" doll was offered by this soft ice cream franchise in limited areas. The following information comes from their publication Tastee-Freez News and Views, dated October, 1955:

"The Western Mass. Tastee-Freez with 15 stores in the territory, did a solid sales promotion job which is offered as a terrific idea to every territory in the country. In David C. Gallano's letter the idea is briefly and effectively stated. He writes: 'This is a picture of our live Miss Tastee-Freez. Her name is Betty Koslowsky. She appeared at a number of our stores for a period of two hours and passed out doll cards. She worked in conjunction with our doll . . and thousands of New England homes are decorated with these lovely dollies. Every town has another "Betty." ' Why not put this idea down for one of your future promotions?"

Whether the doll was free with the cards or sold for a fee is unknown. The doll is the ordinary unmarked plastic 7- 8-inch doll with glued on wig, molded shoes, and sleep eyes. It is dressed in a plaid taffeta dress with lace at the shoulder and hem. Her only identification is on a ribbon worn over the dress. Several costumes were available with this offer.

In 1970 another promotion used the same ordinary plastic doll; a cowboy and an Indian girl doll were offered. Along with a sundae, a coupon was given that was necessary to purchase the dolls. The cowboy wears plastic pants and vest, felt hat, and a plaid shirt. The Indian doll wears a brown suede-cloth dress, headband and painted shoes. The dolls came with a ribbon stamped with the franchise's name.

In 1955 several Tastee-Freez stores in the Massachusetts area offered a 7-inch plastic *Miss Tastee-Freez* doll. The doll is the ordinary type used by so many companies. The redeeming feature of this doll is that it wears a ribbon identifying it as *Miss Tastee-freez*. T. Tripp collection. $4.00.

In some areas free plastic hand puppets named: **Bear of a Burger, Tastee Dog, Little T,** and **Frenchy Fry**, were given to promote certain purchases.

In the mid-1970's well-made plush hand puppets of these same characters were available in limited areas. **Bear of a Burger** is a bear with an open mouth, derby hat, and a neckerchief. **Tastee Dog** has floppy felt ears, vinyl eyes with long lashes, and pompom nose. **Frenchy Fry** is plush with seams on the outside of the fabric to provide the shape of an edible french fry. The features are felt and the beret on its head is also felt. **Little-T** is plush with a pointed felt hat. The puppets are about 10-inches tall.

A chicken puppet also came in this series, which we were unable to find.

The 8-inch *Cowboy* doll wears plastic pants and vest, a plaid shirt, and a felt hat. The *Indian* doll wears a brown suede-cloth dress, and a headband. Both wear painted shoes. Marks: "Miss America's Sweetheart, tastee-freez" stamped on ribbon worn by the Indian doll. L. Yagatich collection, Donald G. Vilsack photographer. $4.00.

In limited areas, Tastee-freez stands offered five plush and felt hand puppets. *Bear of a Burger* wears a derby hat and a checkered neckerchief. Marks: "Bear of a Burger," on front. $3.00.

Tastee Dog, was a promotion of Tastee-Freez restaurants in limited areas. Marks: "Tastee Dog," on felt under head. $3.00.

Frenchy Fry is about 10-inches tall. Marks: "Frenchy Fry." $3.00.

Little-T hand puppet sold at Tastee Freez drive-in restaurants. $3.00.

Tastykake Bakeries. In 1974 the cardboard that comes in packages of Tastykake products included a coupon for a "soft cotton doll dressed as a baker." The 13-inch prestuffed doll cost $1.00 plus the coupon.

Tastykake Bakeries offered a *Tastykake Baker* doll in 1974. The 13-inch doll wears a lithographed chef's hat and a white apron worn over a red suit. The only mark is a "T" on the front of the hat. $6.00.

Texaco Oil Company. In 1973 Texaco Service Stations sold a doll with an oilchange called the **Texaco Cheerleader**. The doll is jointed vinyl, 11½-inches tall, long blonde hair, painted eyes, and a closed mouth. The doll is dressed in a cheerleader outfit with a red knit top and short white pleated shirt. It came in a box with two other outfits: a red raincoat and boots, and a red-checked dress. The box is marked as the **Texaco Cheerleader**, but the doll is only marked "Hong Kong,"

The dolls were primarily advertised on large posters at the service stations and cost $2.00.

In 1973 Texaco Service Stations offered an 11½-inch plastic *Cheerleader* doll for $2.00 with an oil change. The doll is shown in original box in cheerleader outfit with red knit top, white pleated skirt, and white plastic knee-length boots. A red plastic raincoat and a red checkered dress also came with the doll. Marks: "T 30/Hong Kong," on head; "2/Made in Hong Kong,' on back. $3.00.

Texas Dairy Queen Association. This branch of International Dairy Queen, Inc. uses its own promotion dolls. In 1974 three characters from an old-fashioned melodrama were available for 99¢. The hero was the **DQ Kid**, 16-inches and dressed in white like the good guys should be. The heroine is **Sweet Nell**, a 15-inch doll wearing a huge bonnet and carrying a flower in one hand. The villain **Funfighter McDoom** has a patch over one eye of his turquoise-colored face. The dolls were manufactured by J.S. Sutton & Sons, Inc. of New York City.

In 1978 a shapely cheerleader doll was available for $1.00. The doll wears boots, shorts that show the navel, and a bare midriff top. The back of the midrif has an oil derrick, otherwise the doll is unmarked. This doll was manufactured by the Chase Bag Company of North Carolina.

Posters stated "Here is your Derrick Doll available only from Dairy Queen."

The villain of the melodrama series is *Funfighter McDoom*. He wears yellow, green and black clothes and has an aqua blue face. $4.00.

The *DQ Kid* was the hero of the melodrama trio. The 16-inch doll, cost 99¢. Marks: "DQ Kid/Texas Dairy Queen Associ./1974." $4.00.

Sweet Nell is one of the three melodrama dolls offered in 1974 by the Texas Dairy Queen Association. The 15-inch prestuffed doll carries a flower in one hand. Marks: "Texas Dairy Queen Association/© 1974." $4.00.

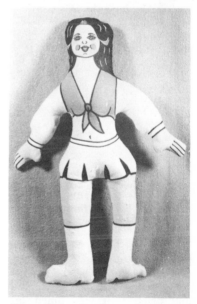

Texas Dairy Queen restaurants offered a cloth *Cheerleader* doll in 1979. The doll wears white boots and shorts with a red, white and blue midrif top. The only mark is an oil derrick on the back. $3.00.

Textile Blueing Co. Both Ladies Home Journal and Delineator magazines of 1901, carried ads from this old blueing company for a **Punch** and **Judy** doll. The dolls were 27-inches tall and printed with oil paints on satteen fabric. The dolls either cost 50¢ or were free for selling 18 packages of blueing.

Thompson's Mail Order Premium House. To quote the offer, "Art Rag Doll **Dolly Dimple** free to every little girl who has answered and complied with the simple condition stated in our advertisement. This doll is free to you. Keep it."

The doll is 13½-inches high, wearing a lithographed red dress with a yellow trim and a blue sash. No marks.

A lovely 13½-inch cloth doll offered by Thompson's Mail Order Premium House. *Dolly Dimple* wears a red dress with yellow trim. No marks. $40.00.

Tide. In 1971 Tide laundry detergent offered a 27-inch bear for $4.50 plus a net weight marker from the package. The brown and gold plush bear was timed for Christmas giving. It had a black pom-pom nose, felt mouth, blue plastic eyes, and a blue ribbon around the neck.

A bear was also offered from October 1976 to October 1977 at limited stores by coupons located at point-of-sale. This bear is 24-inches tall and is brown and tan plush fabric with a plastic nose, felt mouth, and a red bow. It cost $4.95 plus the required coupon, which "may not be assigned or transferred."

The "Tide Bear" is tan and brown plush with plastic nose and eyes and a red bow at the neck. A. Leonard collection. $6.00.

Tillamook Cheese Company. Tillie the Cow is a rubber squeak toy manufactured by Remple in 1958. The cow, 4-inches

Tillie is yellow rubber with brown shading. Marks: "Remple/© 1958/ Enterprise," on stomach; "Tillie/ from/Tillamook," in raised letters on hip. K. Lansdowne collection. $6.00.

high and about 9-inches long, is complete with horns and udder.

Tintair, a product of Tintex. In 1951 two companies manufactured a hard plastic doll named for this brand of hair coloring. Perhaps they observed the Toni doll's appeal to little girls and wanted to share in some of the success. Besides having hair that could be washed, curled, and combed, the Tintair dolls could have their hair colored.

Effanbee manufactured a 13-inch **Miss Tintair.** The doll came with rubber curlers and bottles of non-toxic coloring to apply to the doll's pale blond hair. The doll was dressed in an organdy dress. It is marked EFFANBEE, on the back and has a tag reading: "I am the Tintair doll - An Effanbee Durable Doll."

R & B Company manufactured a 14-inch **Tintair Glamour Girl** doll wearing a rayon dress and panties. It came with a plastic dish, two bottles of coloring, and hair curlers.

Toni, a division of the Gillette Company. Two **Toni** dolls, one manufactured by Ideal and the other by American Character, were sold from retail outlets to little girls wanting to give a home permanent to their doll.

In the late 40's and early 50's, most every female was tempted to try the new Toni hair permanent that could be given at home. A safe home permanent was quite a change from the previous ordeal of receiving a permanent at the beauty shop where it was necessary to sit under a large electric machine with curlers dangling down that cooked the curl into the hair. Besides taking a days time, smelling foul, and being miserably hot, you might discover when the rollers were undone that you have a mass of uncontrollable frizzies or broken strands of hair. Even a trained beautician could get the chemicals, temperature, or timing wrong and produce disastrous results instead of lovely curly locks.

Magazine ads showing twin girls with lovely curly hair ask, "Which twin has the Toni?" This ad was probably shown to alleviate fears that might persist from bad memories of past permanents done at the hairdressers. Toni Home Permanents proved safe and were well received. Many an afternoon was spent carefully twisting up a friend's or relative's hair on tiny rollers.

To capitalize on the home permanent, Ideal patented the *Toni* doll in 1950. The most common size was 14-inches. This doll is 18-inches tall. The dolls have wonderful nylon wigs that can take lots of styling. Not original clothing. Marks: "Ideal Doll/Made in USA," on head; "Ideal Doll/P 90" on body. $35.00.

Both Ideal and American Character saw in this craze the opportunity to sell a **Toni** doll with hair that could be curled by the little owner. The beautiful Ideal **Toni** doll, sculpted by Bernard Lipfert, was patented September 5, 1950. Although the doll may have sold as early as 1948. Thousands of the dolls with their play-wave kits, consisting of wee rollers, a bottle of wave-set (sugar water), and a comb were rushed to stores. The slogan used was: "An Ideal doll with a purpose." **Toni** became the fifth doll in Ideal's history to reach the million mark in sales units. (Other dolls were: Shirley Temple, Betsy Wetsy, Saucy Walker, and Baby Coos.)

The Ideal **Toni** dolls were made of excellent quality hard plastic with swivel head and jointing at

The relatively unknown 10½-inch *Toni* doll is manufactured by American Character and wears a green felt circle skirt, white knit top, and white boots with green piping. Marks: "Toni," embroidered in script on the skirt; "American Character," written around a circle on back of the neck; "American Character," on back. M. Meisinger collection. $20.00.

the shoulders and hip. The glued-on wig was made of luxuriant nylon that could be washed, combed, and curled endlessly with no ill effects. The largest proportion of dolls had pale blonde wigs, other colors were red, brown, black, and medium blonde. Each finger is separated and the feet are flat.

Ads running in 1952 list four prices: $11.98, $13.98, $16.98, and $19.95. Presumably this is for four sizes of doll, although we only found three sizes: 14-inch, 18-inch, and 20-inch.

The eyes sleep, have upper lashes, painted lower lashes, and a thin line represents the eyebrow. Mouth is closed.

Ideal sold several dolls under different names that all used the **Toni** body and some even used the same head but with slight modifications. **Toni** family dolls are: Mary Hartline, Miss Curity, Harriet Hubbard Ayers, and Betsy McCall.

The second, relatively unknown **Toni** doll, was manufactured in the mid-fifties by American Character. Some sizes of this doll are made totally of one type vinyl, others use a hard vinyl for the body and a soft mouth is closed. This doll represents a more grown-up person, as indicated by the high-heeled feet.

American Character's **Toni** came in four sizes: 10½-inches, 14-inches, 20-inches, and 25-inches. The two larger sizes had swivel waists and pierced ears. Included in the doll box was a play permanent wave kit.

Tony's Pizza. Mr. Tony is a molded one-piece doll copied from the trademark. The 8-inch squeezable chef stands on a base, and was available in 1972 for $1.00 plus two Tony's Pizza labels. "The World's Best Frozen Pizza" originated in Salina, Kansas.

Mr. Tony is the chef for Tony's Pizza and was a promotion used in 1972. The 8-inch squeeze toy is white with black and red details. Marks: "Mr. Tony "The World's Best Frozen Pizza," on pedestal. R. Keelen collection. $3.00.

Toys R Us. A giraffe has always been the symbol of this chain of toy stores. The giraffe was first named **Geoffrey** in 1967 and

The 25-inch *Geoffrey* toy wears a red and white jacket copied from the jackets worn by the Toys R Us clerks. Marks: "Geoffrey." A. Wolfe collection, David Nelson, James Giokas photographers. $10.00.

has been sold as an advertising toy in Toys R Us stores for about six years.

Geoffrey is 25-inches tall, including horns, and is made of plush fabric. Copying from the store clerks, **Geoffrey** also wears a red and white striped jacket. It was manufactured by Animal Fair, Inc.

Trailways, Inc. In the mid-1970's when the Trailways bus line introduced their Five Star Luxury Service complete with a bus hostess they also offered a doll. The 12½-inch doll was made of flesh-colored nylon, stuffed, and put on a wire armature. It was dressed in a felt two piece suit and hat copied from the uniforms worn by the bus hostesses. The features are painted and the hair is yarn. The doll stands on its tip-toes and is attached to a round wood base.

In the mid-1970's Trailways bus line offered a doll for 99¢ to represent their bus hostesses. The bus hostesses were part of a service patterned after the airlines and their stewardesses. The 12½-inch cloth doll wears a costume copied from the hostess uniform: red jacket and skirt with matching hat and a white blouse. The large eyes are painted; hair is yellow yarn. Unmarked. B. Glass collection. $4.00.

Travelodge International. This large chain of motels has used the Sleepy Bear symbol since 1954. The first **Sleepy Bear** doll was offered in 1967. Several have been offered since that time.

In 1954 Travelodge was a small chain of motels in California. According to the company, "Someone suggested that since the symbol of the State of California was, and still is, a golden bear, it would be a good idea to associate the chain through that bear with the state. The next step was fairly easy. What was done was to stand the golden bear on its hind legs, extend its "arms" in a sleepwalking position, and add a warm smile with droopy eyelids. That's how Sleepy Bear came into existence."

Since that time the chain has grown throughout the United States, Canada, and Mexico, and the little bear adorns virtually every item found in a Travelodge and every piece of promotion material.

In 1967 the first Travelodge *Sleepy Bear* doll was manufactured and sold from their motel franchise. The 12-inch brown plush bear is wearing his night cap, but is missing a nightshirt. The eyes and mouth are felt, the nose is yarn. Marks: "Sleepy," on cap. $5.00.

Mr. Clayton Beaver, first developed a **Sleepy Bear** doll in 1967. He continues to manufacture the dolls and sells them to Travelodges who either sell or give the dolls away locally.

The **Sleepy Bear** dolls found are similar in that they are made of brown plush, have droopy eyelids and a nightcap marked **Sleepy**.

The 1967 bear is 12-inches high and has a yarn nose.

The next issue of the bear is 14-inches high and dressed in a white flannel night-shirt and cap. It has felt eyes and mouth and a red pom-pom nose.

The next issue of *Sleepy* is 14-inches tall and is manufactured from a shiny plush fabric. The eyes and mouth are felt; the nose is a pom pom. The bear wears a white flannel night-shirt and cap. Marks: "Sleepy," on night-cap. $5.00.

In 1967 a family of bears, two puppets and a pajama bag were available to motel managers. The bears are: **Old Sleepy Bear, Little Bear's Big Sister, Little Bear,** and **Little Bear's Little Brother. Little Bear** is 14-inches high, made of shiny brown plush, except for a tan "face" and orange "feet". Eyes and mouth are felt, nose is black pom-pom. It wears an orange flannel nightshirt and cap and cost $5.99. The other bears in the family are similar; price and size vary. A **Miss Sleepy Bear** pajama bag is also available.

In 1976 a family of bears was available to motel managers to stock and sell to customers. This is *Little Bear*, the smallest of the family, 14-inches tall. The fabric is shiny brown plush, with a tan muzzle and orange feet. The night-shirt and cap are orange. Marks: "Sleepy," across night-cap. Still available.

In 1978 a *Sleepy* hand puppet could be purchased at Travel Lodge motels. Still available.

This costume, large enough to fit an adult, is available through regional offices for special occasions. Courtesy of Travelodge International.

Tropic-Ana. In 1977 a 17-inch pre-stuffed cloth doll was advertised on cartons of this orange juice. The doll is lithographed in three colors on flesh

The *Tropic-Ana* cloth doll was advertised on cartons of the orange drink using the same name. The 17-inch doll wears a removable green felt skirt. Marks: "Tropic-Ana," on bowl. M. Beahon collection. $3.00.

fabric. **Tropic Ana** would be barred from many beaches for her scanty attire, only a green felt skirt and a necklace. One hand balances a bowl containing oranges on her head, the other hand rests on her hip. Black eyes glance to one side. **Tropic Ana** cost $2.00 plus the wording "Tropic Ana" from a carton.

Tru Test Paint. An unverified Tru Test advertising doll has been found. The doll is 12-inches high with a cloth body and composition head. The distinctive face has big round plastic eyes with wobbly black pupils, closed rosebud mouth, and molded hair. The body, arms, and legs are made from a floral print material. A removable mesh fabric hat and vest complete the attire.

A 12-inch doll with a composition head and a cloth body is possibly a 1940's premium of Tru Test Paint. The round plastic eyes have a movable black iris. The body is covered with a floral print material that is also a suit. Over this is a removable hat and vest. Marks: "Tru Test," on paper tag. S. Russell collection. $12.00.

Turtle Candy. See Mr. Turtle Candy.

U-V-W-X-Y-Z

United Hosiery Mills Corporation, also doing business in 1921 as Buster Brown's Hosiery Mills. This old Chattanooga Company used a trademark with two dolls in a circle and the words "Dixie Doll" printed over the top. In 1921 a patent was applied for to use the trademark as a doll. The mill did not keep any of these dolls. The only record we could find was a reference in a letter to the curator of the Buster Brown Historical Society Museum. It states: "One mill superintendent (a woman) recalls the doll as follows: 'The dolls were made of long greige socks stuffed with knitting ravelings, tied in a knot on top of the head (cap covers knot.) The cap is sort of a sailor style. The faces, cheeks, and edges of hair were painted on with oil paint, I think. I don't remember much about the clothes but think the colors were pink, blue, yellow, and red. As I remember the material was flat print."

United Hosiery Mills *Dixie Doll* is 13-inches tall and made of a ribbed knit commonly used to made stockings. The hat, bow, and pants are pink, everything else is white. The face looks hand-painted. Unmarked. $10.00.

314

United Missouri Bank.

To encourage customers, this bank offered a free 22-inch plush tiger to anyone opening a savings account with $300.00 or adding to one.

A 22-inch plush tiger was given to customers opening or adding $300.00 to a United Missouri Bank savings account. Amee Jo De Mello collection. $6.00.

Vanta Baby Garments.

Until into the 1930's babies by the

A lovely example of the 1927 *Vanta Baby* in original outfit. The Amburg Toy Company dolls ranged in size from 11 to 21½-inches tall, each dressed in a complete outfit of the Vanta brand clothing copied from their line of baby clothes. The composition head, hands and slightly curled legs are made of an excellent quality composition. Note the cellulid teething ball worn on a ribbon around the neck. Marks: "Vanta Baby/Trademark Reg./ Amberg Doll." K. Lyons collection.

hundreds were being tied into Vanta baby clothes. Vanta advertised "no pins, no buttons" only nontwist ties. In 1927 Amburg Toy Company manufactured and patented a composition and cloth baby doll named the **Vanta Baby**.

Vermont Maid Syrup.

In 1964 this brand of pancake syrup advertised a 15-inch jointed vinyl doll that was manufactured by Uneeda.

The doll cost $2.50 plus a bottle-top liner from Vermont Maid Syrup.

Vermont Maid doll wears her original outfit consisting of a green jumper worn over a sheer white cotton blouse. The 15-inch doll has high heel feet and rooted braided hair. Marks: "U 22," on back of neck. L. Zablothy collection. $18.00.

Victor Flour.

This flour, milled by the Crete Flour Mills of Crete, Nebraska printed dolls on their 24½-pound sacks of flour.

Animals and a 9-inch **Dutch Girl** and a 9½-inch **Dutch Boy** were printed on their sacks. The **Dutch Girl** and **Dutch Boy** have yellow hair, red and blue clothing, and yellow shoes. The dolls were copyrighted in 1935.

Victors Eucalyptus Cough Drops. During the 1975 Christmas season Victors' advertised a pair of hugging **Koala Bears** for $7.95 plus one 39¢ price circle from a package of cough drops. The fur-fabric bears are 15-inches high and hug with the benefit of bonding velcro. Coupons at point-of-sale were the only means of advertising.

Another coupon was found describing a **Victor Koala** bear that is 24-inches tall and cost $6.95. Date unknown.

The 17-inch *Victor Koala Twins* hug by means of strips of Velcro on their paws. B. Beisecker collection. $13.00.

Victrola, a product of the Victor Talking Machine Company, which was purchased by RCA in 1926. Back when listening to a record meant cranking up the motor first, the trademark for Victrola was a little white dog and the slogan, "His master's voice."

The little dog, Nipper, was the creation of Francis Barraud, an English artist. He'd tried many times to paint his frisky pet, but the dog refused to sit still until Barraud by accident played a record on his gramaphone. The little dog listened intently to the sound coming from the morning glory horn. Barruad began to paint. After the painting was completed he tried to sell Nipper's picture, but no one seemed interested. Thinking the picture needed color Barraud went to the Gramophone Company (name was later changed to the Victor Talking Machine Company) to borrow a fancy brass horn. The manager took one look at the painting and sensed it was the perfect trademark for his product. The artist was delighted and even came up with a slogan, "His master's voice."

In 1929, when RCA purchased the Victor Talking Machine Company it was with the stipulation that Nipper come too. For 80 years Nipper was used to advertise everything from gramophones to stereos. In 1971 RCA decided to retire Nipper, but apparently reconsidered because a four-ton replica has been installed on top of their plant in Albany, New York.

Many sizes of *Nipper* have been manufactured to use in displays and to give to customers. This 3-inch dog is made of chalk. Marks: "RCA VICTOR," in raised letters on base. $8.00.

December 22, 1915, a patent was registered by J. Henry Smyth, Jr. of Philadelphia for Victor, "His Master's Voice," for dolls and stuffed toys. Another patent was registered the same day by the same man for Victrola Vic, **The Phonograph Dog** for dolls and stuffed toys. We found a 12-inch and a 22-inch plush likeness of **Nipper**.

Vigortone.

Vigortone Pig, 17-inches was a premium of this pig feed company. Marks: "Vigortone," on back. V. Rasberry collection. $6.00.

Viva Towels, a product of Scott Paper Products. A free teddy bear was offered for 15 seals from Viva Towel wrappers. The 15-inch plush bear is brown and gold with a pink bow at the neck.

Vlasic Pickles. In 1977 a 53-inch inflatable **Vlasic Stork**

The *Vlasic Stork* is a 4-foot, three-inch inflatable used primarily for display in stores carrying Vlasic Pickles. The stork has orange legs, white body and wings, and wears a blue cap marked "Deliver." Marks: "Vlasic," on front. $4.00.

was created as an advertising premium to coincide with a complete advertising program that included TV commercials and magazine ads.

Voortman Cookies.

Voortman Cookies offered an 8½-inch plastic *Dutch Girl* doll from 1972 to 1973. The doll has blonde wig, sleep eyes, and wears a Dutch costume that includes wooden shoes. $4.00.

WITN Television of Washington, N.C. This station apparently used a 14-inch cloth doll

An interesting 15-inch cloth doll was used by channel WITN of Washington, North Carolina. One side of the doll is a clean-cut announcer wearing a brown suit, white shirt, and tie. The other side is an unkempt fellow with patched suit, beard, and big glasses.
Marks: "witn tv 7," on front of suit $6.00.

lithographed with an "establishment" announcer on one side and a "hippy" announcer on the other side.

Welch Grape Juice. A 9-inch plastic hand puppet of **Wally Welch** was given free at the resort area of Silver Dollar City in Missouri.

Wally Welch hand puppet was given at resort areas in the Ozarks. Puppet advertises the grape drink sold by Welch Foods. J. Varsolona collection. $1.00.

Western Union. Western

"Congratulations" was one of the original four *DollyGram* dolls used by Western Union to send messages. The other dolls in the original series were "Happy Day," "Happy Birthday," and "Please Cheer Up." Nineteen other messages were added later. The 6-inch dolls are made of velvet with raffia hair. A pocket across the front was used to hold the message. $3.00.

Union inaugurated a novel way to send a message February 16, 1975, with their doll-by-wire service. Instead of just a printed telegram, a **DollyGram** would convey the message.

The doll chosen for the **DollyGram** was made at a farm in Chittenden County, Vermont by Editions Limited, Inc. Western Union considers the handmade dolls "Early American folk art brought up to date."

Westinghouse. To promote hot water heaters, Westinghouse used the trademark, **Cozy Glo Kid**, a small child standing nude with a towel modestly held in front. It is not known when the trademark was produced in doll form.

The *Cozy Glo Kid* was used by Westinghouse to promote their hot water heaters. The one-piece composition doll is 12½-inches tall with molded/painted features and towel. Marks: "Cozy Glo Westinghouse Kid," on sticker. C. Haenggi collection. $150.00 to $200.00.

In the late 30's Westinghouse Mazda Lamps offered a cloth doll patterned after a figure used in many ads. **Lotta Light**, 16½-inches, is primarily lithographed in blue and black on white fabric. **Lotta** is a school girl with pigtails and she carries a slate.

The 16½-inch *Lotta Light* cloth doll was offered by Westinghouse in the 1930's. She is dressed in a short blue and white striped dress with matching stockings and carries a slate under one arm. The braided hair and eyes are black. P. Coglan collection, Harry Sykora photographer.

In 1976 Westinghouse used a full-page color ad to promote a tan plush fabric **Kangaroo** with a baby in the pouch.

Westinghouse used an 18-inch plush kangaroo with baby to remind customers "to keep spares on hand." Courtesy of Westinghouse Public Relations. $8.00.

In 1978 a stuffed green plush **Turtle** was offered to promote Westinghouse Turtle-Lite Bulbs. The **Turtle**, 11-inches long by 6-inches high, cost $4.50, and was available until March 1979.

White Front Stores of Seattle, Washington.

The White Front Stores in Washington offered a 16-inch *Friendlee* doll. It is a cloth elf with side-glance eyes, pointed ears, and unusual hands with only one large finger and a thumb. He wears a red cap and shirt and yellow pants. Marks: "Friendlee ©," on back; "® 1972 White Fronts, Inc.," on one foot. $5.00.

Whiteshine Shoe Polish. This English product offered a cloth **Jimmy Whiteshine** doll that was manufactured by Deans.

Wrigley's Gum. According to Plaything's Magazine the **Spearmint Kiddo** and **Spearmint Kid** dolls were manufactured in 1912 and 1915.

The **Spearmint Kid**, 1915, had composition head and hands with a composition body and wood legs. It is very similar to the figure in the trademark.

Spearmint Kiddo, 1912, resembles a child and was manufactured by Amberg & Sons. The doll should be easy to identify because its molded/painted hair was decorated with molded/painted mint leaves. The mouth is open/closed with a few teeth showing.

Wurlitzer. To promote the new Funmaker Sprite line of easy-play organs this company offered a 15-inch **Funmaker** cloth doll.

The 15-inch cloth *Funmaker* doll was a promotion for the Funmaker Sprite line of easy-play organs manufactured by the Wurlitzer Company. The doll wears green. Marks: "Funmaker," on brim of hat. $5.00.

Yukon Flour Mills of Yukon, Oklahoma. Three small cloth dolls depicting animal characters from the popular children's books by Thorton Burgess were used to advertise this old brand of flour. The dolls

A frightened looking *Peter Rabbit* doll was used to advertise Yukon's Best, a flour milled at Yukon, Oklahoma. The 7-inch doll wears red trousers, aqua vest, and brown jacket. Both sides have a face. Marks: "Peter Rabbit/Pat. Pend./ Yukon's Best." E. Davis collection. $10.00.

are printed in several vivid colors, so they were probably not printed on the flour sacks; usually flour sack dolls have few colors and they are dull.

According to a resident of Yukon, Oklahoma the dolls probably date prior to 1915 because the mills were closed about that time.

The three dolls are: **Peter Rabbit** 7-inches tall, **Mrs. Peter Rabbit** 7½-inches tall, and **Unc' Billy Possum** 6-inches tall.

Zee Toilet Tissue, a product of Crown Zellerbach Company. It was only natural that Zee offered a **Li'l Softee** doll to make further use of their clever trademark. The doll we obtained was 5½-inches tall. Some ads were for a 7½-inch doll, so apparently **Li'l Softee** came in two sizes, both cost $1.95 plus 2 Quality seals from Zee Nice 'n Soft bathroom tissue.

In 1975 Zee Toilet Tissue offered a *Li'l Softee* doll. The 5½-inch doll has a soft vinyl body with straight legs and hard plastic head and arms. The unusual mouth is an H of black paint defining the molded smile. Hair is light blonde and rooted. This brazen child wears only a blue plastic hat with a floppy brim. Marks: "Hong Kong," on one foot; "CCZ," on the other. K. Lansdowne collection. $3.00.